Dancing on the Stones

Dancing on

Selected Essays

the Stones

John Nichols

University of New Mexico Press
Albuquerque

TO MOTHER, and all the Gleasons, who, with much love,
gave me a world rich in literature, music, family gatherings,
movies, nature, and a wondrous curiosity.

Mil gracias to ANDREA OTAÑEZ, who helped shape
this collection at the start, and to BETH HADAS,
who saw it through.

Also by John Nichols

Fiction
The Sterile Cuckoo
The Wizard of Loneliness
The Milagro Beanfield War
The Magic Journey
A Ghost in the Music
The Nirvana Blues
American Blood
An Elegy for September
Conjugal Bliss

Nonfiction
If Mountains Die (with William Davis)
The Last Beautiful Days of Autumn
On the Mesa
A Fragile Beauty
The Sky's the Limit
Keep It Simple

© 2000 by John Nichols
All rights reserved. First edition

Library of Congress
Cataloging-in-Publication Data:
Nichols, John Treadwell, 1940–
Dancing on the stones: selected essays
John Nichols—1st ed.
p. cm.
ISBN 0-8263-2182-8 (cloth: alk. paper)
ISBN 0-8263-2183-6 (pbk: alk. paper)
I. Title.
PS3564.I274 D36 2000
814'.54–dc21
99–006983
CIP

"To Be of Use," from Circles on the
Water, by Marge Piercy.
Copyright © 1982 by Marge Piercy.
Reprinted by permission
of Alfred A. Knopf, Inc.

Photograph on page 107 by Maestri Smith

Photograph on page 165 from John Nichols'
family collection

Drawing on page 205 by Rini Templeton

All other photographs and drawings
by John Nichols

Designed by Sue Niewiarowski

Contents

It is not a matter of any one particular time being
a million-to-one Now, but of doing what best we can
with our own particular bit of time. . . . And yes,
there is mostly defeat and frustration. In the head,
that's bearable because that necessarily implies struggle
and purpose. In the heart, it's bearable because of
those we love, and greet, and share with . . . and in the soul,
because of the sheer wonder of the world we live in,
halfway between electrons and quasars, fucked over,
enduring, the indescribably beautiful world.

—Rini Templeton

The author at Big Arsenic, north of Taos.

Introduction

In my younger and more vulnerable years, I really could flit across Rio Grande boulders like a gazelle. And in the dark, too, if I felt like it. I was an agile lad. I had more balance than a mountain goat and usually felt twice as high, a real giddy person proud of his coordination. Hell of a trout fisher too, if I do say so.

Sure, the boulders were dangerous, and sometimes I slipped and fell into the river or crashed among a pod of rocks that almost broke my ribs or put a dent in my noggin. But that never slowed me down for long. In the parlance, I've always been a "gamer."

Later I developed Ménière's disease, which is an inner ear problem. And through a series of not exactly felicitous circumstances the condition became oscillopsia, which is a *real* inner ear problem. Lacking any serious vestibular reflex makes for an interesting equilibrium deficiency. Tack on a heart condition that requires digitalis daily, and you're talking some major limitations. They don't keep me off the boulders yet, but now I move like a rickety snail when I'm casting the waters for trout. I'm taking my life in my hands . . . but that's the way I like it. Risk lies at the heart of true vitality.

I'm a sucker for that water, those stones, that gorge. So it's no hill for a maudlin stepper like me to merge them into a metaphor of my existence. River of Life, the Rio Grande, with its high-spirited currents crashing through glistening fat lumps of basalt, which I've decided stand for ideas and adventures and confrontations along the way. Each rock is different, and they're all landmarks on a path toward my own imminent conclusion. You don't have to be

Wordsworth to draw that kind of a longbow. Any fool can do it to justify the title of a book.

A labored analogy, sure, but absolutely sincere. These essays, speeches, ruminations—*articles,* if you will—are stepping-stones on my journey (though not at all chronological). That's me hopping from one "rock" to the other, so obnoxiously full of pizzazz. It's been a chaotic trip so far, all over the map, but what else is new? On any fishing expedition I go up the river and back. Sometimes I cross over. I fish on my side, then across the way, then maybe in the middle. It depends. I never claimed I could pick the water clean. Nor that my system was logical. I've had good days and bad days, whether in 1971 or 1993. The mood is constantly changing. But it should be obvious that I've had a lot of fun.

Some of these pieces were written for magazines like *Audubon, Natural History* or *Outside Magazine,* and that means they were fairly polished from the git-go. Others were semi-off-the-cuff lectures I gave to groups as diverse as the Rocky Mountain Association of Collegiate Registrar and Admissions Officers and the Sierra Club, and they required big-time pruning and "cleaning up" to become even halfway palatable. A handful have never been seen in public before and may be a trifle shy, so please read them with consideration.

What does it all add up to, these stepping-stones in the river of my life on the way to a no doubt cantankerous end? A pretty interesting day on the water, I hope.

In the old days I hiked out of the gorge each evening with a gunnysack full of slimy critters. You can't do that anymore, the rules have changed: it's a catch-and-release world we live in. So when you're done, pilgrim, pass along this book to a friend. Literature belongs to the people.

Hasta la palabra, siempre!

Taos, March 1999

Part One
My Little Infinity

Stock pond on the Taos mesa.

I was raised all over this country, but my roots are in New Mexico and it's been that way since 1969. All but one of the essays in this book were written in my hometown of Taos.

I love where I live, an environment both heartrending and beautiful. At its most simple and primitive, Taos is about landscape and weather. Then it gets complicated, as we shall see later on.

But in the beginning, for the moment, there is simply wonder. . . .

I Never Met a Cloud I Didn't Like

I'll wager I live out west because of clouds. Truly, my heart leaps up when I behold. There's a billion miles of Big Wide Open to gambol in that never feels cluttered. Even when this vast dominating space is blank, I feel it's just one grumble shy from rarin' to go. The sky *will* explode at any minute. Up here in Taos that tension is endemic.

At times I lead a chaotic life, full of theater and emotion. The air over this valley properly reflects my diatribes. But what can a writer like me say about clouds that isn't a hackneyed stereotype or reminiscent of the lyrical words on a best-selling record by Judy Collins? Not much. They're fluffy and fleecy, big and booming, utterly diaphanous, charmingly puffy—

Excuse me, but, um, gee—y'know? It's like calling dogs Spot and Fido and Rover, cows Bossy, and cats Puss Puss or Garfield.

Doesn't matter, though, does it? Let's exempt atmospheric verities from a demand for original rhetoric. So: Each day, each hour, clouds reinvent the sky, serene as silk, big as hippos, loud as choo-choo trains. Their Greatest Show on Earth can create a brand-new postcard shot faster than I can whistle for help backward.

Clouds frighten; they enlighten. They kill people with lightning and floods and freezing shadows in January. They also soothe my soul, causing me to catch my breath and think of J. M. W. Turner or Georgia O'Keeffe or Maxfield Parrish. They make me want to lie in a hammock and float indulgently, more lazy than a dandelion, more placid than a sheep.

I climb Tres Orejas Mountain in the middle of our sagebrush

plain. There's a rock shaped like a half shell on top of the south-ernmost peak. There lie I, a humanoid embryo curled into a basalt egg, staring straight up past the drifting buzzards toward some vast theory of relativity, azure colored and without a single bit of vapor marring its "perfection."

Has to be pretty windy up there, however. For suddenly a blink of white appears *out of nowhere,* and, like a magician's handker-chief, that raggedy cloud unfolds in size a dozen times over in the shake of an icy invisible wrist. Whoa, boy! Check out that albino blast of vapor growing so huge in shape, it ultimately casts a shadow that actually makes me shiver. Then just as abruptly it evaporates, sucked back into a bright blue hole with hardly a protesting quiver: *poof.*

For years I have photographed clouds in all their splendor, bombarded by sunshine, glorious or inane. They are always ea-gerly willing—like enormous slavering puppies forged of cotton candy—to cater to my sense of melodrama.

"Money in the bank!" the mercenary *moi* cries gleefully every time those big vapor bozos go bonkers in cliché spasms almost too rococo to record on Kodachrome. And I reach for my camera, point-ing the lens at heaven.

Weather. We all spend our lives schmoozing about the weather. We look up; we frown; we calculate the *cabañuelas.* It's gonna rain, gonna be a hard blow, an early winter, a gosh darn drought. I sup-pose everybody loves sunny skies except *me.* Sorry, but I hate dawdling along underneath a bland canopy. I want my heavens puckered by enormous cirrus feathers. Better yet, give me a heap of scary thunderheads looming up like Pittsburgh's Steel Curtain or the Dallas Doomsday Defense. Frankly, I grow mega-excited when the sky starts lookin' for a fight.

Yo, I'm game, bro—toss *everything* you got at me. Rain, thun-der, lightning, cauliflowers the size of Norway, swollen cumulous giants, cumulonimbus *abuelitos* or La Llorónas aching for a rum-ble, nimbostrati going ape, crystal smudges changing effortlessly into atomic columns—*oh, I do love a parade, Mame!*

Sky and cloud, what's not to adore and worship and gawk at?

Massive and dark and bright and powerful: you can't say a mysterious greater power isn't trying. Or if that isn't your cup of tea, how about Gerard Manley Hopkins?

> . . . up above, what wind-walks! What lovely behavior
> Of silk-sack clouds! Has wilder, willful-wavier
> Meal-drift molded ever and melted across skies?

Fair enough? I hope so. If you're a Spanish speaker, you might reply, "*Órale,* Geraldo—*tu y las nubes me traen muy loco.*"

Or Native American?—"Lovely! See the cloud, the cloud appear! Lovely! See the rain, the rain draw near!"

But what if you're a just plain goofy guy like me?

Well, I have often declared: "Give me this day my daily cloud . . . and I'll not have need of wine."

Now *there's* a promise as true as wind and sky and provocative nebulosity.

New Mexico Magazine, *September 17, 1999.*

Short Season

Summertime in Taos, New Mexico . . . but the livin' ain't necessarily easy.

It's a short season in a high country, wedged between springtime snow flurries and September frosts. Vegetables that we don't dare plant until mid-May grow up paranoid, racing to reach maturity before getting mugged by an early icicle. I remember a freeze one year on August 7 that nailed all my squash.

Still, summer always begins with such high hopes, so many plans. I am divorced, and in June the kids arrive. Instantly my little adobe house is a mess. But I'm prepared this year—with countless jobs, exciting excursions, fascinating camp-outs. So Tania promptly falls from a tree and breaks her leg. Then Luke crashes while doing BMX wheelies in the driveway and fractures his collarbone.

It rains each afternoon. The crippled children track indelible mud into the house until everything is filthy. My asthma attacks increase. Luke festers, building airplane models; Tania would like to ride a horse but can't. So we go to the drive-in movies, but the film is horribly vandalized by all the lightning chattering overhead. And while we are out, commando cows storm up the driveway and trample the budding garden.

Later, mysterious night animals start eating our baby broccoli and young cornstalks. We leave a radio (playing punk rock music) out there all night long to protect the trembling beans and cauliflowers.

Crises abound. Every year a brood of flightless fledgling magpies winds up whining in the lilacs, stalked by our cat. We chuck them into our magpie cage and dish out food for two weeks while hordes of adult *urracas* perpetually screech at us from surrounding cottonwood trees. Then we remove the youngsters—who bite our fingers in appreciation—and toss them into the wind . . . off they swoop, cat-proof forever.

Duke (the cat) captures one, two, many field mice daily, carts them into the bathtub where they can't escape, and bats them around for hours. Often I wake up in the morning and step on mangled water snakes. Then Duke tangles with a skunk, staggers blindly through the cat door into the kitchen—and we immediately drench him with tomato juice!

On hot afternoons we go swimming in the Rio Grande or traipsing over that river's opulent boulders with fly rods in hand. I am after trout: Luke and Tania would rather catch lizards for one of the many terrariums at home. Afternoon showers leave astonishing rainbows astride the sheer walls of the gorge. At dusk, hundreds of bats flutter above the river. And canyon wrens release their eerie diving calls as we lug burlap sacks full of good eating up the trail.

Driving home on the mesa's rutted roads, I constantly swerve to avoid kangaroo mice and jackrabbits. An occasional deer bounds into the sage. Burrowing owls fly up. Nighthawks gather insects above our heads. Coyotes howl over by Tres Orejas Mountain.

After dinner I may type at the kitchen table while the children cavort outside in the dark, playing Ghost in the Graveyard. Or I may spend the night irrigating the back field. At dawn, I lean wearily on my shovel and lazily regard blackbirds and magpies plucking insects exposed by the water . . . and the peace feels almost religious.

Sometime in July the last patches of snow disappear from the surrounding mountains. Usually the slow snowmelt keeps the Rio Grande muddy all through the summer. Often the water *never* clears up until the weather is so cold that the trout aren't biting anymore.

For a moment the valley simmers in a lush swoon. Wild sunflowers sprout and blossom everywhere. Road shoulders are made indigo blue and mauve by chicory and purple asters. And in the evenings killdeer fly low over hay and alfalfa fields, screeching mournfully.

There's so much daytime activity. So much growing and constructing and vacationing to do in so little time. Dust clouds kicked up by recreation vehicles hang over town. And then, abruptly, it's over. It seems leaves have just barely fluffed out . . . when they begin to wither.

Always, during the last half of August, I can feel autumn in the wind. Nights are cool. In the morning, up at Williams Lake beneath Wheeler Peak, one is apt to discover a thin layer of ice on the water. Twice I have been chased out of the mountains on Labor Day weekend by budding blizzards.

One day in late August the kids simply vanish into thin air, back in school. On a Monday the crab apple tree is full of siskins headed in a southern direction; on Tuesday the tree is deserted. Next a light powdering of white appears on Taos Mountain. And I stand in my back field, bewildered, wondering . . . *What happened?*

Outside Magazine, *June 1983.*

Dancing on the Stones

I have never been to the Grand Canyon, I fear it's much too crowded. I'm told the Snake River is fabulous, but it's very far away. Rifle Gap in Colorado has been wrapped by Christo, which sort of turns me off. And although some say Big Bend is a real treat, I don't like muddy water.

Fact is, I'm an infinity-in-a-grain-of-sand kind of guy: I get my jollies at home in Taos County, northern New Mexico. So when it comes to dramatic canyon walls and a river that courses between them, the Rio Grande Gorge just west of me is the rift that I adore. I've been roaming it since 1969, from Chiflo Mountain twenty-seven miles north of Taos to the tiny town of Pilar, fourteen miles south of me. And so far I've never been bored.

Norman McLean said it for many of us in *A River Runs Through It:* "I am haunted by waters." To begin with, my Rio Grande receives much of its immediate liquid sustenance from the high country above my home in the Sangre de Cristo Mountains. For decades I've hiked the local watersheds, and I know well the principal streams that tumble into the canyon. When I'm in the gorge, I can feel those high country origins emanating from the water. In frothy cascades I see bear and elk, I hear wind in fir trees, I feel the brutal weight of snow.

Often I sit, ecstatic almost to the point of senility, on a rocky promontory at the rim of the gorge. From this lookout I contemplate the visible world: Picuris Peak down south, Taos Mountain to the east, Tres Orejas west of me, and nothing but sagebrush in between. Cliff swallows dart everywhere, and bats keep jiving around my head. There are nighthawks booming and vultures always circling. Ravens sail quickly by below me. On even the quietest evening there's a remarkable turbulence of motion—and emotion—taking place. Noise from the river 650 feet below is a music that keeps the excitement growing.

Usually I enter the canyon on steep bajadas that most others shun. In earlier days these narrow paths down sometimes dangerous fall lines were used by Spanish shepherds taking their sheep to water. They pounded their names and dates into the rocks. Along the river there are also pictures that Indians carved into the boulders. My favorite is a diminutive hunter with a bow and arrow pointed at a couple of deer that resemble llamas.

The bajadas are difficult; they keep out the riffraff. In fact, once upon a time I had this cleft in the earth almost to myself. I and only twelve other guys in the valley fished the hard-to-reach stretches of the Rio Grande in Taos County. We weren't afraid of rattlesnakes. Willingly we risked our lives on the treacherous rock formations. And we were not deterred by the occasional lunatic who showed up on the rim and started firing his rifle into the canyon. We depended on being alone in a massive and deserted place.

Then rafting came along and changed the mood on part of the water. Given my druthers, I'd outlaw river running. Making an impregnable place accessible to every Tom, Dick, and Harriet with a double sawbuck in their pocket makes me grumpy. Didn't Ed Abbey once say something to the effect that if you couldn't walk there you didn't *belong* there?

However, I admit I'm an unreasonable crank; so I've made my separate peace and I still love the mighty Rio. I just pick my spots more carefully.

When I head out in September to the Wild River section near Cerro, I am entranced by the gaudy yellow rabbitbrush and radiant purple asters lining the route. On warm days I scramble down to the water almost stoned on the vanilla redolence of ponderosa pine trees. And I listen to Townsend's solitaires and Clark's nutcrackers while lizards scramble out of the way.

Boulders are the heart of my experience in this place. I dance on the big slick stones like a happy satyr, always in motion, moving up and down the churning river, casting to brown and rainbow trout. I never sit still on the Rio Grande. When the water is low I cross to the other side by leaping from rock to rock. I misstep occasionally on wet basalt and tumble into the river. Or I trip into heaps of wicked stone and nearly break my arms and legs. Once I plunged headfirst into a thundering pool, losing fishing rod and eyeglasses and nearly my life in the bargain.

But I honestly do not care. The romantic inside my body cries, "Let the boulders kill me, I know I'll die content!" Then I jump back up and keep on dancing.

I have even developed an affection for the shoreline's rampant poison ivy, which turns such beautiful colors in autumn. I always pause to marvel at fireflies around Big Arsenic Springs, where I am also bedazzled by the bright blue darning needles that proliferate in August. Eagles have nested on the high walls for centuries, and occasionally I get to salute them. Beavers and muskrats leave their crawfish-laden deposits on the rocks. And I particularly like the ouzel nests of mud clinging to the sides of enormous stones.

For years, around Easter time, I climbed down a bajada to an ancient aerie. I scaled a small but dangerous cliff to reach the ledge where centuries of raptor droppings, owl castings, and rabbit and lizard bones littered the cliffside-cave floor. Back in a recess I always found a pair of great horned owl fledglings. When I drew close for a few seconds they clacked their bills at me. Hurriedly, I went away. But I returned the next year—just to make sure they were there again—and for many years after that. I was never disappointed.

I can't make it to the ledge these days—too dangerous, and besides, I've grown a tad frail. To be truthful, I do not cavort on river boulders anymore with such a careless disdain for danger. Instead, I move on them a bit more cautiously as befits a man pushing sixty. Sometimes I even pause briefly and press my chest to the hard stone, feeling the sun's warmth, sucking up the vibrations from pounding currents.

I'm a sucker for all the *work* involved in my canyon/river affair.

Climbing out in the dark I curse the steep bajadas, sweating until I'm soaked, pausing to glance at the moon and all the stars while gasping for my life as an owl hoots nearby. In October the Milky Way runs directly overhead, north and south along the gorge like a reflection of river in the sky. Coyotes yip. Maybe a few mule deer, gone below to drink at dusk, climb out ahead of me.

On my slow hike up toward the rim I often recall that there was an upswelling in the earth's mantle millions of years ago, a rift occurred, then a river cut down through it. And the majestic fissure reminds me of our galaxy, the solar system, time and timelessness.

Inevitably I return from my rambling expeditions exulting in my own exhaustion. My hands stink of sage from grabbing the bushes to haul myself up the arduous trails. I sit on the tailgate of my truck, eating a sandwich, dangling my feet, smelling juniper, and ogling the constellations. And I am as happy as a man can be—

In my little infinity.

Audubon Magazine, *March/April 1998.*

The Holiness of Water

When I was five and living in Montpelier, Vermont, at the end of World War II, I often visited a tiny pond in a small meadow overlooking town. The Tadpole Pond. It had a few cattails, maybe a lily pad or two, and lots of green algae. I was fascinated by the tadpoles, the dragonflies and darning needles, by the water skeeters and other aquatic life. The pond was only thirty feet across, a mere saucer of water. But it teemed with life. And I liked the scale, which was just my size as a child . . . and has remained so ever since. I don't know if that means I never grew up or if I am simply a spirit who sees most clearly when the view is limited and self-contained.

Today, at fifty-six, I am still connected to small puddles of water. I live in a dry country at high elevations far from Vermont. Mountains rise to thirteen thousand feet above my hometown and there is a fabled river gorge only a few miles west of the village plaza. Stretching for miles on either side of the river is a sagebrush mesa. Scattered across this parched land are a few stock ponds built ages ago by small ranchers in our valley. Three of those ponds, located within several miles of each other, have captivated me for years.

There are no trees beside the diminutive watering holes. The sun beats down without quarter, and when water accumulates it evaporates quickly. The tanks are splendid in their isolation, totally exposed to heat and wind and dust.

In a wet year I have seen them filled to overflowing, and the cañadas in which they lie boast turbulent muddy rivers. In a dry year the ponds are forlorn empty bowls, lackluster and desolate.

It does not seem life could ever take hold in such a brutally mundane setting.

Yet I am drawn to these places of water in a sere landscape: the simplicity turns me on. The ponds are a metaphor that is clean. And I have visited them in all seasons, discovering countless beautiful moods.

Some days on the mesa the wind blows until the air is laden with grit. Then it grows quiet and the sun beats down and even the sagebrush wilts. In the gut-wrenching heat, grasses wither and die and the air seems devoid of sufficient oxygen for breathing. It's hard to believe that animals, bugs, or birds could inhabit such alien country. There's no water in any of the stock ponds.

An impersonal majesty defines the arid realm, a kind of arctic desolation. But I can never travel through it without experiencing an almost desperate yearning for rain. So my heart leaps up when I behold that first threatening puff of vapor in the sky.

All stock ponds are slave to this sky. They gain their being from springtime snowmelt or from sudden rain squalls when an entire small watershed delivers the goods. Thunderheads roll across the blue atmosphere like bison grazing a prairie; wind and lightning follow. When the clouds burst tons of moisture splatter to earth, but it takes a heap of rain to create even the tiniest pond. Imagine an atomic explosion whose energy is translated into a few square feet of water. The gods throw a virtual flood at the earth in order to create a single mosquito.

I have seen a pond fill to forty yards in length and half again as wide. On the mesa, that is a veritable lake, capable of breeding Loch Ness monsters. But for the most part my puddles remain small and are gone in several weeks. During that truncated season, however, all hell breaks loose.

One day many small white moths fluttered over a dry stock tank moments before it rained. Later, as water tumbled out of a shallow arroyo to splash against the dam, those peppy insects dived into the flood like joyful kamikazes. Who knows why the mass suicide took place? I know it must be part of the birthing process, a statement of life itself.

The day after a puddle is born, that statement is made vividly by tracks in the mud: of horned larks, a coyote, rabbits. But the message really goes up the next night after the Creation when spadefoot toads crawl from the earth and raise their incredible mating racket. Suddenly pinkie-sized toadlets are crowding every square foot of water.

A spadefoot passes all its days underground until the moisture arrives. Then it scrambles to the surface, eager to procreate. After a swift and noisy orgy, millions of eggs are laid. Immediately the adults tunnel back down to their eternal hibernations. Meanwhile in the pond a vertiginous evolution from egg to adult takes place in eleven to fifteen days. Carnivorous tadpoles devour each other in order to reach maturity before the puddle evaporates. In the middle of the growth cycle you can dip your cupped hands into the water anywhere and scoop out a dozen pollywogs.

Coyotes feast on the tadpoles, as do hawks and other birds. Robber flies suck them dry. Snakes gobble them like Jujyfruits.

The tadpoles constantly gasp for air on the surface. Or perhaps they are eating mosquito larvae. One year there were so many adolescent spadefoots in my favorite pond that I could hear a burbling like beer foam prickling, caused by all their mouths constantly breaking the surface.

Spadefoot babies eat each other and graze for microorganisms in the muck and knock off mosquito larvae by the billions. Every stock pond is a supermarket full of special treats. Most prolific are mosquitoes, then come the fairy shrimp and the clam shrimp. Overnight, the water is teeming with these critters. The egg sacs of estivating fairy shrimp may have been waiting in the dust for years. But give them a shot of H_2O and you almost have to jump back out of the way to avoid being trampled in their rush to propagate.

Fairy shrimp and clam shrimp are invertebrates, crustaceans, brachiopods. Their appendages function as both mouths and gills: they eat and breathe through their feet. Their eggs are stored in a brood chamber whose walls are transformed into a protective capsule called an ephippium. When the shrimp molts, the capsule sinks to the bottom and lies dormant. If the pond evaporates, no harm done. The ephippium is impervious to drying or freezing. Wind often blows the egg sac miles to another location. The being inside simply snoozes along in suspended animation, waiting for a new puddle; its egg sac is the brachiopodal version of a transmigrating soul.

But mosquitoes are the real workhorses of the stock pond food chain. A clarion call goes out and immediately the water is reeling with their larvae. Soon after a pond is created I can sit on the dam and marvel at the insects taking flight. Usually it's a trompe l'oeil situation. Not a cloud in the sky, and no wind either: a day placid as milk in a glass. But raindrops are falling onto the surface of my pond. Correction: not raindrops; it's only mosquitoes being born, hundreds of bugs hatching off the surface every second.

From the start mosquito larvae abound, clinging upside down to the underside of the water's surface skin. Pretty soon they pupate. But they are transparent and I cannot directly see them. However, sunlight reflected through their translucent bodies casts their shadows against the ooze a few inches below. One wriggles and then—*pop!*—it is gone . . . airborne . . .

. . . and instantly devoured.

They fall victim to a horde of minipredators, an aggressive Wild Bunch of hyperactive protein-scarfing machines. At twilight time my favorite hunters go to work.

Nighthawks are the most laconic snipers, openmouthed, systematically seining the air for food. Bats jitterbug back and forth, amazingly adroit with their echolocation techniques. Cliff swallows dart and dive gracefully. Their beaks just barely tweak the water—*tick!*—then the bird is away, leaving delicately expanding ripples in its wake.

The dam is honeycombed with kangaroo rat tunnels. Rabbits live among the gully rocks below. A modest prairie dog village is not far off: two of their tunnels are home to burrowing owls. With the advent of water, all these critters wake up and get active. Suddenly a marsh hawk appears, cruising low over the sage, scrounging for tidbits. Rattlesnakes naturally gravitate to the area. Water is like coffee, cocaine, crystal meth: it makes everything *alert*.

I soon discover animal scat everywhere. Big blobs, little splashes, calciferous bird droppings—I inspect all of it with interest. Coyote scat is intriguing. I've seen it full of ants, piñon nutshells, apricot pits, mouse jawbones, lizard tails, and even small stones. Owl castings are apt to show up near the water as well.

One sweltering afternoon I stumbled upon the skull of a skunk. What was *it* doing way over there?

Lizards pop up from the rocks and dust. My favorites—the collared kind—run on their hind legs like toy dinosaurs. Obnoxious grasshoppers are all over the place, fluttering, crackling. I spot a shrike in a rabbitbrush bush. Wee spiders zip across lichen-covered rocks. Enormous tarantula hawks land in the slime and strut about busily. When a meadowlark warbles, I *listen*. Crickets strike up their monotonous concert at dusk.

How can such a small dab of water generate so much *noise?*

Once a year I almost step on a rattlesnake at a stock pond. I park my truck and start walking toward the water. Inevitably a sixth sense impels me to glance down just as my left foot is landing two inches from a coiled serpent. For some reason I never scream or jump away. For some other reason the snake never rattles or strikes. Naturally, my heart always does a dive. When I am past the snake I stop and turn around. I consider the dusky rattler and marvel. I respect and admire the danger. They create a landscape that declares, *Don't tread on me.*

Rattlesnakes: the mesa's testosterone.

Killdeer provide the schmaltz. The baby ones, that is. Put water in a mesa stock tank and just watch the killdeer assemble. Their chicks are dandelion seed fluff balls walking on toothpick legs, positively adorable.

The most disturbing stock pond inhabitants are guajolotes.

A guajalote, in Nahuatl, is a turkey. A guajolote, in our local idiom, is the newt stage of the tiger salamander. They run rampant in northern New Mexico ditches and lakes and sewage plants. Nobody around here cottons to guajolotes. They are voracious predators. They're *ugly*. In past summers my kids and I caught them at Bernardin Lake and kept the beasts in an aquarium on the kitchen table. We fed them grasshoppers at lunch. That was cruel and fascinating "fun." Guajolotes demolish grasshoppers with brutal efficiency, striking like snakes and ingesting their victims accordingly.

But how do they wind up in a temporary stock pond out on the mesa? I have never solved this riddle.

Vegetation created by the magic wand of water includes wild sunflowers. And nettles on the dam. And profusions of gramma grass and ring muhly and western wheat grass. Also prickly buffalo burr, wild milkweed, Russian thistle, and even a few stalks of scarlet gilia. Winter fat flourishes, and rabbitbrush blossoms golden, exuding a skunklike odor.

Monarch butterflies are attracted by the milkweed. There are always hera moths and darning needles and dragonflies and honeybees. I recall a brief explosion of ladybugs. And I have found minuscule Day-Glo pink water mites shining in the mud.

In a wet season you can always count on hummingbirds. Seven years ago a billion cicadas were born. But I doubt water had much to do with them. They occupied every sage bush growing within ten square miles. The ground was pockmarked with their exit holes. They made a nonstop racket for two weeks, then disappeared.

In good years a pond might hold water in September or October. If so, it becomes a powerful magnet to migrating birds. Mourning doves fly in at dusk and walk about on the damp shore, daintily sipping water. They are timid and blend with the landscape, almost invisible.

Avocets come specifically to fatten up. They are thin-legged birds with long upturned bills who work together in shallow water, three or four abreast, heads bowed and bills swinging back and forth like pendulums, stirring free the food with metronomic persistence. They rarely glance at me.

Once at a pond I flushed an ibis, a weird creature flapping off like a pterodactyl. I have jumped many small ducks: bufflehead, goldeneye, teal. If I sit down quickly and don't move, they'll fly in a circle around me once, twice, then set their wings and return to the water, gliding in a fluid line out of the sky down to a graceful landing.

Phalaropes appear also, nervously quartering the shrinking pond with bobbing heads, spinning in circles to stir up food. They never quit: back and forth, hither and yon, swimming . . . *swimming*. Like all other eating machines that abound in this sudden water, they are so full of energy. They *never* sit still.

One evening I found sharp little hoofprints near the water. The only explanation? There'd been antelopes in the arroyo.

Everything flourishes quickly at a stock pond, where all life is a race against time. Overnight the pollywogs lose their tails, crawl free of the water, disappear back into the earth. Each day the pond's surface area diminishes. The bats and nighthawks and swallows hunt faster. The guajolotes thrash about. Coyote paw prints at water's edge double and triple. Fairy shrimp and clam shrimp grow more frenetic in their zipping as the water races to dry up. Once there was a pond here; now there is a puddle. The skies stay blue, relentlessly azure. And the wind never rests for a minute.

Soon the puddle is no larger than my kitchen. The rains have ended; the sky remains desperately clear. Sunflowers dry up and wither. Grasses crackle underfoot. Mud splits open into chips and peels backward. Russian thistles become tumbleweeds. Wind blows ring muhly grass stems into a golden halo around the stock pond shore.

The wind sucks up the water, giving no mercy. The sun shines blindingly, killing every plant rising from the soil. There are no shadows to hide in. Dying now becomes an urgent business with the water drying up.

I want to cry, "Stop!" but I keep my mouth shut. Respect for nature is a commandment with me. What's "heartless" is uniquely human; what's impervious is strictly natural. I believe this death is wonderful.

Next thing you know, the swallows are gone. And no more bats, nighthawks, mourning doves, or killdeer. A duck wouldn't land in this fetid splash of goo, let alone an ibis. Dragonflies head for greener pastures.

I can still take a picture of clouds reflected in my postage stamp of water . . . but a day later it's over in the wink of an eye.

A sluggish guajolote tries to wedge itself into a damp crack in the bottom of the dry pond. But to no avail—the thing will die. Gnatlike bugs are flitting around its skin, preparing to feast. A nearby cluster of clam shrimp shells is glaring in the sun, all emptied out inside.

On the dam the nettles bake and turn brown. Wind erases footprints in dust the way it never could obliterate the tracks in mud. The grasshoppers are gone. So too the ladybugs and robber flies. I blinked and everything went to seed and only the sage remains. A landscape drab and dull, without fluttering beasts or cricket music at night. The air grows colder, sharp and dry.

Geese fly by overhead . . . and sandhill cranes. But there's no water anymore, and nothing *but* water could call them down to earth.

In the end my stock ponds lie barren, empty, quiet. I visit a final time and sit on the dam as wind ruffles my hair. An entire universe has evaporated, a community disbanded and traveled elsewhere. I know seeds and fairy shrimp ephippiums lie in the dry dirt and thousands of toads are hibernating under the sage. But it's certainly a dreary landscape now that the water's gone.

I enjoy the mesa in any incarnation. Yet what most gives my heart a lift is the startling intensity of aliveness when water gathers briefly in the desert.

Water is the one true power and glory that defines our universe of life. The heavens may twinkle with vast fires of exploding hydrogen, and the rocks on Jupiter may hold within their dark hearts the secrets to gravity and time, but—

But water gave rise to the only living web we'll ever know, and water created my active imagination. Consciousness and soul owe their incredible being to every drop of moisture that ever fell from a cloud and awakened a spadefoot toad, called forth a mosquito, or birthed a dragonfly.

Written in 1996 for a proposed photo-essay, currently unpublished. Portions appeared in New Mexico Magazine, *July 1992.*

Trout Up the Gazot

Little did I and my Philadelphia friend Mike Kimmel know what lay in store for us when we set out one bright summer afternoon last year on a three-day pack trip to the Latir Lake high country of northern Taos County, right on the Colorado border. Armed with a few raisins, a bag of stale granola, a bottle of whiskey, and a couple of Shakespeare Wonderods, we planned to survive in the wilderness on our wits and fishing expertise alone.

Though we might have been described as total neophytes at alpine angling, we were positively brimming over with confidence and chutzpah.

We began auspiciously . . . by striking out at Cabresto Lake just above Questa. In three hours we caught a single four-inch-long rainbow trout. We blessed the tyke and wrapped it in fine Irish linen, then hiked four miles up to a campsite a few hundred yards below Heart Lake (which is a gorgeous pond at nearly twelve thousand feet). There we fried the fish and ravenously nibbled on it, then relaxed for a long spell, contented and happy, just Mike and me thinking about Hemingway, "The Big Two-Hearted River," and that bottle of old J.D.

At the crack of dawn we tramped up a pine-needle-strewn path toward our first rendezvous with high country cutthroat. At stake?—breakfast, of course, and perhaps the rest of our trip. We were Anxious and Jittery as we crept, hunched over and nearly breathless, across that last long cornflower meadow leading to Heart Lake.

In both our minds loomed the ugly specter of Defeat . . . Utter Rout . . . Zero Trout. If we couldn't catch fish, what were we going to survive on in the desolate alpine tundra for three days—grubs? Dandelions? Stale granola?

I closed my eyes momentarily and hallucinated a gigantic tin of Spam.

Then we poked our heads cautiously over the Heart Lake Dam. The pond was quiet; streams of mist curled slowly, almost menacingly across the water. Nothing else stirred. In the remote mountain saddles above us patches of snow gleamed mysteriously. A marmot whistled—

On our bellies (so as not to spook the trout) we slithered forward into position. With an infinitely delicate flick of my wrist I cast into some nearby reeds. Gritting his teeth in determination, my pal fired his lure into more open water. My fly and his spinner touched down at the same instant and, *"I got one!"* we both cried simultaneously, excitedly horsing to shore a couple of nine-inch beauties.

Wow.

We cast again. This time I had a fish on my fly *before* it hit the water. *"I got another one too!"* Mike shrieked enthusiastically.

Both of us stood up, giddily throwing caution to the winds. And in thirty seconds we had creeled four ten-inch cutthroats that we subsequently ate before 7 A.M.

After breakfast, to while away the morn, we made book on the cast-catch ratio at Heart Lake, which turned out to be one fish hooked for every cast. In short order we threw back fifty skinny trout, then took a breather.

Whew.

Next, trying to make it sporty, we flipped in a bare hook with a buttercup stuck on the barb, and the fish demolished that the way Amazonian piranhas attack crippled, bleeding tapirs.

I popped the head off a stem of timothy grass and they gobbled it while the lure was still six inches above the surface of the water.

An elephant falling into the lake they probably would have stripped to bare bones in less than a minute.

It would have required enormous skill, patience, and preparation *not* to catch a trout.

Mike sat down, shaking his pitching arm to loosen out the kinks while flexing his cramped fingers. The one thing we'd forgotten to bring was a large tube of Ben-Gay or Sloan's liniment.

After disassembling our rods and packing up, we started a short hike over the mountains to the magical Latir Lakes we'd heard so much about. I hadn't brought a map, but I told Mike, "Don't worry, it's a piece of cake, everybody said we can't miss 'em. They're only a half mile away."

Six hours later, utterly exhausted, petulant, and filthy from bushwhacking through impenetrable forests and impossible stretches of aspen blowdown, we reached the Spam-and-Dr.-Pepper-can-littered shore of Little Baldy Blue Lake, a modest puddle only seven miles off our course. Cursing blackly, Mike guzzled a third of the Jack Daniels and then cast into the crystal clear water: *Bam! Whack! Crunch!*

Supper caught, we ate. Then we played a game: Who could catch and release the most fish in nine minutes? I landed and returned fourteen, but Mike won handily with twenty.

Come the dark, we lay side by side in our sleeping bags, lulled by the sparkling firmament. Was that a bear who snuffled across the tiny lake? Neither of us slept a wink.

Next day we continued taking wrong turns. I led us downhill five miles in order to walk back up seven miles to the Latirs. When we finally achieved Lake 7, Mike glowered at me dully from out of his bloodshot eyes and spat the name he would call me for the next four weeks—"Wrong-side-of-the-mountain Nichols!" Then he keeled over backward in a dead faint.

Well, what did I expect? He was just a half-pint sea-level Philly kid who'd tramped more than twenty miles (most of them *up*) at 11,500 feet in two days.

Come morning, we climbed a picturesque cliff to Lake 6, caught a few twelve and thirteen inchers simply to keep our hands in, and then sat down, marveling at the plethora of cutthroats dimpling so often it seemed hail was pelting the water. Fire a bullet into that turbulence and you were bound to kill at least a half dozen adolescent fish.

The pine trees were cluttered with noisy jays. We tippled a few more spirits and munched stale granola while chatting dreamily about life and literature. Soon clouds settled over the mountains and a wind rose, causing aspen leaves to shimmer blithely. And as the first refreshing drops splashed in our outstretched palms, we realized that life would probably never be as good as this again.

After a while we got up and left the Latirs and walked back to Cabresto Lake in the rain.

First published in a slightly different version in Southwest Magazine, *Albuquerque, November 1972.*

Part Two

Down in Guatemala

Reies Tijerina, Española, NM, October 1971.

When I visited Guatemala in the spring of 1964 I was twenty-three and that country changed my life and my writing career. Put simply, I was "politicized." Polemics entered my literature and have remained there ever since. If it weren't for Guatemala, I never would have come to New Mexico.

I was drawn here in part by the deeds of Reies Tijerina, a fiery organizer of the 1960s. His Alianza Federal de los Pueblos Libres demanded justice for Chicano people and a return to them of their original land grants held in private hands or by the U.S. Forest Service. Following an armed courthouse raid (in June 1967) at Tierra Amarilla, two hours west of Taos, Tijerina was arrested and jailed in federal prison for over two years.

The essay "Down in Guatemala" is clumsily written, one of my first attempts at political commentary. After Guatemala, I never felt comfortable or safe again. Most people on earth live in fear of hunger, sudden disruptions to their lives, lack of justice. These stories touch on all that.

Down in Guatemala

A piece of frayed rope separates inland Guatemala from Mexico. Exactly underneath this rope the Mexican section of the Pan American highway ends and the Guatemalan section begins. The Mexican road is paved; the Guatemalan section is dirt—rubble, you might call it. It is very hot there in March; everything is dusty because the rainy season has not quite begun. On either side of the rope are two customs shacks, and on the Mexican side there is a thatched sunshade over the corpse of a restaurant. A few Mexican and Guatemalan petty officials preside fussily over the details of passports and luggage.

Two years ago I descended from a Mexican bus and walked up to that rope. On the other side a yellow school bus built by Germans in 1934 waited to take me to Guatemala City. It had two flat tires and an Indian mechanic sat on the ground, sipping a soft drink, looking at them. I went through customs, ducked under the rope, and chose myself a seat.

Three hours later our bus took off carrying seven passengers and a mustachioed guard with a .38 revolver stuck in his belt. We went about three hundred yards up a rise, turned a corner, got another flat, and coasted downhill to a garage, the first and last one until Huehuetenango.

The Indian boy fixed the tire, and when again we started up we were on the road for good, rattling and banging at breakneck speed along this skinny travesty of a "highway" strewn with boulders.

When Indians walking beside animals appeared in the middle of our path, the driver leaned on his horn and accelerated. Dust choked us as we careened along, passing many crosses hung with flowers that said, *Here died the family so-and-so, whose car* . . . Only when we were climbing was there relative peace and no fear of immediate doom. We rose at a crawl and the sun sank slowly. Deep in one ravine I saw natives bathing in a river. Clutched to the hillsides were plowed fields, symmetrical and Stone Age, fierce and pathetic, but above all beautiful.

I had expected jungles and butterflies in Guatemala, and for brief seconds there was all of that. But for long hours it was nothing but dust and donkeys and chickens and people scrambling to keep from being flattened by our yellow heap.

As we drew nearer to Huehuetenango the bus frequently stopped to pick up Indians. A woman sat down beside me, her baby in a sling round her shoulder, and I spoke with her in Spanish, which is the national language of her country. She smiled shyly and giggled, muttering a reply I did not understand. Then she continued in a Spanish that consisted of perhaps ten words, plus *sí* and *no*. Later I learned that most Indians, who constitute three-fourths of the country's population, speak Spanish poorly or not at all.

I entered Guatemala as few people do—on a bus—and I stayed in the country for one month. I learned a few things, among them how to barter, because nothing in the markets has a fixed price and you fight for what you get. One day I returned jubilantly to the apartment where I was staying and bragged to my friend's maid that I had purchased a dozen carnations for only fifty cents. I had worked the seller down to that ridiculous price from the original one she had suggested—two dollars. The maid was properly incredulous: "But you should only have paid *three cents!*" Afterward, I asked my friend how much he paid that woman, who cleaned the four-room apartment, scrubbing the floor with rags and brushes. She also did all the cooking we wanted, did the laundry, and worked steadily from 9 A.M. to 5 P.M. twice a week. My friend said he gave her one dollar a day.

That is the Guatemalan economy, where the average Indian earns as little as ten cents a day, yet a pair of shoes would cost him what they would cost in New York. Hence shoes in Guatemala have come to denote a difference in class: If you have them, you are middle class; if you don't have them, you are poor. Many people in the capital city don't have them, and almost all the Indians in the countryside go barefoot.

The citizens of this poverty-stricken nation live with vultures. I remember a street in Chichicastenango where a dead dog lay and some fifty of the huge birds hopped and clucked over the carcass, their wings rattling like bones. Behind them drunken Indians in town for market day snoozed in doorways or lay on the sidewalks, their goods sold, their heads obliterated by cheap Indita liquor.

There are also human vultures to be found in the Ladino ruling class, epitomized by the last president, who sent millions of dollars from the country, then took a powder himself. The Ladinos drive peasants in open trucks down to the coast to pick bananas for virtual slave wages. Ladinos own shoes and farms and buy food and televisions in special markets and pay United States prices for all their goods . . . and speak impeccable Spanish.

But there are stirrings in Guatemala. Several nights before I left, a jeep full of angry men with machine guns drove by a bus stop one block from where I slept and fired at a few small-time officials waiting for an uptown conveyance. My favorite bar was situated just behind the bus stop, and next morning I counted twenty-one bullet holes in the whitewashed facade. Two men had died and a third was seriously wounded, and I figured it was time to leave Guatemala. I had dysentery, and I was tired of beggars and open sewers and poverty . . . always poverty and the constant fight for a price.

Once more I traveled by bus, going north. When I entered Mexico there was a rise in the standard of living hard to believe because I'd always pictured Mexico as poor. The major difference, I think, was that the Mexicans were a unified proud people, and their country was their own country. Whereas the Guatemalans were abjectly plodding along under the rule of a few rich people and a government that was the enemy.

But after a while, as Guatemala receded, Mexico became more destitute. The land in the north and along the west coast was arid and the towns were small and broke. During the last five hours of my trip I sat beside a man who was planning to shoot across the U.S. border illegally—a "wetback"—to work in California. Again and again he brought up his family, of which he was very proud. It consisted of fourteen brothers and sisters, and eleven were still alive and working.

When I reached Tijuana, night had fallen. The town was quiet. I ate a final Mexican supper, carted my bag through customs, and got on a Scenicruiser bound for San Diego. Behind me piled on about twenty American boys—tall, muscle-bound, crew-cut guys between the ages of eighteen and twenty-five—drunk as coots and heading back to the naval base at San Diego. They swore and pitched about the seats and cursed the bus driver, who handled them with bored professional hatred. They were dressed in plaid short-sleeved shirts, khakis, white socks, and loafers. One of them started barfing. The others spoke only in obscenities—in fact, their vocabularies were more limited than that of the Indian woman who'd sat beside me as I entered Guatemala.

Once under way our tires hummed on the freeway and there wasn't a jounce in miles. With incredible speed we moved toward our destination.

Nobody ragged or dirty sat on the bus. Maybe they had a few hundred newly acquired crabs or an infant case of the clap, but otherwise the passengers on that Scenicruiser were just very drunk . . . and very clean.

In the darkness I thought of Guatemala and the vultures and the machine-gun holes and the open cesspools and the lack of shoes. What a contrast to these boys, who were as representative a product of our culture as anything else. But eventually I sat back, thinking, *To hell with it,* because who's to say which poverty is worse? And how do you measure corruption, anyway?

In 1966 I wrote a column (as an alumnus) for my college newspaper, The Hamilton Spectator, *called "A Star and a Half." This one appeared on March 4, 1966.*

A Butterfly Bomb in Taos

Taos Plaza, Thursday, May 4, 1972

It's 9:45 on a sunny, cool spring morning, and the Plaza doesn't look much different from any other morning. The pigeon population is lined along the adobe rooftops, idly preening. At the east end of the square a few blanketed Indians are seated on a low adobe wall, smoking, waiting for the Pueblo taxi. Lilac trees are finally green after an erratic high country spring; a few evergreens are parched and dusty from lack of rain. I see no snow on the mountains beyond.

There's a difference to the Plaza this morning, however. A few gay balloon clusters are hanging along the portal eaves down at the west end. And, wearing a change apron and a purple Lions Club beret, local realtor Charles B. Brooks is in the street, hawking mops and brooms for the blind. On the tiny bandstand, which is actually the roof over the subterranean Taos Police Department headquarters, a local high school band called the Springtime Drifters is tuning up while KKIT announcer Ray Trent fiddles with knobs and dials on his electronic equipment, preparing to broadcast live, from the Plaza, this morning's special activities.

Today is a nationwide Emergency Moratorium Day to protest the air war in Vietnam. In Santa Fe an estimated 250 people are going to congregate in the Plaza to hear speakers decry the present conduct of the war. Among them will be La Gente barrio organizers, Attorney General David Norvell, United States House candidate Gene Gallegos, and *New Mexico Review* editor Jim Rowen.

In Denver, many demonstrators are going to stage a silent anti-war vigil around the New Customs House. And in Kent, Ohio, a hundred Vietnam veterans will lead Kent State University students in a mute parade protesting the war and memorializing the four students shot to death by the National Guard two years ago.

But even though War Resisters' League member Craig Simpson was in Taos less than a week ago with a slide show that detailed the horrors of laser-guided bombs and anti-personnel ordnance whose pellets are made out of plastic so they won't show up on X rays (making operations impossible), the air war is *not* foremost in the minds of Taoseños on this lovely spring morning.

Today is "Balloon Day" in Taos. It is the opening round of the "Shop Taos First" promotion. Any minute a plane is going to fly over town, releasing a thousand balloons, many of which will contain Free Gift Certificates for one dollar, five dollars, ten dollars. There will even be a certificate worth One Hundred Dollars (!!!) redeemable anytime between now and Saturday at the store of the participating merchants involved.

In fact, right this instant, at ten o'clock on the button, here comes a half-pint red-and-white plane streaking toward the Plaza. It's piloted by airport flight service manager Orren Ohlinger. Beside Orren is Rick Griffin, head of the Taos Merchants Association of the chamber of commerce, who's getting ready to give a thousand balloons the old heave-ho. Near them both is Nancy Stadler, *Taos News* art editor, right on top of the scoop.

Down below I'm standing by with my daughter, Tania, in tow alongside friends George and Jeri Track and their daughter Darlene and their granddaughter Pollen Shorty. All of us are casting jaundiced aspersions on the momentous Something-for-Nothing event about to occur. We gasp when a string of balloons is released from the plane, popping out in an awkward trickle, maybe thirty in all about the size of goat turds or colored fish eggs. Weighted with sand, they come twirling earthward slowly, growing bigger, some taking as long as thirty seconds to arrive. Green and pink and gold, they float past the outstretched hand of a hard-hatted worker atop Harvey Mudd's Sunshine Restaurant and Movie Theater. On the Plaza clusters of three to five people gather, arms upstretched, grabbing, jostling, pushing, laughing. Most of the balloons explode from being manhandled, spraying sand—but no certificates—onto the eager jostlers.

George Track and Darlene retrieve two balloons, but we can tell there's only sand inside.

"You bust 'em," Darlene says. Obligingly I stab them with my pen, leaving George and his daughter holding a couple of tiny rubber rags, their hands full of sand, and with no more belief in the Great American Dream of Get-Rich-Quick than they had when they entered the Plaza . . . or when they were born, for that matter.

No time for philosophizing, however, because here come ten more balloons from Orren Ohlinger's second pass overhead. While the Springtime Drifters leap into "Proud Mary," a blue globe falls between elm branches, its transparent shadow bobbing against the small war memorial that was recently beautified by an ugly chain-link fence to protect it from vandalism. The balloon continues toward a noisy group of five excited citizens with upstretched hands . . . only to get caught in a branch six feet above everyone's head.

I perform my civic duty for the day by chucking a piece of bark at the errant balloon, dislodging it, and the bauble bounces off eager fingertips to the ground, exploding when pounced upon.

Too bad—nothing but sand inside.

And that's all, folks. The balloon drop is over. I look at my watch. It took seven minutes.

But the Springtime Drifters are going strong, and in between their American and Mexican pop tunes Ray Trent is bopping around the roof of the police department, mike in hand, plugging Shop Taos First Week, rattling off the names of the merchants involved and looking for a winner. Twenty preschool kids from the Taos Pueblo are seated on the flagstones in front of the bandstand. Don Vigil, last month's COC Sales Person of the Month, an employee with Taos mayor Phil Cantu's furniture and hardware store, is kibitzing during his coffee break. Camped on a nearby bench with a friend is Ralph Suazo, an Indian sculptor who's pleased as Punch because he just sold a sculpture piece to a guy from Minnesota. Up on the bandstand Mario Pizii, ad manager for the *Taos News,* is photographing the crowd for the paper. And five cute ragamuffins hanging on to the eastern railing of the bandstand are gaping at the musicians.

Pretty soon the winners begin trickling in. Actually, Oliver Romero comes exploding onto the scene, grasping in his hot little hand the magic piece of paper worth a hundred dollars of goodies that all of us were hoping for.

"I'll let my wife do the picking," he blurts happily into the microphone. *"I called her up and she couldn't believe it!"*

But most winners are toting one-dollar certificates. Like a tiny bambino named Ralph, who found his prize over by the post office, good for a buck of eats from La Cocina Bar and Restaurant. Well, Ralph's not old enough to drink, and there's not much in the way of a meal you can obtain for a dollar at La Cocina. So Ray Trent says, "You can take your mother in and she'll buy you something real good to—"

Ralph glares at his certificate as if the picture on it is of Benedict Arnold or that Norwegian turncoat, Whosamadig Quisling.

Another winner is a boy named Sean Jenkinson, who bagged a one-dollar certificate for Gamble's Hardware. He stands proudly beside the mike while Ray Trent explains to him the catch-22 of Something-for-Nothing, American Style: "Sean, if you find a more expensive item you want, you can apply that certificate to the purchase price. . . ."

And so, ladies and gentlemen, in one paragraph or less:

THE SAGA OF SEAN JENKINSON'S
RELENTLESS SEARCH FOR HAPPINESS ON
LESS THAN A BUCK!

"We went to Gamble's together," recounts his mother, Kathy Montgomery, a teacher at Da Nahazli school. "To begin with, there were only about four things in the store that cost less than a dollar. So the salesman kept going around suggesting more expensive things, like a punching bag, which I think cost nine or ten dollars, and Sean kept very reasonably trying to tell this man that those items cost more than a dollar. Whereupon the salesman said, 'Well, I bet your mom'll help you out.' I said, 'Oh no, you don't. . . .' And in the end Sean got an eighty-eight-cent battery-not-included stunt plane. I told him I thought we had some batteries at home that would make it work. . . ."

Shortly thereafter I drift from the Plaza to the nearby *Taos News* parking lot, and I'm standing in lazy, bright sunshine talking with the paper's editor, Tom Day, about an Operation Breakthrough meeting last night while my twenty-month-old daughter, Tania, plays in the dirt at our feet. A short distance away the drunks are gathered in the shade between Vigil's Liquors and the *News* office, swilling rotgut.

It's a peaceful morning and fun to chat—small town, warm and friendly. Jenny Vincent stops by, urging me to attend the local production of *Antigone,* in which her son has a starring role—the play has been sold out three nights hand running. No sooner does she leave than here's Eddie Barboa, state senator from Bernalillo County, dropping by to press the flesh with Tom Day and give us his card. Just before he departs he wants to know whose offspring Tania is, and when I say mine he reveals, "I lost a little girl last year, you know. Maybe you read about it in the Albuquerque papers? She was suffocated in the back of a camper trailer. . . ."

And he strides off, a broad-shouldered, rough-looking man in a mod striped suit on his way to a rally in Clovis.

Then I'm walking home, feeling good, with Tania on my shoulders sucking on an Eskimo Pie. My pockets are stuffed full of letters from friends that I picked up at the PO. Halfway out Ranchitos Road we cut under a fence and head across alfalfa fields toward our house. There are meadowlarks in our path, cattle, too, and a killdeer that runs away on the ground, feigning a broken wing. Piñon smoke is rising from the Upper Ranchitos church, behind which cottonwood trees are faintly leafing out, gauzy and golden.

Sixty yards from home I can tell our turkeys have spotted us because they're gobbling up a storm. Our greyhound breed Tubby, the fastest and most moronic dog in the West, comes galumphing crazily through fields and fences to meet us, scattering dozens of butterflies—

Suddenly things slow down and the sunshine grows hot and bright as the day freezes for a second. It becomes strange and awkward and threatening as I remember back to Craig Simpson's slide show and a picture of a tiny bomb—made by Honeywell Corporation—that floats on the wind like a leaf. The Vietnamese call it a Butterfly Bomb because it looks so much like a butterfly that children have actually chased after it and caught it, only to have their fingers blown off.

That's all the freeze is, though, just a momentary stutter in an otherwise smooth and cheerful morning, one of those brief but scary little tics that keep popping out of nowhere all the time to bug me. Maybe today it's from a slight twinge of conscience, or perhaps the result of an insight into the upcoming plans of Richard Nixon. Then again, it may have been caused by the actual infinitely faint concussion and shock waves traveling across the seas from an explosive dropped somewhere, onto someone, in Vietnam.

When I settled in Taos, I began to write articles for The New Mexico Review, *an investigative journal. The work was voluntary but invaluable to me. This is from June 1972.*

The Wounded Deer

On the second weekend in November, I went fishing with my friend Sylvia Landfair and her daughter, Kendy. No clouds punctuated the cold blue sky. Snow lay on the ground, and bright sunshine made it an almost soporific day.

We drove a few miles up the Rio Grande del Rancho and parked on a dirt road beside a long meadow through which the small creek, only inches deep and rarely more than ten feet wide, meanders. Sylvia and Kendy started fishing upstream at the truck; I walked downstream several hundred yards. The water was clear and very cold. Crusts of ice scalloped the riffles; slim sandbars lay half buried in snow.

Though expecting to catch nothing, I promptly landed a small brown trout on a beige fly. With that, my interest pricked up and I began to concentrate, creeping stealthily along, casting carefully, making certain that I did not spook the river.

Occasionally I paused, glancing around, absorbing the wonderful serenity. No vehicles appeared on the nearby road. The world was silent and calm. I felt young, lighthearted, and happy to be alive.

Squatting in the river, my rump almost touching icy water, I prepared to cast into a wide pool. Suddenly an enormous deer flowed from the willows into the exact spot where my fly was destined to alight. He halted and I froze. For an instant the six-point buck did not spot me. I had never before been that close to such a majestic wild animal.

My initial impression was of liquidly sculpted muscles on a pow- 41 erful frame. Then I realized something was wrong. The buck gasped a little—his broad chest heaved. His mouth hung open, the tongue trembling, and the eyes looked hurt.

The deer remained immobile and I held my breath. Agony radiated quietly from the animal as it panted. I could have reached forward with the fishing rod and touched his beautiful flank.

He glanced sideways and our eyes caught. Immediately, his body literally exploded. In a garish spray of water, he bolted out of the river and straight up a six-foot embankment onto a ledge, then thundered frantically away in a jerky bounding run. His rear right leg had been snapped in two a foot and a half above the hoof. Attached only by some skin and sinew, the hoof flapped uselessly as he fled. My stomach lurched.

Despite what must have been excruciating pain, the deer moved fast, leaping off the ledge back across the stream onto a sandbar. Then he flashed around a bend, disappearing behind a stand of russet-colored willows.

I was shocked and deeply flustered by that grotesque flight. Of course the buck was doomed. I climbed onto the ledge, where garish splashes of blood stained the snow. Following the deer's tracks, I jumped onto the sandbar, rounded the corner, and searched for the cripple. I even picked up a hefty stone, thinking, "He can't go far, he's losing too much blood. If I find him, I'll put that poor bastard out of his misery. . . ."

But I lost the trail. Apparently he had stayed in the water. Whether ahead or behind me I could not tell. So eventually I gave up the hunt and sat on a log, calming down. Nothing about the bright blue day had changed. A Steller's jay fluttered across the river, landing in a spruce tree.

When I resumed fishing, my heart wasn't in it. The image of that doomed animal moved up the creek ahead of me. I cast my line onto the clear water, but I had lost concentration—the fly alighted clumsily. The day remained sweet and remarkably peaceful.

I had advanced a hundred yards when all hell broke loose. High-powered rifles started blasting and out of sight up ahead Sylvia screamed. Echoing off steep hills on either side of the meadow the

shots sounded like huge bombs going off. The noise was so violent it seemed as if I had been struck by a bullet, and my body
shivered, expecting to be spun around, knocked flat. Excited men
hollered and kept pulling triggers. My first impulse was to hit the
dirt. But immediately I thought, "If I duck, they'll think I'm a deer
trying to hide and they'll kill me."

Up on the road, forty yards away, hunters in red vests and crimson caps sprinted toward me like soldiers charging a machine-gun
nest, firing helter-skelter, their high-powered blasts rocking my
body, almost physically bruising me. I dropped the fly rod and waved
my arms while screaming, *"Don't shoot! Don't shoot!"* But they continued to lay down a withering field of fire. Each report punched
my body like blows. I *knew* I would be hit. They were shooting
both in front of me and directly *at* me. Repeatedly I screamed,
"Don't shoot!" absolutely convinced that those crazed gunners intended to slaughter me. I had forgotten the wounded buck, which
was obviously fleeing back downriver in my direction.

As the saying goes, the barrage "seemed to last forever." Within
ten seconds I had made myself hoarse ordering them to cease and
desist. About five men galloped along the road, firing their guns.
Behind them came three trucks piloted by more beer-drinking
people. Miraculously, I wasn't hit. And I never saw the three-legged
deer as it bounded past behind me, unscathed by their fusillade.

Men scrambled down the embankment, humped by me, and
crossed the stream, shouting to each other. I was literally stupefied
by what had transpired. Then I realized a couple of men were in-
censed at *me*. "Why the hell aren't you wearing *red?*" one guy
snapped. "We could have shot you!" The implication was that they
should have popped me for not sporting a crimson outfit.

I yelled, "I'm wearing a white sweatshirt, for pete's sake! You
morons can't see a white sweatshirt?"

"If you aren't wearing red," growled a surly commando crunching along with a cocked .270, "you deserve to get shot."

Mouth agape, heart still thundering, I watched them canvass
trees on the far hillside, searching for the maimed buck. They
laughed, cracked jokes, and cursed and had a grand old time.

But I had no desire to stick around and hurriedly climbed up the slope to my truck. Other men on the road chuckled and gestured buffoonishly; they thought my predicament had been funny. Guns were everywhere. I started the Dodge and drove east to fetch Sylvia and Kendy, who limped toward me, ashen faced. The wounded deer had been a few yards behind them when the cannonade began.

We swung around, heading out, and as soon as we turned a corner the day grew serene again. Lucid sky, warm sunshine, silvery spruce trees. The tiny stream burbled nonchalantly westward. A chickadee called . . . a chipmunk skedaddled . . . and the ringing left our ears.

Only then, finally, and for the first time that day, did I remember it was hunting season.

The Dallas Times-Herald, 1982.

Those Are Skinny Horses

There's hardly any people in the landscape, driving down fast heading south in New Mexico along highways lined with brown beer bottles sending out bright glitters of sunlight—blipblipblip—roaring past this church and its Welcome signs and those Whiting Brothers billboards jittering between the Jesus Saves and the "I'm Gonna Be a Country-and-Western Hippie" songs on the radio. Watery mirages pulse on the road up ahead, and the wash of passing semis causes a static splash on the radio in the middle of a chorus. There's lavender-gray sagebrush stretching forever and yellowy grass hissing softly and cream-green liquid tarnished with oily rainbows in stagnant water holes. Windmills, too, and some Indians in a pickup with a TV in the back wrapped up in a beautiful woven blanket, and then a deserted ragtime rodeo grounds that's nothing but a two-bit corral full of tumbleweeds, and nearby crouches a bunch of ravens over a rabbit carcass. More tumbleweeds lope across the asphalt in the wind, and Finger-Lickin' Good Kentucky Fried drumsticks with Pepsi blares out of the speaker, and a one-room beauty salon squats in the middle of the hard-core desolation. Behind it is a bleached HELP IMPEACH EARL WARREN sign. Later it's Whoppa Burgers and Lotta Burgers, buzzards and flattened prairie dogs, edgy sparrow hawks on shiny telephone wires, and the abrupt ratcheting thump every time the car hits a cattle guard. Main Street in Lordsburg is lined with deserted store windows all quiet and dusty and displaying dozens of dead black beetles, flies, crickets, and even a few bumblebees. South of Lordsburg butterflies come fluffing over the windshield or they crash into the radiator, and what sage there is is colored a dusty beige, and pieces of exploded tires line the narrow shoulders like smashed crows. By the time the no-account town of Rodeo starts glinting ahead in the panorama, bright sulfur splotches of bugs litter the entire windshield.

Rodeo is a Shell sign, a train trestle with no tracks on it, a few crumbling adobe hovels, and dirt yards pocked with occasional tufts of colorless grass. Dead bushes have garbage hung up in them. An outhouse is horizontal. Chickens and snoozing dogs are visible among the rusting auto bodies up on blocks with no wheels and bullet holes through the windshields. There's no sign of human life in a dark bar-restaurant, a general store, a post office, and a few sagging yellow Santa Fe R.R. shacks full of nesting bluebirds. Huge shattered blown-over cottonwoods lie everywhere. The air is full of white cottonwood fluff too, and there's soft drifts of the stuff across the highway, drifts that swirl up and break apart every time a pickup blasts through at sixty miles an hour. Then weeds, more useless machinery, a few windmills, Hamm's Beer, the jagged Chiricuahua Mountains to the right . . . and finally the road beyond is lined with yellow flowers and cattle grazing.

Then in the silence of the one-gas-station-nothing-else ghost town of Apache a mourning dove is hooting.

The close-by Geronimo Surrender Monument is a high stone phallus at a roadside rest area sporting a stone latrine, a couple of picnic tables under a sunshade, Arizona Highway Department litter barrels, and a fence made of barbwire.

Near here, Geronimo, last Apache chieftain, and Nachite, with their followers, surrendered on Sept. 5th., 1886, to General Nelson A. Miles. U.S. Army lieutenant Chas. B. Gatewood, with Kieta and Martine, Apache scouts, risked their lives to enter the camp of the hostiles to present terms of surrender offered to them by Gen. Miles.

After two days Gatewood received the consent of Geronimo and Nachite to surrender.

The surrender of Geronimo in Skeleton Canyon on that historic day forever ended Indian warfare in the United States.

This memorial erected A.D. 1934 by the city of Douglas, with Federal C.W.A. Funds. U.S. Gov't Property.

As I cruise the lonely Arizona countryside, all thoughts are about "the end of Indian warfare in America." Corrugated tin and tarpaper shacks pop up and recede into endless miles of yucca, a few saguaro, and acres of oily puke green greasewood trees. Sometimes there are dead cars in corrals, as if people had once hoped they were horses, those cars, treating them like horses instead of machines, feeding them hay in place of gas, and firing bullets through their front hoods when the gas ran out and the tires went flat.

Between a bitter arroyo and some forlorn desert washes, exactly one million miles from God, Mom, and Apple Pie, stands a dilapidated TV repair shack, the whole front of it and both sides heaped to the roof with old picture tubes and other mechanical guts interspersed with snow-white deer antlers. Beside the front door, still throbbing, is a Coke machine. But nobody's stirring in any direction; no motion, no noise. Except from the car radio. "Here comes Mr. Green and his gang," babbles the disc jockey. "How's your gang, Green?" Followed by a pause for news: the bombs are falling, falling, *falling* in Vietnam.

And Chief Dan George, a seventy-two-year-old actor who achieved fame in the film Little Big Man, says, "It is hard for me to understand a culture that spends more on war and weapons than for education and welfare. Man must love all creations or he will love nothing."

Another song on another station: *"Olvidemos la mañana, porque nunca llegará."* Then: "Sally Was a Good Ol' Girl." And more golden goodies, Stonewall Jackson singing, "Help Stamp Out Loneliness." In between you better play Super Bingo, my friends. And don't forget to shop at Piggly Wiggly. And the road signs: Stock on the Highway. And: Dip. And: Flash Flood Area Next 10 Miles. Smashing through a cloud of small birds the instinct is to duck, expecting a thousand painful thumps against the windshield, but the car doesn't clobber a one.

Up in San Carlos, at the end of San Carlos Avenue, there's a goddamn jet fighter plane sitting atop a pole casting a shadow across the lives and the history of all Native American people everywhere. Who the hell thought of that?

A fifty-two-year-old chairman of the Miccosukee tribe in the Florida Everglades, Buffalo Tiger, says, "Now we have to obey the state hunting *regulations for deer and whatever game is left, and we're not allowed to hunt alligators at all. The white man kills off most of the game by killing the animals and draining the swamps. Then he says, 'You Indians can't hunt anymore.' When they took our hunting away, they made us slaves to jobs we had to take to support our families."* But: "We never were defeated," Buffalo Tiger adds, "so we have a kind of pride in us. We don't think we're better than anybody else, but we give people respect and we expect to get respect from them. We live with nature, not against it. . . ."*

Farther north, in Carrizo, buzzards cast their gliding shadows over a bunch of yellow and green shacks and a rattletrap orange school bus. Then it's on toward Show Low and Snowflake, White Cone and Keams Canyon and Tuba City. It's intimidating, that incredible flatness and unfathomable wideness and desolation and solitude. All open range, no fences, and no limit on human despair, either.

A man half asleep in a sand dune has been waiting all night for a ride. His face is scarred, he's wearing a colored jacket, he's going to White Cone. In the passenger seat he folds his arms and remains silent, except for once, as we're speeding past some gaunt animals, when he observes: "Those are skinny horses." That's his single comment for over a hundred miles, his explanation of life on earth. In due course he asks the car to stop and gets out in the middle of a god-awful barren landscape with no human sign, no roads, no structures, no nothing, and he begins walking across the rocky earth toward some savage gray hills a century and a half away.

At the Cochiti Pueblo of New Mexico, Governor Celestino Quintana announces that this year the pueblo will sell no dove-hunting licenses to outsiders. "I think we have enough of our own people to hunt the reservation," he says. "I think we don't want to ever again engage in allowing outsiders to hunt on our lands."

Here: a scarecrow in a patch of bedraggled cornstalks that aren't even knee-high to a grasshopper in a patch of sand in the middle of the shit-for-brains desert. There: a lone weird woman on the plain in a bright blue-and-red blanket, like a rainbow beach ball in that infinity of bleached burnt umber that flows into piles of red boulders that change into enormous soft gray-green piles of rock and sand that are like melted elephants and squirming in the heat.

Far to the east in Lawton, Oklahoma, the mother of two Indian boys in elementary school, Ms. Francis Wise, threatens to file suit to force her sons' school to drop its hair code so that her boys, who have shoulder-length hair, can attend classes. A youth coordinator of Oklahomans for Indian Opportunity, John Truedell, who was prevented from speaking at a high school's Indian Club because of his shoulder-length hair, backs Ms. Wise, saying that Indians have a right to long hair "because that is their heritage."

A half-dozen dust devils swirl across the land, threading among big chunks of anguished-looking russet rocks in a violent frozen jumble at the foot of vermilion cliffs.

And far to the south at an Inter-American Indian conference in Brazil, a delegate from the Santa Clara Pueblo of New Mexico, Dave Warren, tells the people: "Some communities are no longer willing to be studied by anthropologists."

Suddenly the road leaps up into the Kaibab Forest among the tall ponderosa pine with wind roaring like the ocean in overhead branches. Snow is everywhere on the ground, and it's absolutely wonderful.

Written between 1970 and 1972 for The New Mexico Review *but never published.*

A Man Like the Northern Weather

It is three o'clock on a sunny Sunday afternoon in Española, and after two years in jail Reies Lopez Tijerina is back speaking to the people of the north. Dressed in a conservative gray suit, he is standing in front of five hundred men, women, and children in the JFK Junior High School gymnasium, and pretty soon, if you ever doubted that the old magic was gone or had been muted by the prison years or by a tumor rumored to be in his throat, your doubts are going to be dispelled.

Tijerina has changed, some people say. Because he is on parole, because his hands are legally tied his message has become quieter and unclear. Others are puzzled by strains of what they consider to be a new mystic bent in the land grant leader's line. Across the mountains, at Highlands University in Las Vegas, a histrionic fight is developing over the amount of Tijerina's October 12 speaking fee. And there are even rumors that today he will be on the other end of a citizen's arrest for allegedly misusing or misdirecting land grant organization funds.

But in Española on a Sunday afternoon during the first week in October, it is Tijerina as the people have always known him.

In the beginning his voice is low-key. He jokes. He is lighthearted and happy. Noting all the brown faces in the audience, he assumes they want him to speak in Spanish. Nevertheless, he calls for a vote. Close to five hundred hands demand that he speak in their native language. Four people timidly ask for English. And so Reies addresses the people of the north in their own language, and with that there is a warm feeling in the gymnasium, a feeling that Tije-rina is really home.

Sadly, now, he tells of "taking part in your interests and dreams." Stepping back, enumerating how many poor Chicano men and women have died over the years, he speaks of having seen the people's tears; he remembers how the prayers of the poor, begging for justice, have been sounding day and night in the churches down through the years.

Whereupon all at once his voice explodes, his hands sweep out, up, down, his knees bend, and he is shouting about the land his people have lost since the war between the United States and Mex-ico, and he ends in a booming climax:

"One day the Treaty of Guadalupe Hidalgo will be as popular as the Constitution of the United States!"

And the crowd bursts into applause.

Tijerina becomes soft again, weaving words in and out. "On this planet, *hermanos,* gold and silver are difficult to find. It took them more than twenty-five hundred years to discover the atom and to convert it into energy. But what is difficult still to discover and personify and give life to is—"

And he shouts out the word suddenly, violently, catching every-one off guard: *"Justice!"*

Grimacing, shifting his hands to and from his pockets, he an-nounces triumphantly: "I want to discover the secrets of the Treaty of Guadalupe Hidalgo!"

Quiet again a moment later: "When I was in prison, I lost 765 days. Yet in another sense I didn't lose them at all. In fact, they were the greatest days of my life. I would never change them for the forty-three years of my life outside of prison. I have received letters from people who say, 'Mr. Tijerina, you are in prison for us; you are in prison for our language; you are in prison for our brav-ery and for our history; you are in prison for our pride. . . .' And, *mis hermanos,* I am thankful to have had that privilege!"

The voice dies down and for a moment he appears sly, vaguely contrite about his role in recent New Mexico history. But suddenly his right hand bangs the lectern two, three times to emphasize a point and then again, softly, quite softly, letting his words out on a string:

"Our land is a very poor land. Our people are very poor. Long ago we said, 'Come in,' to strangers. We offered them water, coffee. We opened our hearts and our arms—"

The arms spreading wide, encompassing the crowd, holding it a welcoming moment—

"And"—(banging the lectern so hard it makes people jump)—*"they left us with nothing!"*

With that he is abruptly relaxed, philosophical. "Well, God may take a while to do the job, but He never forgets. . . ."

Once more he is talking about the Treaty of Guadalupe Hidalgo, the document that ended the Mexican-American War in 1848 and theoretically guaranteed most descendants of Spanish land grants the rights to their communal lands. But those lands have been taken from them in one manner or another these past 123 years. Tijerina's hands fire up toward the ceiling, face twisting angrily, calling down the wrath of God on the robber barons who stole it all. Yet just at a moment when it seems the people will bolt up angrily from their seats, he glides off in another direction, settling the audience down a little, chuckling and telling a story that makes them laugh. And you think of the northern weather these past months: sunny, then suddenly raining, thunder and lightning, and a minute later there's a tranquil pink horizon, then hail and snow, and freezing temperatures followed by a profound and brilliant lightness.

"I want the schools to teach the history of what happened between 1860 and the 1920s," he says, referring to the manner in which Chicano communal lands were ripped off or lost to rigged taxes or to the notorious Santa Fe Ring. And, drawing guffaws from even this bitter pill, he jokes that in exchange for the land they "gave us powdered milk. If you put hot water in it, it isn't as cold, but it sure isn't justice."

Next it is, "*Hermanos,* we are going to document our culture. We are going to bring together letters and books and the old laws. Many of us don't know where we ourselves, and our history, came from. This is because of a conspiracy." And only if the people become interested in the land grant documents and books, the laws and cultural history of La Raza, can they "get rid of the chains of this conspiracy!"

His hands form circles; they reach out and tenderly draw in the people. "We must revolutionize; we must popularize justice," he tells them, going on to explain: "Justice is one thing; written law is another thing. You can have sex without love, and you can have written law without having justice. . . ."

Shoulders hunched, he works on the metaphor, developing it, joining his powerful hands together in front of his face, graphically interlocking his fingers to demonstrate first conjugal love and then a right union of justice and the written law. He pulls his unbuttoned coat together, lets it fall open, seems to sink back momentarily, halfway dazed, and then bursts joyously at the crowd, loudly proclaiming that he has established an institute for the research and study of justice.

"*Hermanos,* we are going to *document* our culture! There are some who investigate the stars and the planets, there are others who probe the seas, but I dedicate my time to *the investigation of justice!*"

And the people are with him. They are loud in their approval at the end of his speech, and then they make a long line in order to pass by Reies and shake his hand and say a few words with him. Then everyone is out in the glaring Española sunshine, with the certain knowledge that a force that has been absent from New Mexico for these past two years has indeed returned.

The New Mexico Review, *November 1971.*

Part Three
Some Thoughts on Humiliation

Between 1965 and 1973 I had a hard time laughing. I was pissed off, deeply involved in the anti-war movement and other struggles, and shell-shocked by North American venality at home and abroad. However, somewhere toward the end of that era I realized I could catch more flies with honey than with vinegar.

Truth is, if you can't laugh, you'll never survive the daily holocaust. The essays in this section aren't all set in New Mexico, but in spirit they certainly relate to the area and its problems.

The Six Greatest Museums in the West

One

Last year I spent a really delightful afternoon at the William F. Cody Buffalo Extinction Museum in Tarp, Wyoming, at the foot of the Wind River Range. The impressive old building that houses the displays was originally financed and erected by the local chapter of the Daughters of the Eastern Star. Today the museum is maintained in a financially stable condition by the hard-earned dollars of patriotic American citizens who choose to check the William F. Cody box on their 1040 tax returns.

The building—set in the picturesque grasslands of Wyoming with a backdrop that includes beautiful, snow-capped mountains year-round—is as large as an enormous manufacturing warehouse in, say, northern New Jersey or maybe at the Brooklyn Shipyards. The displays inside this building are directly to the point.

A tastefully illustrated circular given to you at the door by Verna Smallwood (the museum's curator for fifty-three years) explains that her museum contains the skulls and skeletons of eight hundred thousand buffalo shot by William F. Cody (aka "Buffalo Bill") between March 1871 and July 1872. And that's all there is in room after room, huge heaps and piles and stacks of buffalo bones, massive, calciferous, and magnificent. A narrow path leads through the ossuary, and walking it is like navigating through a blinding white maze. The building is almost a half mile long and thirty yards wide. At the exit door is a small rack with postcards of starving Native Americans and pieces of literature for sale. I bought a copy of *Gung Ho* magazine and the Fortune 500 illustrated edition of Adam Smith's *The Wealth of Nations*.

Two

Another wonderful place to visit is the Bradbury Science Museum at the national laboratory in Los Alamos, New Mexico. I like to stand in the main exhibit room there, contemplating Fat Man and Little Boy, thinking about what they did to the Japanese and what they have done to all of us since 1945. I ruminate on the history of physics, the story of Los Alamos, and the evolution of science and human values in the twentieth century.

My favorite museum demonstration is the chain reaction booth at Los Alamos. Bouncing Ping-Pong balls keep entering a clear plastic chamber at a frenetic pace until it seems as if the chamber will explode, spewing Ping-Pong balls all over the museum. I enjoy that little k-fuffle—it's a metaphor for my own life, which is full of ever accelerating demands and obligations that multiply incessantly and threaten to destroy me. Those hyperactive Ping-Pong balls are a perfect metaphor for the modern world, with technology going berserk, creating more cars and more air conditioners and more people and more wars until I suppose the entire atmosphere will explode . . . and that'll be that.

Three

The anticipation I felt for years whenever I thought of visiting the International Museum of the American White Man on the Sioux Reservation in Rosebud, South Dakota, was nothing compared to the ecstasy I experienced when finally I got there. I made a pilgrimage to Rosebud with my two kids on the Fourth of July, 1989.

This is definitely one of the nation's most respectful museums. Some of the dioramas are spookily realistic. Take, for example, the reproduction of the Keystone, New Jersey, Tastee-Freez, circa 1957. The flattop haircuts of teenagers, the Clearasil-camouflaged pimples on their freckled faces, even the details in their braces will bowl you over, for sure.

Another diorama features the stuffed bodies of a blond, blue-eyed man in a gray-flannel suit, his perky snub-nosed wife in a pretty shirtwaist dress, and their two spoiled children at a Sunday meal of pot roast, mashed potatoes, string beans, applesauce, and gravy with pasteurized milk on the side. I swear it is so realistic you can almost smell the gravy.

There are thousands of interesting artifacts in this museum. Coke bottles from the 1930s, a Maytag wringer washing machine, a football helmet, a Fruit Of The Loom jockstrap, several cans of Spam in pristine condition, and even a petrified loaf of Wonder bread.

More controversial are the two dozen shriveled Anglo scalps, allegedly collected at the Battle of the Little Big Horn. These scalps have created a controversy (in recent years) that you may have read about in your newspapers. Descendants of George Armstrong Custer, Charley Reynolds, and other white people killed during the battle have petitioned the courts for the return of the scalps so that they can receive proper burial. The museum's trustees are sensitive to this problem. They have entered negotiations in good faith, and rumor has it the issue will soon be resolved to the satisfaction of all parties concerned.

Four

The National Pesticide Museum in Cornell, Idaho, is pretty wild. The two front rooms are full of dead bugs: dead corn weevils, dead boll weevils, dead sorghum mites, dead cutworm moths, dead turnip borers, dead carrot ants, dead parsnip aphids, dead centipedes, dead grasshoppers, dead locusts, dead claw beetles, dead fruit flies, dead banana spiders, dead tomato worms, dead squash bugs, dead sucker flies, dead horseflies, dead blowflies, dead pop flies, et cetera.

The next two rooms are full of dead birds: dead robins, dead ravens, dead chickadees, dead song sparrows, dead grosbeaks, dead warblers, dead hawks, dead ospreys, dead condors, dead nuthatches, dead woodpeckers, dead vireos, dead mallards, dead wood ducks, dead geese, dead wrens, dead grackles, dead cowbirds, dead swallows, and so forth.

The last two rooms are full of dead people. Dead white people, dead brown people, dead pink people, dead red people, dead green people, dead black people, dead corn farmers, dead real estate agents, dead tractor salesmen, dead housewives, dead children, dead grandmothers, and even a couple of dead molecular physicists from the Dow Chemical Company.

It's all modestly done and not as morbid as you might think. The curator, Thaddeus Columbine, is always happy to answer questions. And his white frame farmhouse just across from the museum has recently been converted into a three-star bed-and-breakfast.

Five

If you really want a hit of "morbid," please visit the National Tourist Museum in Dalhart, Texas. I went there in 1992 and had a ball. The building is made out of aluminum siding, fiberglass-asbestos panels, and Velcro molding. The museum's centerpiece is the only known specimen of the Giant Sperm Winnebago, which stretches over 190 feet long and in its heyday got minus thirty miles to the gallon. Another display in this oddball joint features the matching his-and-hers, blue-and-pink jumpsuits worn by Mr. and Mrs. Clyde Rumple of Soybean, Oklahoma, who are reputed to have eaten meat loaf, wax beans, and peanut brittle at every Stuckey's in America.

One whole wing of the museum is full of interesting artifacts discarded by flocks of transients on this nation's interstates, including two tons of soiled Huggies, one ton of plastic foam McDonald's containers, and five thousand pounds of crank bait for bass, also a fair gaggle of mangled dirt bikes.

Six

The Sandhill Crane Museum in South Platte, Nebraska, is about as special as a museum ever gets. It boasts over a dozen lifelike dioramas of migrating cranes eating corn in the surrounding fields or doing their special mating dance on the sandbars in the nearby river. The front lobby features three mechanical dancing cranes the kiddies can ride on if you drop a quarter into the slot. And the cafeteria serves an imitation craneburger, made from a mixture of soybeans and rabbit meat.

If you go there on April 5, during the annual celebration of the Dance of the Cranes, you can witness an event, sponsored by the museum, that has to be one of the great tourist attractions of the American West, guaranteed. On the evening of the fifth, and repeated again on the morning of the sixth, is a reenactment of the mating dance of the cranes. Local Friars, Lions, and JCs dress up in real crane skins they shot from the skies years ago, and, down on the last remaining sandbar in the river, they perform the fabled dance.

All dancers are also members of Lodge 72 of the Legal Order of Sandhill Cranes, and they pay particular attention to authenticity. So much so that it is easy for the observer to forget that *real* cranes are extinct, and it's actually human beings under all those feathers.

In Conclusion

To my way of thinking, these are the six greatest museums in the West.

Adapted from a keynote speech to The Mountain-Plains Museum Association in Albuquerque, New Mexico, autumn 1991. Reprinted in El Palacio *(the magazine of the Museum of New Mexico), spring 1992. This is a seriously abridged version.*

Rafting? Schmafting: *I Want My River Back!*

The last thing I promised my dying mother I never would do was go down the Wild River section of the Rio Grande Gorge in Taos County in a raft. Why? Because I am a fly-fishing enthusiast, and there is about as much good blood between denizens of this specialized trade and river rats as there used to be love in the Old West between cattlemen and sheepherders.

And besides, *my* gorge is a deserted, nearly inaccessible, and luminous canyon devoid of all humans except me, the solitary angler. In the autumn I descend a dozen secret *bajadas* to fish for trout in an ambiance that is shimmering and prehistoric. I stop often, holding my breath, awed as I absorb the beautiful loneliness. And I always know I am the first human intruder in that spot for centuries.

Nevertheless, life is convoluted and full of contradictions. In my case, love made me do it, pure and simple. I hate to admit it, but a trusted friend lured me onto the wild river in a large rubber raft.

Her name? . . . Betty Read. Her métier?—beagle, mouthpiece, law books . . . specializing in domestic relations. Her disarmingly simple come-on? "Wouldn't it be fun to take a raft trip down the Rio Grande?" Lightly she touched my shoulder, causing my heart to flip-flop.

"Isn't it dangerous?" I waffled.

"It's exciting," she replied.

"You're not scared?"

"I'm scared, but it'll be *exciting*," she insisted.

Not long afterward I spied a guy named Seaver Jones seated at a smoky bar in Taos. The Ragtime Kid was playing a song, so nobody occupied the neighboring stool. I flopped down like a fool beside this large and boisterous man, downing some potent amber concoction in swift neat gulps. "Seaver," I whispered, "I know you are a river runner. Tell me all about floating the gorge from Arroyo Hondo to Pilar. . . ."

For an hour that born-again evangelical water sprite calmed my fears and pricked my interest indeed. He spoke of Canada geese and their delicate goslings, of once domestic goats running wild among the boulders, of bald eagles cruising overhead, and of the thrill to be had in Powerline Rapids. When at last I skulked stealthily from that murky bucket of blood, I was a believer. Posthaste I telephoned some fellow travelers in Denver, and, after I painted a glowing picture, Rod and Mari and Wayne and Debbie agreed to join Betty and me for this once-in-a-lifetime escapade.

And at 8 A.M. on Memorial Day, 1983, with our hearts in our throats, our cameras in hand, and a serene early morning sun pulsing warmly overhead, the six of us found ourselves gathered in the Tennis Ranch parking lot north of Taos, nervously awaiting our destiny in the shape of a big old ramshackle yellow school bus.

Far Flung Adventures had a reputation for being one of the best companies on the river in Taos. I had chosen it for that reason, and also because they advertised an early launch time. I wanted to float in morning purity, long before other rafters had polluted the Rio's precious bodily fluids. "Go early," Seaver Jones had intoned, "and you will see the Canada geese and their goslings. You might spy the wild goats among the rocks. And perhaps you'll even catch a glimpse of a bald eagle."

Right on time, here came the lumbering bus (full of jabbering recreators) loaded on top with four rafts and rowing frames and plenty more erudite paraphernalia.

"Howdy," the head honcho, Steve Harris, said.

Jovially masking our queasiness, we hopped on board. It was good to feel safe in the hands of an expert like Steve, a lanky and leathery man, brown all over, and right friendly to boot. He had an aura of being in control: professional, good-humored, no nonsense.

Brimming with overconfidence, then, our conveyance rumbled off from the Tennis Ranch parking lot.

Three miles south of Arroyo Hondo a howitzer shell clobbered us. The bus shuddered, rattled, and swerved. A rubber raft spun off the top and bounced in the roadway. Another raft flip-flopped upside down, slamming into the western windows, and dangled there. A steel rowing rack clattered to the pavement as we skidded onto the shoulder. Somebody connected to Far Flung Adventures muttered with alarm: "Holy cow, *this* never happened before."

Our guides worked feverishly to change the blown-out tire and clear dented detritus off the highway. They clambered over the bus, jockeying clumsy rafts back into position, lashing them down tightly. Meanwhile dozens of buses, trailers, RVs, pickups and assorted four-wheelers chugged by us full of jeering tourists and hooting oarsmen from other outfits.

But quickly we hit the road again. And as we descended the winding dirt path toward the John Dunn bridge west of Arroyo Hondo, I clasped Betty's hand tightly, worried about the danger involved. What about the terrible Ski Jump rapids and the hellacious Powerline maelstrom? Maybe our venture was foolhardy, doomed, snakebit. Perhaps we should cancel out at the last minute and—

Betty squeezed my sweaty fingers. "Don't worry, John Nichols; all is well."

On that cue, we turned a corner onto the bridge and entered a scene that I can only compare to the sacred Ganges at Varanasi in India at ritual burial time.

As our bus inched slowly backward down a side road west of the bridge toward the launching beach, I stared in horror at a riot of buses, Jeeps, RVs, trailers, motorcycles, and children. My God, *look at all those big adults, fat adults, half-dressed adults, apprehensive adults!* Twenty rubber rafts of various dimensions and colors were lined toe to toe along the shore. Swarms of tanned, healthy river rats in shorts, sandals, and yellow rubber boots were trying to act good-natured in this traffic jam, bumping into each other and jostling for room, obviously desperate to get on the water. Boys from the Bureau of Land Management, jaunty in government shirts and ironed shorts, scurried hither and yon, fretfully checking people in, casting aspersions, issuing veiled threats, and wondering how in hell things had come to such an impasse.

The guides hustled rafts off the tops of buses and began to pump them up, loading gear, tying down ammunition boxes for cameras, heaving in coolers of beer and sandwiches for lunch. Gas generators wheezed and coughed. Skinny and fat and perplexed and pink people were lined up twenty deep, waiting to use portable outhouses supplied by our friendly government agency in charge of the fiasco. Transistor radios played heavy metal music, country-and-western ballads, good old rock 'n' roll. Everybody was choking to death on the dust. One hyperactive little kid kept firing a toy machine gun.

Steve Harris wrestled a rowing frame onto our raft, secured it expertly, and slipped in the oars. In the background animated human beings wearing tank suits, Bermuda shorts, purple sweat suits, yellow diving suits, tattered blue jeans, cowboy hats and baseball hats and magenta bandannas took thousands of pictures of each other taking pictures of each other applying suntan lotion to each other. Offshore, a bunch of kayakers, sleek seals compared to us ungainly whales, slithered on the wide, passive river, warming up, doing rolls, spinning around, floating sideways, checking their gear, their muscles, their egos.

Rod and Wayne and Mari and Debbie went for a climb in the rocks to see if they could, just before departing, inadvertently step on a prickly pear cactus or brush their palms against a nasty cholla.

The plethora of kids carelessly prancing through the turbulent scene caused me to remark to myself: "You know, maybe this isn't as all-fired dangerous as I thought."

Betty wandered off a ways, lit up a Kent, then coolly surveyed the zany carnival scene. Finally, by way of comment, she said, "Huh."

Suddenly Steve Harris called, "Okay, let's go." In seconds we tumbled into the raft, pushed off, and were riverborne. My heart began racing again. I grabbed the hand straps and tensed to hold firm and weather the white water, screaming in excited frenzy as we plummeted through billows of angry waves just inches from certain death among jagged boulders.

Instead we began to float south with almost somnolent stateliness, a sensation about as exciting as snoozing on a water bed.

The river was high and muddy. In the bland blue sky the sun shone brightly. It was eighty degrees. And rafts similar to ours stretched bumper to bumper fore and aft as far as the eye could see, like a train of barges toting a corpulent and noisy cargo of Texas beef toward New Orleans.

"This is nothing," Steve said. "One Labor Day, I eddied up and there were so many boats on the river, I couldn't get back into line for an hour."

Rod, Mari, Wayne, Debbie, and Betty glared at me, The Organizer. I shrugged, pointing ashore: "Look at the geese." Sure enough, there they were, those fabled Canadian honkers and a couple of goslings, resting peacefully near the old Manby Hot Springs. They stared as we floated by.

"Throw 'em some peanuts," I heard a voice say. "Anybody got any peanuts?"

Apparently not. But the party that swirled laconically up on our starboard side had bags full of Cheez-It crackers, fried pork rinds, barbecue chips, and Doritos, which they were washing down with lite beer. The handsome guide at the oars called with cheerful sarcasm, "Hey, gang, aren't we having fun?"

We responded, "You bet . . . yessir . . . *wow!*"

My pulse really slowed down; my heart quit fibrillating. Betty Read, master of the subtle remark, observed, "I should have brought my bathing suit." Wayne hollered, *"Pass me back one of them brewskis, cowboy!"*

We opened the cans and drank a toast to Rod, who perched nervously on the gunwale of our Avon Pro. He was outfitted in a cute green rubber suit intended to protect him from the splashing water.

We drifted for five monumentally uneventful miles and then tragically ran out of beer. Our oarsman advised, "Keep your eyes open for beer cans. Sometimes they fall overboard. They look sort of like bubbles. If they're low in the water, grab 'em, because that means they're full of booze."

Steve Harris is an amiable guy. He talked about his life on rafts in the Big Bend of Texas; he outlined plans for an Alaska float later this year. Betty bummed cigarettes from Steve, and Wayne regaled us with tales of his truck-driving days for the Teamsters. Mari and I took pictures of other rafts and rafters taking pictures of us. Rod began to feel pretty stupid in his green rubber suit that was absorbing sunshine and drenching him in sweat.

I yawned. In fact, I could not stop yawning. An hour passed . . . and then another.

We scanned the shore for other rare fauna, but all that came into view were rafters eddied up, noshing cookies, drinking beer, burping, slopping on the suntan lotion, climbing rocks, masticating pensively, staring back at us.

"You know," I said, "this doesn't exactly feel like a wilderness experience to me."

As yet one more raft filled with tubby jovials consuming baloney and cheese and Schlitz malt liquor twirled lazily by us, Steve pointed upward: "Are those eagles?" We squinted and agreed that yup, those two minuscule blips soaring eight thousand feet above our heads were probably golden eagles.

Then *that* thrill was over and the day settled back on top of us like a bottle of liquid Valium.

"I bet there's a coyote around the bend," I joked. "Preening on the bank, checking out its coiffure in a mirror, begging for little cans of bean dip, slices of white bread, and Hershey bars."

We decided the rafting companies had chipped in to rent the wild geese we'd seen earlier. Pretty soon a couple of trained beavers in Lycra miniskirts would be doing a cancan dance on the beach while five dozen tourists filmed them. After that, a pet deer with scurvy might appear munching on Bunny bread wrappers. And a mangy raccoon, at the end of a tether, would pluck salami from our greasy fingertips, then gleefully smoke a cigarette.

Some clown started yodeling, *"Oh, bury me not on the lone prairie. . . ."*

Abruptly Steve warned, "We're approaching a rapids. Keep your eye on the right, and around that rock outcropping you'll see a nesting water ouzel."

Biff, bam, bumpety-bump, the raft squizzled into some white water. We woke up and searched for the "water ouzel nest" but found nothing. The rapids lasted two and a half seconds.

"That's *it?* That's a *rapids?*" Suddenly I yelled, *"I want my money back!"*

"Oh, there are better ones up ahead," Steve drawled. "You'll like Ski Jump."

But as we approached Ski Jump, I griped, "This isn't Ski Jump. This is the Big Trout Riffles south of Caballo Trail. Right here in low water there's a beautiful island of white stones in the middle of the river. I usually wade over to the island in water up to my thighs and fish the riffles on both sides. They're full of brown trout. Then south of the island there's a wonderful rock garden of fast-riffle water. I always hook a big one."

Today there was no island, no rock garden, no distinguishing features at all. Just the high muddy river boiling along carrying four dozen floating cocktail parties composed of obnoxious cultural imperialists wearing orange life jackets, Bermuda shorts, and yellow John Deere caps. Our raft heaved up, slewed sideways, bounced left, spun crazily, lunged and bucked twice, then skidded into smooth water again. We had just started to shout, "Eyeow!" when it was over.

Mari cried, "That's it? That's Ski Jump *rapids?*"

Steve explained that there are different classes of rapids, numbered one through six. What we had just come through was a

Class 3 rapids. We immediately demanded some Class 4, 5, and 6 rapids; we wanted some *action.* Steve said, "Well, there's Power-line still. But right now we're gonna dock the raft and eat."

We nosed in among a flotilla of lolling boats and toddled ashore like good children. They fed us baloney and cheese and salami sandwiches with imported mustard and mayonnaise, lettuce and tomatoes and sliced ham, apples and oranges and various juices and more beer. Then we lounged on the rocks with eighty other Joe Blows from Peoria ordering kayakers, "Do a roll, do a roll!" Usually they obliged, tipping over, then flipping upright again. They grinned as we clapped and cheered.

"Reminds me of the Colorado," Steve said. "Sometimes it gets real crowded. Often when we ran out of beer, we'd send the kayakers over to the big rafting camps and have them do rolls in the river for beers. The campers would cheer and toss in the cans, and they'd bring 'em back to us."

To Betty, I murmured, "This scene is so goofy and bizarre, it's downright campy." Betty glanced sideways, letting smoke trickle provocatively from her mouth, and, with just the hint of a sardonic smile, she whispered, "That's right, John Nichols."

A teensy cloud appeared in the bright blue sky. We munched on apples as Steve recounted a dream that a fellow guide, Del DuBois, had once had. Del was rowing a raftload of people down river. The gorge was quiet. All of a sudden he peeked into the water and blinked—what was *that?* For a ways he tracked a float-ing object and finally realized it was a Butterball turkey. Puzzled, he let it pass by and disappear downstream.

He had not progressed much farther, however, when—what was this? Another one? And sure enough, a big plump Butterball turkey twirled lazily past the tips of his dripping oars. Next a whole drove of the plucked birds bobbed into view and disappeared downstream. With that, Del realized the gobblers were prizes, re-leased by the government as rewards to the rafting companies that deigned to tackle this sleepy river. Trouble is, when he plucked them out of the water they were always a tad rotten.

At which point he woke up.

Another diminutive cloud shyly appeared and a faint breeze riffled the water as we clumped lethargically back into our raft. "What's this bailing bucket for?" I joshed. "In case somebody vomits from boredom?"

And off we sailed on the lazy currents, accompanied by dozens of other jocular rowdies who by now had a thorough buzz on. Violet-green swallows darted gracefully over the water. I grumbled dourly, "If I had a cane pole and some chicken gizzards soaked in vanilla extract, I'd start jigging for catfish."

Pretty soon we noticed some rafts had stopped along both shores and people were changing clothes, donning wet suits and other rain gear.

"What's that all about, Steve?"

"Oh, they're just preparing for Powerline."

The sky went black: BOOM! A stiff wind leaped upriver against us. The temperature dropped thirty degrees in five minutes. *Ouch.*

But we still felt pretty wiseapple. During our next scoot through mild white water, I stood up, snapping pictures. Wayne rode the back hump of the raft like a bull rider, grabbing a loose rope with one hand, his other appendage swinging free, while we screeched, *"Don't touch the bull with your left hand!"*

Then Powerline arrived. I had just begun to rise for another candid snapshot when we did a nosedive into an eight-foot-deep gulch. Betty lurched two feet into the air; I pitched across the bow as Rod toppled toward me, and we collided; I clobbered him on the head with my camera, knocking off his glasses, and we both swallowed a gallon of water and fell to our knees as the raft pitched riotously, slithered and bounced over a dozen mammoth boulders, and Wayne—none too soon—grabbed his loose rope with both hands, both knees, and, no doubt, both buttocks.

"Man overboard!" came the cry from a trailing raft.

"We got a swimmer," Steve Harris observed. "Let's haul him in quick. And bail your asses off, please."

Expertly, in the churning water, he waffled us sideways and

reached the swimmer; Wayne and Debbie hauled him over the side. The guy was exhilarated. Steve barked, "Come on, bail harder— I can hardly control the boat."

So I bailed, then Betty bailed while Rod fumbled in the water for his glasses. Nobody wisecracked about using the bucket for boredom vomit. The swimmer, a complete idiot, chortled, *"Whee!"* at every lunge and buckle. Wayne pitched forward, then lurched backward, then jerked sideways: "Yikes!"

Powerline endured only a moment, then we had to eddy up again. A teenage girl in another boat had broken her collarbone. She'd lost her grip in a whirlpool and slammed into an ammunition box full of cameras. Steve and Debbie (a doctor) leaped out . . . and they set her arm in a sling while I scrambled up and down the boulders, trying to get warm. The suddenly dark day had turned bitterly cold. I was drenched, rain was falling, icy wind whipped against me. I had goose bumps the size of nipples on every inch of skin. My fingers had lost their feeling up to the *elbows*.

Looking mildly concerned, Steve returned to our raft. "That's the first I ever had a swimmer *and* an injury at the same time," he said. "Come on. Hop in. Chop-chop."

Back on the river our journey became excruciatingly painful. We bounded, flopped, and twirled, taking wave after wave in our faces. Most of us wore only T-shirts, shorts, and sneakers. Everybody turned blue. Tossing and twisting and bailing frantically, we hung on for dear life. I gave up trying to snap photographs. Every time we chucked out the water we'd hit another pocket, spin, splash, and sputter like spastics, take on more river, gulp traumatically, and commence bailing again.

"More!" we cried deliriously. "Come on, Steverino, give us something better and *bigger!* We want some *Class 5* water, man. Isn't there any *Class 6* hereabouts?"

Waves smashed into our teeth, driving water like splinters down our throats, into our crotches, against our ankles . . . and hypothermia became a serious consideration.

I noticed—in the middle of all this—that Steve Harris was

working *hard* at those oars, trying to keep us under control. And I realized—*duh!*—that maneuvering a boatload of half-snockered smart alecks safely through all that angry water was not easy. It took strength and know-how and plenty of moxie, too.

One rapids followed another, now, fast and hectic. We bounced high, bounced hard, held on; Betty almost got thrown overboard. We would have enjoyed it a whole lot more if we hadn't been so stinking *cold*. Rod's weenie rain suit didn't seem all that stupid anymore. My very *bones* shuddered. How come nobody had instructed us beforehand to dress up like rubber penguins?

The last rapids (*Finally. Thank Christ!*) occurred where the Pueblo River joined the Rio Grande. A hundred spectators populated the shore, taking photographs: I shot them a birdie. One last chilly thrill elicited a final shriek—then we arrived at the takeout point a few yards beyond the Route 96 bridge north of Pilar. By then we were so soggy and frozen our tongues had turned *white*.

Another amazing zoo awaited us. Boats lolled everywhere. Bewildered, frozen, drenched-and-catching-pneumonia tourists stumbled dazedly from the rafts. Bedraggled, completely disorganized, the ensemble onshore could have been a decimated Normandy landing, or perhaps a comical retreat from Dunkirk filmed by Mel Brooks. Rain pelted down unmercifully. My chattering teeth sounded like frantic tap dancers.

With numb fingers our palsied crew grappled for drenched gear and ruined cameras as we floundered clumsily from the raft. "Bye," Steve chortled. "Thanks for choosing Far Flung Adventures." We staggered through the miserable crowd, searching for our bus. But when we got there we couldn't leave right away, because it took ages to maneuver the broken collarbone girl on board. Then a hobbling kayaker appeared, his thigh all bandaged, probably hiding a broken femur. He collapsed on the seat in front of me. "Where did it happen," I asked, "at Powerline?"

"Naw, I negotiated that fine. Then I was just standing on the bank, watching the others go through, when some klutz climbing the boulders up above me kicked loose a rock and it bounced off my leg."

We made the return trip in a blinding deluge. The windshield fogged up and our driver could scarcely see. We remained seated, stunned, dripping on the slimy floor. Rain harsh as hail clattered against the tin roof. The exhausted passengers stared vacantly ahead like concentration camp zombies.

Mari and Debbie rasped hoarsely, "We're staying at the Sagebrush and they have a hot tub. We are gonna get off there and just lie in that warm bubbling water for hours and hours and *hours.*"

The bus halted to set them free. They invited Betty and me, but we declined; I had to pick up my truck at the Tennis Ranch. Our fellow travelers wobbled bowleggedly toward the hotel like football players after losing the Super Bowl. Betty Read remarked coquettishly, "They're thanking you for this experience, Johnny."

We next stopped at Holy Cross Hospital. Helped by a pretty Far Flung Adventurer, the wounded limped inside. When she returned, the blond aide murmured, "Jeez, there's all *kinds* of victims in there. One lady busted her nose rafting; her face is a royal mess."

Finally, totally burnt and drained, we reached the Tennis Ranch. Betty and I crawled painfully inside my truck, turned on the whirring heater, and headed home, feeling keel hauled, bruised from guggle to zatch, achingly cold and defeated.

"Well," I chattered triumphantly, "did you like *that,* Betty Read?"

She glanced at me, sticking her svelte tongue pensively between her teeth. Then her eyes sparkled with a mischievous gleam and her lips turned upward in a sweet, mocking smile: "Sure, Johnny. I had a ball."

At home, I called Rod and Mari and Wayne and Debbie at the Sagebrush Inn. "Boy," I told Mari enviously, "I bet you all really enjoyed that wonderful hot tub."

"No, we did not," she whimpered. "The damn thing is broken."

I suppose the River Gods had tried to teach me a lesson—and perhaps they succeeded. In a pinch—yes—I could understand the lure of white water. Nevertheless, I had lost something precious on that trip down the Rio Grande: a sense of place, inviolate, majestic, solitary. In just a few hours the "wild" and "inaccessible" gorge had been made smaller and more mundane for me. Too many people with nonchalant attitudes had used the river for thrills that had nothing to do with the awe and respect I had built up for it since arriving in Taos years ago.

But folks like myself are an anachronism. No doubt beauty ought to be shared, even if the sharing destroys the mystery that made it lovely in the first place.

And anyway, human perturbation is transitory. Nature always heals herself. To prove it, last night I had a dream.

It was autumn again, the river low and clean and clear. All rafters were gone, silence reigned, and the trout had begun to rise. Alone, I descended a steep *bajada,* rigged up my rod and reel, and, dwarfed by the magnificent high walls of the deserted canyon, I cast once more into the tumbling breakers. In no time, of course, I hooked a big one and played it for long minutes, scrambling spiritedly over boulders as it dragged me downstream—

Until finally, triumphantly, I swung my mammoth and noble adversary into a shallow alcove. Then I reached down and grasped gently and lovingly by the gills . . . *one of those friggin' Butterball turkeys!*

Adapted from Impact Magazine, The Albuquerque Journal, *June 23, 1983.*

Some Thoughts on Humiliation

I have been a tourist in many places. I don't think that makes me a devil or a careless person. I know one can travel with positive intentions that don't necessarily lead to hell.

At the same time I know that tourism—proclaimed the largest industry in the world and growing—is largely an indulgence of affluence. It rubs the noses of the poor majority in the reality of the unequal distribution of wealth on earth.

I have the great good fortune to come from a family with tri-cultural roots: in America, France, and Spain. I was raised with an awareness of those roots going back for centuries and with a respect for the languages, cultures, and histories involved. My mother, a Frenchwoman raised in Spain, died young and I had no opportunity to discover my European roots until I was twenty. But in the summer of that year I visited my grandmother in Barcelona. It was a fabulous learning time. I began to speak both Spanish and French, and I became a bullfighting aficionado. I attended the festival of San Fermín in Pamplona, studied the avant-garde architecture of Gaudí, and made a pilgrimage to the Goyas at the Prado Museum in Madrid.

A friend of my grandmother's gave me a copy of Garcia Lorca's *Romancero Gitano,* and she whispered to me stories of the Spanish Civil War. I read several books about that conflict and moved through Spain very much aware that it was a dictatorship and the people had limited freedom. In Barcelona, the capital of Catalonia, it was forbidden to speak Catalan, and books and newspapers in that tongue were banned. The poverty in Spain disturbed me.

In her apartment my grandmother had three servants: a cook, a chauffeur, and a maid. I had never been waited on like that before and was terribly uncomfortable. I hated riding in a chauffeur-driven car. I created flaps by making my own bed, shining my shoes, and fashioning my own sandwiches in the kitchen, much to the consternation of the maid and the cook. I loathed servant-master relationships. Though I was white and middle class, I did not enjoy exercising such obvious power over others. This was a gut reaction, as I had no political sophistication at the time. But it helped lay the foundation for a class consciousness that eventually followed.

And as a tourist I became an ambivalent human being.

After graduating from college I returned to Europe and spent a year with my grandmother, working on a novel. I taught English to earn a living. On several occasions I visited a girlfriend in Paris. And I *loved* Paris. It seemed like the most wonderful city on earth. Wherever I went, I always had a map and a dictionary in hand. Each morning I translated articles from the newspapers. I pressed myself to speak with strangers, ask questions, learn. I visited aunts and uncles and grew more familiar with my European roots. Out of a grand mishmash of language, history, personality, and impressions I was constructing another couple of souls to join with my American spirit.

I was not some kind of politically correct and sainted Yankee in a foreign land. But I felt that I operated far from the negative arrogance of an ugly American. I was eager to speak foreign languages and to immerse myself in a brand-new culture and history. I was proud to honor the countries in which I lived. Increasingly, however, I clashed with my grandmother over servants, power, the privileges of class, her indulgent lifestyle. Yes, I accepted her generosity toward me and was grateful for it. But when we parted company I was tremendously relieved to escape from her world, where the inequalities were so clearly defined and observed.

In the spring of 1964, a year after I had returned from Spain to live in New York City, I took a bus to Guatemala. I visited a friend who was on a Fulbright grant, studying illiteracy. I approached Guatemala as an adventure and a lark, without ulterior motive or preconceived opinions. In effect, I was very much the tourist.

That experience *really* changed my life. Spain had been rich and free compared to this Central American country. I was unprepared for the poverty and brutality of Guatemalan society, though in the beginning, I'll admit, I was fascinated by Guatemala's raw energy and colorful despair. It was a "quaint" and dangerous place, and very exotic.

Most especially it was a land of prostitutes—available women, paid-for sex, the "real" thing. To a puritan of my limited experience the availability of these women had great allure. My power as a moneyed North American was pretty heady stuff. And for a moment, in my excitement, I ignored the embarrassment about privileges that had characterized my sojourn in Spain.

Near my friend's apartment was a street of hookers. The women occupied narrow storefronts with Dutch doors. You could walk up and down the sidewalk, assessing the goods. The price was fifty cents a pop. One night I cruised the street and found a woman I wanted. A six-word conversation struck our deal. I entered the cubicle and followed her around a thin partition. She was young and pretty, wearing a simple dress and no sandals. I took off my clothes and hung them on a peg, but the girl simply lay on her back on the cot, hiking up her dress. I felt foolish for shedding my outfit; I was exposed and profoundly *naked*.

Failing to perform, I became excruciatingly embarrassed. And not just because I was impotent. Suddenly I saw the situation for what it was—appalling. And humiliating to both of us. So I gave up, and, making an attempt at reconciliation, I tried to kiss the girl. She turned her head away.

That ended my lust for whores in Guatemala. And it began a process of education that radically altered my future. Guatemala was a cesspool, and the United States, I soon realized, had made it so. The economy and the oligarchy were controlled by Yankee corporations. I read Guatemala's Nobel laureate, Miguel Angel Asturias, whose epic works like *El Señor Presidente* and *Viento Fuerte* castigate the United Fruit Company, which once controlled much of that land. I conversed with many indigenous people who hated my country. They told me about the CIA-led coup a decade earlier that had overthrown their democratically elected president. And the shame I had felt with that youthful prostitute was multiplied considerably.

Almost twenty years passed before I traveled south of the border again. In the meantime I had moved to Taos, New Mexico. It was common for my Taoseño friends and neighbors to vacation in Mexico, in towns like San Cristóbal, San Blas, San Miguel de Allende. But after Spain and Guatemala, I could not see myself as a tourist in the Third World. I knew that the minute I crossed the border, I would feel like a blond, blue-eyed agent of North American imperialism. To take leisure in countries where the human misery was so pronounced seemed to me like an act of depravity. Even without malicious motives, how could a person feel comfortable floating around in their affluent, protected bubble while the people attending their every whim were in dire need of food?

In 1983 I went to Nicaragua. I had political reasons. I wanted to learn firsthand about the Sandinista revolution so that I could be a more credible voice against Ronald Reagan's policies in Nicaragua. Before leaving, I read books about the country to give myself more background. Then I spent eight days touring with a group of twenty other North Americans. We spoke to finance ministers and liberation theologists, union organizers and nurses. I took notes, filling up two hundred notebook pages. I think we were ideal tourists because we had a purpose and the conscious intent *not* to exploit Nicaragua.

When I returned to New Mexico, I wrote a long article for the *Albuquerque Journal*'s Sunday magazine, explaining my favorable take on the Sandinista revolution. In following years I gave dozens of interviews and speeches on behalf of Nicaragua. In the end this did not stop the United States from destroying the Sandinistas. But our effort to halt the injustice was important. And what I learned in Nicaragua still informs the politics of my existence and is useful in other struggles.

My final "tourist" adventure (to date) occurred in 1987. That year my second wife and I spent two months in Europe. Juanita is half Dutch, so we began in Amsterdam. Given the wealth of Holland, my conscience did not feel totally remiss—though I still felt like something of a cultural imperialist because I could not speak the language. We got a sense of the country, visited Juanita's cousins, demanded very little service, and spent every minute learning.

In France we hit all the museums and I shot the breeze to my Gaulic heart's content, relearning French. We traveled out to Giverny and bicycled to the home of Monet. We paid homage at the grave of my great-grandfather, Anatole Le Braz, visited family in Port Blanc, ate oysters in Cancale, chewed carrots at Mont-St.-Michel, and scarfed sandwiches on a cliff overlooking the ocean at Chateaubriand's tomb on the Grand Be at St. Malo.

Heading south to visit relatives in Spain, we stopped at Ouradour-sur-Glane and walked through the burned-out town that Nazis had destroyed in reprisal for underground activity during the war. It isn't a tourist attraction, advertised with billboards and refreshment stands. And there's almost no comment within the empty village, just a few plaques commemorating where most of the people were herded together and shot.

Europe is an education, and I guess that always saves the day. In the end, though, I was glad to return home. I was tired of trying to be a responsible tourist, which can often seem like an oxymoron. Somehow, the fact that I was rich enough to be traveling thousands of miles from home among people who could not travel at all always muted the fun.

Given my attitudes about tourism, it is probably odd that I have chosen to live in a village that survives by being a major Southwest tourist destination. I moved to Taos in 1969 and I like it here; I plan to stay for good. We have scenic mountains, pretty mesas, and the dramatic Rio Grande Gorge. People can hunt and fish and camp, visit museums, buy paintings in some seventy art galleries, and stay in a like number of B&Bs or in more upscale hotels and Swiss-style chalets. They can ski in winter at several top-notch areas and visit Taos Pueblo, whose main dwellings are advertised as the oldest continuously inhabited buildings in the United States.

Taos promotes itself as a tricultural community where the three main ethnic groups exist in harmony. Sixty-five percent of the population is Spanish speaking, 30 percent is Anglo, and the rest is Native American.

Sounds interesting, and it is. There's one problem, however: After decades as a tourist mecca, Taos is still poor. Put bluntly, it is a picturesque rural ghetto. Despite ski areas, galleries, and national forests, our socioeconomic stats are alarming. Official unemployment often rises above 20 percent. Underemployment, much of it close to minimum wage, is a fact for most of the workforce. Many workers are "unskilled" and nonunionized and are prone to layoffs depending on visitor volume and spending habits. The glamour of Taos is supported by an army of workers earning limited wages for scrubbing toilets, washing dishes, and changing bedsheets.

Tourism, a seasonal, service-oriented, and menial industry in this area, has always promoted a poverty culture. Hence we have all the attendant problems that go with such a culture: alcoholism, burglary, battered wives and children, poor health care, broken families, instability within the community. Many of our resentments and tensions relate to race problems, since the class differences— and there are great discrepancies in wealth here—break down principally along ethnic lines. The middle-class, largely Anglo minority controls much of the wealth; the Chicano majority is poor; the Indian people suffer most.

Nevertheless, a community long existed here. If it was not always harmonious, that community was a vital and self-sufficient organism more or less in balance with the surrounding landscape and with the resources—the biological capital—of the valley. That balance is going by the boards today. Like most everywhere else in the world, Taos is caught in an upheaval from which it is unlikely to recover. Growth and development, largely around the tourism and recreation industries, are disenfranchising longtime locals and forging instability in the educational, agricultural, economic, environmental, political, and civic arenas. All that was once solid is melting into air.

Our beauty has a new look, one more akin to that of a streetwalker making herself attractive to transients and outsiders who could care less about our personality, history, or aspirations. Whatever their surface intentions, tourists basically visit this country much as I entered Spain or Guatemala years ago. They just want to have fun.

My dictionary defines *tourist* as "a person who travels, especially for pleasure." In our culture pleasure is usually translated as the search for entertainment, and entertainment is most often achieved through consumption. So the tourist is encouraged not to participate but to consume. Tourists expect to be pampered, waited on, and deceived all in the name of comfort and convenience. That's what the money they spend is all about.

To make it palatable to visitors, our living culture in Taos is sanitized and presented much like a diorama in a museum: picturesque and safe. Tourists would rather not know that in many respects life here approximates the way four-fifths of the globe survives. The relationship between Taos and the tourists who support us has all the egregious class and cultural conflicts that disturbed me in Spain and Guatemala. It is as if both sides of the human interaction have been programmed to create a humiliation similar to the one suffered by me and the young prostitute in Guatemala City.

The working people of Taos understand their humiliation and resent it. But they keep a low profile, because even if the work is demeaning it is needed. And tourists rarely experience overt shame because they have been raised to accept the unfairness engendered by the class nature of our economic system. Most visitors do not even know that their passively racist attitudes exist.

Wherever commerce and social interaction focus on transients, local culture and responsibility die. The town itself adopts a transient soul. Everybody is scrambling for dollars from strangers instead of from each other. That changes the social contract. It eliminates respect and accountability. Merchants who wouldn't gouge their next-door neighbor will gladly join with that neighbor to gouge a stranger. Climax tourist exploitation leads to profit as the sole motivation for work.

A change in attitude can only begin with education. I know that my travels seriously shaped my life and my politics and all the books that followed. My eyes were opened and my sympathies with other cultures were powerfully reinforced by those trips around the United States, Europe, and Central America. So the tourist experience *can* be rich with possibilities. It is up to both travelers and host communities alike to realize those dreams.

In August each year I help teach a photography workshop in Taos. Ostensibly, the fifteen participants wish only to photograph northern New Mexico landscapes. But I always begin our sessions with a talk giving an overall view of Taos. I speak of our community, the economic disparities, the problems of race and social decay. I detail our building environmental tragedies and caution the shutterbugs not to eat fish caught in our rivers because they may be full of mercury. I talk about local groups striving for economic, social, and environmental justice.

I describe the acequia system that waters our valley, and I elucidate specific land and water struggles around issues of development, pollution, and resource mismanagement. Because the Pueblo is a main attraction for photographers, I pull no punches as I describe the appalling conditions out there. I also outline our recent history. I suggest books and pamphlets the photographers can read in order to become better informed. I list organizations to which visitors can contribute money, explaining that these local groups are determined to defend the natural and human resources that draw visitors to Taos in the first place.

All during the workshop I continue with a similar patter. It is the only way I know for workshop participants to make a valid landscape image.

I hope to send my photographers home full of information and inspiration. My goal is that Taos should be for them like my Guatemalan adventure—a challenge and an education.

In my book, that is how modern tourism should work. Not as an act of prostitution, but rather as a preamble to understanding and commitment.

From Discovered Country: Tourism and Survival in the American West. *Edited by Scott Norris, 1994.*

Whole Lotta Fun in Kansas

Hey, kids, you wanna go to Wild Animal Auschwitz in Dardanelles, Kansas? You wanna see big, beautiful, majestic bison incarcerated in tiny pens suffocating in knee-high mud and their own meadow muffins while cars zoom by behind them on Interstate 707? Do you just *love* the thought of gooning at cute old Wile E. Coyote and his mate trapped in a claustrophobic mesh cage with a concrete floor? How about demented rattlesnakes entombed in a deep wooden box you can peer into, or an eight-thousand-pound cement prairie dog you can take a *leak* on when your parental units aren't looking?

Or would you like to traipse around right in the middle of a *real live prairie dog village* and poke at the sick ones until they topple over and slide backward down into Prairie Dog Oblivion with their four little legs up stiff in the air? It sounds like fun, right?

Hey, check it *out,* little dudes and dudettes! Lace up those Air Jordans and clasp on that Batman cape. Dardanelles, Kansas, is only a hop, step, and a jump from your home and mine out here Where the West Begins. And Wild Animal Auschwitz is right at the *heart* of everything all of us have always believed in.

No, they don't have Mickey Mouse and Pluto walking around on stilts handing out Daffy Duck lollipops, but they *do* have something a whole lot better: beautiful pheasants pacing in two-by-three cages. Real live bobwhites chirping merrily from their diminutive cells. A badger staring at you dumbly from his cramped wooden box. A gorgeous bobcat—Mr. Kansas Puddy Tat himself—lying on a concrete slab with no place to go but crazy!

Wow, isn't *that* exciting?

Did your mom and dad let you see *Schindler's List?* Better yet, did you ever rent *Porky's* and *Porky's II* when the Mommy Gestapo wasn't looking? And then did you really blow chunks in fear terrified that she'd find out and tell Daddy Gestapo to go fetch the *Gott mit Uns* belt?

No? You didn't have the *guts?* You were terrified of getting *spanked?* Shame on you! But okay, that's really not a problem— here's the good news. *You don't have to do naughty, rotten, corrupt, pornographic things to get your rocks off anymore!* Just figure out a way to get Mom and Pop in that Vanagon headed east on I-707, and the rest is duck soup. Wild Animal Auschwitz is *perfectly legal!* Parents *love* it! What's more, it's *cheap*—only four bucks at the door, *free* for the *chi-chi*-slurping papooses. You can even take your throwaway Instamatic inside for some candid pics of fainting goats, baby pigs, a miniature donkey, and a giant fifteen-pound Flemish rabbit.

Unfucking *forgettable!*

But here's the best part. For the diaper set *and* the old folks alike, Wild Animal Auschwitz at Dardanelles, Kansas, has a huge gift shop where you can do *all* your Xmas shopping. Wouldn't Grandpa like a real, honest-to-goodness stuffed jackalope? There's *tons* of them. Or how about some hillbilly toilet tissue for Grammie?— three tiny corncobs in a Baggie! *Cute squared!* Oh, she'll laugh until her lorgnette falls in the eggnog on Xmas morning with a gift like that—guaranteed! Who says glaucoma stops all the fun?

Or how about big brother Bobby? Wouldn't he just go mental on Xmas morning if he found a rubber rattlesnake in his stocking? Or a can of Kansas-Style Delicately Smoked Fish Assholes? Or maybe one of Wild Animal Auschwitz's world-famous Kansas Pasture Pies? I bet all his frat brothers at the Greek Geek House would go ballistic with envy if he showed up back at school with a plastic pig snout, a roadkill toupee, or a package of pinto beans labeled "Bubble Bath."

Yo, Bobby, *gimme five and that's no jive!*

They also have the perfect gift for Mom and Dad. No kidding—

you really wanna blow doors scoring brownie points with the moldy oldies that begat you? Then save your allowances and buy Mom a *Roadkill Cookbook*. She'll love you for teaching her how to prepare creamed possum, raccoon stew, skunk fritters, and armadillo croquets sautéed in buzzard blood.

Believe me, they have *everything* for sale at Wild Animal Auschwitz, from rattlesnake skin jockstraps to rubber tomahawks. Also exquisite posters of beautiful wild animals in their exquisite natural settings that I'm sure you'll want to give to gnarly old Uncle Ben (the stupid tree hugger Dad wishes a couple of Wise Use groupies would terminate with a gas-operated Mark II fragmentation grenade one of these days before that dang old spotted owl turns America into a communist country!).

You'll have a blast at Wild Animal Auschwitz, I promise, or your money back. You and Mom and Dad and Sister Carrie can all join hands out in the yard when your visit is over and sing "America the Beautiful" and "Home on the Range" to all the desolate, deranged, and depressed wild animals hunkering down on their atrophied legs in their suffocatingly diminutive cells. The insane desert swift fox in its stark box will thank you for the gesture.

Or maybe you oughtta sing, "Deutschland über Alles."

But whatever you do, *don't wait any longer!* Right now, right this minute, *immediately* go tell Mom and Dad to gas up the Caravan and hit the old roadeo, because time's a-wasting. Believe me, that big, fat, eight-thousand-pound prairie dog ain't getting any younger. And those oversized bison are liable to sink beneath the ooze if you don't get there pronto.

Wild Animal Auschwitz is fun, it's educational, it's totally *awesome*.

Visa and MasterCard accepted . . . of course!

Written (unsolicited) in June 1996 for the Colorado Springs Independent. *I'm still waiting for my pal Kathryn Eastburn to publish it.*

Part Four
What Is to Be Done?

One of the following pieces was written in 1985; the other three are products of the 1990s. But they all represent how I first learned to think and believe in the 1960s after that trip to Guatemala. My understandings of how the planet works haven't changed much since 1965, though I do have a more sophisticated "environmental awareness."

The Writer as Revolutionary

In a book called *Chicago: City on the Make,* Nelson Algren said: "I submit that literature is made upon any occasion that a challenge is put to the legal apparatus by a conscience in touch with humanity."

Heinrich Heine, the great German poet, put it this way: "A poet should have on his casket not a wreath but a gun, to show that he was a faithful private in the liberation struggles of humanity."

As a writer myself I have made much of my work overtly political. In most other countries the artist is by definition political. You cannot separate art from social responsibility in France or the Soviet Union. That's why so many writers outside our borders are suppressed or executed, or they wind up living in exile. But here in the United States of North America it is said that being "political" is not "artistic."

Yet all art involves choices that are "political." All *action* is political, and literature is action. There is no such thing on earth as an a-political human being. Of course, when our cultural Brahmins denigrate politics in art, they are talking about "left" politics. Their prejudice developed most strongly in the McCarthy period of the late 1940s and 1950s during the establishment of the Cold War.

Recently a proponent of that myth has been Nobel laureate Isaac Bashevis Singer. In *The New York Times* he said, "No Marxist has ever written a good novel." Singer further stated that a Marxist "has never written a good novel because a writer must have roots, and Marxism is against roots. Marxism is cosmopolitanism, and a cos- 89 mopolitan cannot write a good work of fiction—because a writer belongs to his people, to his clan."

When asked, "Do you feel that a writer ought to commit himself in political or social affairs?" Singer replied, "It's unhealthy. I have never seen a single political novel, or a single novel that has to do with sociology, that really came out well. Sociology deals not with a single person, but with masses of people, and in a way this is true of all the sciences." He added, "The writers who don't discuss character, but problems—social problems or any problems—take away from literature its very essence. They stop being entertaining."

Not according to Thomas Mann, who believed that "unity of humanity, the wholeness of the human problem, permits nobody to separate the intellectual and artistic from the political and social, and to isolate himself within the ivory tower of the cultural proper."

Jean Renoir, the French filmmaker who directed *Grand Illusion* and *The Rules of the Game,* wrote in his autobiography: "Our present-day religion is the bank and our language is publicity. The key word is output, by which we produce more. When the world market is saturated we start another war to get new customers. The aim of warfare is no longer conquest but construction. When the building is destroyed, the wheels turn again. We build skyscrapers in the ruins of pagodas and this fills the belly of the workingman, who would otherwise revolt."

According to Hans Koning, author of *The Revolutionary:* "If we're to survive against the state, and against Them, we want a constant, a day-and-night militancy on everything, every single damn issue. Nothing is uncontroversial and nothing they suggest is innocent. Every word is a stone and every plan a barricade. The Bastille has to be retaken every single bloody day. Sounds pretty exhausting and a bore, but what other chance would there be of self-preservation?"

My point is simple. Artists need to be activists. A writer's job is to create in defense of this globe. So let's develop a revolutionary consciousness, then take to the barricades in whatever ways we deem ourselves most effective. Our dream and intention should be of one day seizing power, in order to move the colossus in a different and healthier direction.

Adapted from a talk at the Old Southwest/New Southwest Conference, Tucson, Ariz., November 14–17, 1985. Printed in Old Southwest/ New Southwest: Essays on a Region and Its Literature. Edited by Judy Lensink, 1987. This is a radically abridged version of the published essay.

The Case for a Social Ecology

I have watched with dismay some recent conflicts in northern New Mexico between "environmentalists" and the indigenous population. Specifically, I'm thinking of the court case between the Sierra Club and Ganados del Valle, and the injunction (out of Arizona) against logging that excluded some firewood gathering and caused a major flap in Truchas last autumn. This led to a public confrontation between Ike de Vargas and his loggers from Compania Ocho and the Forest Guardians in Santa Fe. Such antagonisms are not new to New Mexico. I've been aware for years of a long-standing suspicion held against individual ambientistas and environmental organizations by many of my friends in the north.

Since I arrived in Taos in 1969, most of my orientation toward water, forest, and sierra has been guided by local population: ranchers, farmers, activists, and other members of a majority Spanish-speaking population. Much of this culture has been working class and economically deprived. It has had a strong sense of community and a tradition of responsible land management. No, that hasn't included promotion of wilderness areas. Livelihoods were gained from irrigation farming in Taos County, firewood gathering, small ranching operations dependent on grazing leases in the national forests, and a low-key economic hustle that has defined this area for centuries.

The environmental movement in New Mexico has grown out of the inmigration here over the past thirty years. Environmentalists tend to be relative newcomers and middle class. During the twenty-seven years I have lived in Taos, changes caused by the influx of outsiders have really accelerated. A highly competitive profit-oriented economy has been imposed on a valley with strong roots in communal property and sustainable endeavors.

Excessive capital, wielded by middle-class newcomers, has created harsh divisions between locals and immigrants. It has highlighted ethnic tensions, destabilizing ancient communities and their value systems. In the north today a critical class struggle is taking place and the environmental movement is in danger of being on the wrong side.

Anyone who lobbies for changed policies in a national forest ought to remember that much of that forest was taken from native folk less than a century ago, and the resentments are still deep. Modern environmentalists are not responsible for those injustices, but to ignore them is to imperil any positive act we espouse. Barry Commoner said, "The world will survive the environmental crisis as a whole, or not at all." If the majority (Spanish-speaking) population of northern New Mexico does not work with us toward conservation goals, there will be no valid environmental movement here.

When we deal with environmental crises anywhere on earth, it's important to keep in mind that most of the crises have been created by the consumptive activities of the ruling and middle classes. I am a member of the middle class but try to effect a simple lifestyle. The first question I'd ask any environmental activist is: "To what extent do you *truly* lead a life of voluntary simplicity?" I would also note that in New Mexico most longtime residents lead lives of simplicity, though it's not usually voluntary. Across the north poverty is a bitter fact of life. That poverty—multiplied around our globe—is the basic environmental problem on earth.

Not long ago I compiled a few articles that should be of interest to us all:

The April 14, 1996, New York Times had an obituary for Sydney Howe, a man described as "an early fighter for clean soil, water, and air who was one of the first to balance the needs of the environment with those of poor people in the cities." According to the obit, Howe "lamented what he saw as a form of discrimination among conservationists. 'We are today a racially segregated profes-

sion, heavily populated by so-called rugged outdoorsmen,' he declared at a 1967 conference. 'Conservation must now be of and for
increasingly urban environments and their people.'" He continued:
"'People involved in social issues wondered how I could spend my
workdays at conservation and nights at their meetings, because
conservation goals sometimes ran against such things as adequate
housing for poor people. . . . But there are larger purposes in life in
which conservation and social equity must go hand in hand.'"

Wes Jackson, head of the Land Institute in Salina, Kansas, recently published an article called "Wilderness as Saint." In it he
wrote: "Harlem and East Saint Louis and Iowa and Kansas will have
to be loved by enough of us or wilderness is doomed. Those who
struggle for social justice by working with the poor in cities and
those out to prevent soil erosion and save the family farm are suddenly on the same side as the wilderness advocate. All have joined
the same fight, so to speak."

The May 20, 1996, *Nation* had a book review of *Divided Planet*,
by Tom Athanasiou. The reviewer was David Rothenberg. He quotes
Athanasiou: "It is past time for environmentalists to face their own
history, in which they have too often stood not for justice and freedom, or even for realism, but merely for the comforts and aesthetics of affluent nature lovers. They have no choice. History will
judge greens by whether they stand with the world's poor."

The spring 1996 issue of *The Workbook,* put out by the Southwest Research and Information Center in Albuquerque, has a number of book reviews relevant to these concerns. One long review/
commentary is by James Elkins, of *Environmental Justice: Issues,
Policies, and Solutions,* an anthology of environmental writings edited by Bunyon Bryant. The book discusses how "the movement
for environmental justice is unprecedented in the way it brings together social, economic, political, and scientific concerns and communities of interest and in how it has established the clear relationship and commonality of interest between poverty, racism,
disease, and the environment."

James Elkins emphasizes that the book points out this most important fact: *"An environmental movement that does not reach out to working-class people, indigenous people, and people of color has no sustainable future."*

In that light, we "environmentalists" should recognize that Compania Ocho and Ganados del Valle are among the more important community—and environmental—organizations in northern New Mexico. Certainly their members are as crucial to local environmental health as anybody working on behalf of Carson Forest Watch or Forest Guardians. Obviously it is distressing when the Sierra Club is cast as an ogre in the community it wishes to help, yet this should be a learning experience, an important wake-up call, a demand for expanded horizons.

If the environmental movement can develop an understanding of and a sympathy with social, economic, and cultural issues, wildness—and community—stand a much better chance. I hope we can learn to base our future struggles on this social ecology, where conservation and human equality go hand in hand.

Adapted from a talk to the Sierra Club at the Unitarian Church, Santa Fe, May 21, 1996.

An Elegy for Armageddon:
A Tongue-in-Cheek Disquisition on Our Maniacal Lust for Excess

Not long ago, the brilliant egghead philosopher, Woody Allen, had some observations on the future of humanity that I thought insightful. Perhaps they are germane to the occupation in which most of you here today find yourselves, as employees of the Breckenridge Environmental Not-in-My-Backyard Progressive Democratic Coalition for Peaceful Dismantling of Rampant Development Excess in Rocky Mountain Tourist Towns.

Near as I can recall, Allen said (and I paraphrase): "Humanity has arrived at a fork in the road crucial to its very existence. One way leads to utter devastation and despair; the other to extinction. Let us hope we have the wisdom to choose correctly."

I often think of these words when the Pope gives yet another speech prohibiting the use of condoms; or when the Tobacco Lobby rises up in righteous indignation, protesting that nobody has really proved beyond the shadow of a doubt that smoking is bad for your health; or when the Republican Contract on America proposes to solve unemployment by jailing everybody without a job; or when scientists insist there really isn't enough information about the hole in the earth's ozone (ten thousand miles wide and fifteen thousand miles long!) to conclude that at some vague future date it will compromise the quality of life on earth—

I mean, we live in a world where nothing makes sense if you are worried about the survival of intelligent life in Breckenridge or on earth. We all support an economic system based on the Orson

Welles diet. Every day we wake up, inoculate ourselves with five cups of Maxwell House heroin and a pound each of Froot Loops, Boo Berries, and Sugar-Coated Junk Wheat, then we hop into a tin coffin responsible for forty thousand deaths a year and drive off to the office. There we click on the air-conditioning (so Peabody Coal can fire up those DC-7s, annihilate another hundred acres of Arizona, and send more stockholders to vacations in Tahiti). Once comfortable, we eat a couple of strawberry Danishes and a box of Mallomars, guzzle more heroin, smoke five Marlboros, and settle down to work. Two hours later, our 390-pound bodies start grumbling for more fuel. So we pop out to Bob Obesity's Carcinogenic Grease and Lard Fast-Food Diabetes Emporium for a couple of cholesterol hush puppies soaked in hot fudge gravy on a bed of Sodium Plus Anxiety Chips and Banana Creme Waffle Syrup, which is a *real* wake-up call.

Next, we waddle into the bathroom and drop a doughnut the size of an NCAA Official Regulation Size Basketball into the city sewage system, which, sooner or later, will carry it to the Gulf of Mexico, where it can mate with an oil spill and kill a half dozen whooping cranes just for the fun of it.

After that, we open *The New York Times* to check on our investments. Oh, goody, Chrysler rose another two points; Dow Chemical is going through the ceiling; Amalgamated Dioxin is strong; United Chlorofluorocarbon is up a half point; Ligget and Myers is worth $200 a share; Nestle's Third Word Breast Cancer Stimulant is at an all-time high; sales of Disney/Mattell's new Death Squad Doll are through the roof and still rising like an intercontinental ballistic missile; Rwandan Machete, Inc., is double what it was last year at this time; Israeli Galil is more profitable than ever; Breckenridge DWI and Liquor Enhancement No-Load Securities just went public, split its stock, and doubled your money overnight; and it looks like those new Rhino Bullets are a *hit*.

Moral—? You can't keep a good investment portfolio down on the farm, not in our country.

Then (back at the old job), when the factory whistle blows at 5 P.M., we rush downstairs and outside to Paddy's Shamrock Inebriation Chophouse for a quarter bottle of vodka and a splash of OJ before heading home to the latchkey kiddies. Of course, some of our stellar comrades like to bypass the tedium and annoying social congress of getting blind drunk in dimly lit buckets of blood, so they simply pop a few DDT tablets and wash them down with Alar during the commute home. This will deform a person's cellular structure a lot more efficiently than alcohol.

At home, after we feed the backyard cows (who keep up our daily quota of methane gas emissions into the suffering atmosphere), all of us spend three to five hours in front of the tube absorbing dreck, our shoulders slumped, our mouths agape, our brains in suspended adulation.

Pretty soon it's the weekend, and what do most of us do? Well, we grab an ax, a few guns, a house cat, a carton of cigarettes, some bottles of tebuthiuron, a jug of Clorox, a box of Tide, some pressurized paint cans and a little Red-Devil paint remover, along with various containers of raw ether, asbestos, ant poison, weed killer, and birdseed soaked in cyanide. Then we hop onto our diesel backhoes and run amok for forty-eight hours, whacking down trees, bleaching the pulp to be used in *People* magazine, passing out Camels to teenagers, building prefab houses from plywood soaked in carbon tetrachloride, herding befuddled songbirds into cat traps, spraying paint remover through a hose at all our neighbor's mailboxes, washing clothes with Tide and Clorox, pouring ant poison into swimming pools, inhaling polyurethane fumes just for the fun of it, dumping old cans of WD-40 into the ocean, ordering starving workers from Mexican sweatshops to make us more basketball sneakers faster and cheaper, flying our private jets down to El Salvador to drop napalm on the Coffee Workers Union's headquarters during an important meeting, and in general playing Enviro Death until the bell rings on Monday morning and it's time to go back to work, start the heroin cycle, flip off Superfund, and push a button every twenty minutes that either (1) explodes another atomic bomb in an Olympic Peninsula forest, or (2) by clever remote control crashes another two-hundred-yard-long oil tanker into jagged rocks off the coast of Brittany, cracking open the hull, or (3) scoops up everybody in Grand Central Station, New York

City, and inoculates them with either squamous cell cancer or AIDS, or (4) creates a small earthquake under Rocky Flats (Colorado) so that whatever is *up* there can drain into whatever's *down* there, or (5) lifts up the entire Houston Shipping Channel and drops it into Chesapeake Bay.

Now: I know that all of you good people here today are sincerely interested at least in saving Breckenridge, if not the planet. You support the EPA and the Clean Air and Water Act, you recycle your cans and bottles and newspapers, and you are appalled by the 1872 Mining Law, the Bosnia-Herzegovina of American mineral extraction policies for over a century. And most certainly you do not advocate the scenarios I have just painted so deftly in my taciturn, reserved, and rather timid manner.

So what's the problem? A pivotal question you all are probably asking yourselves right now is: What's a nice guy like me doing in a chipper upscale little resort town like Breckenridge on a pleasant afternoon like this, ranting and raving like Paul Ehrlich and Barry Commoner high on crank trying to sodomize Jesse Helms?

Okay, no more shilly-shallying. Let me explain myself. Put simply, I'm here hoping to make you laugh so hard that when I'm gone you'll go home and question all the values you live by, all the goods you consume, all the ridiculously overblown conspicuously consumptuous houses you live in, the insane automobiles you drive, the *sauve-qui-peut,* upper-class friendly, lethally competitive, mega-devouring and sadistic economic principles you're brainwashing your kids with . . . and furthermore, of course, I'm also hoping that after I'm gone none of you will be able to smoke another cigarette, or look at your lawns filled with weed killer, bug spray, and toxic fertilizers without seeing them as Superfund cleanup sites cleverly disguised as "living" Astroturf in a peaceful nothing-can-go-wrong suburbia from hell.

I'm hoping also that you'll realize nothing any of us does is innocent; therefore it behooves all of us to *stop*—in the name of Love . . . Canal—and begin to change everything we do from the ground up so that pollution, inequality, greed, and intolerance will not annihilate the earth.

My problem, clown that I am, is I can't even look at our material well-being without concurrently visualizing the catastrophic devastation—both human and "natural"—that is creating the Armageddon disguised as that well-being. I see some cute curly-haired yuppie white kid bopping along in her Nike Air Jordan pump-up skid-proof ninety-dollar brothel creepers and immediately the innocence of that vision for me is shattered by a countervision of a whole gaggle of Mexican or Taiwanese *maquiladoras* pumping out carcinogens in a toxic wonderland where brown people getting paid starvation wages are choking to death on a poverty that is keel hauling the entire globe while they stitch up the pump ups that little kid is wearing.

I can't even look at a shiny new Dodge Neon without going into paroxysms of macroscopic overload, picturing the Mesabi Range strip mining that unearthed the ore that went to the smelters to create the tin that was plated by chemicals that sickened the rivers that were dammed to create the hydroelectric power to drive the factory that made the bulldozers to strip-mine the soft coal that went into a slurry line fed by the diversion of an entire river to carry the coal to a power station (emitting a four-hundred-mile-long plume of trace metal smog) that makes the electricity to run the auto plant that builds the Dodge Neon that emits the carbon dioxide and monoxide that causes the greenhouse effect and the ozone holes that lead to ultraviolet radiation that kills all the frogs and causes the melanomas that cripple so many of us who rely for our survival on radiation, chemotherapy, and prohibitively expensive engines of salvation that themselves require billions in material destruction to build and maintain—and so forth, ad infinitum.

Towns like Breckenridge, and Taos, where I live, and Denver and Santa Barbara are founded on shit heaps of collapsing natural and human infrastructure the likes of which our planet has never known. It's not impossible to imagine this, but when we're leading the good life we choose *not* to imagine it. We think of development as "good for business, great for the community—look at the jobs." Just so long as they don't destroy *our* pretty forest to get the wood to build the condos. Just so long as they don't pollute *our* pretty rivers to fill the slurry lines to carry the coal to fire the power plants that render operational our ski lifts and help create all the plumbing and stovepipes and radiators and air conditioners and sewage lines and restaurant furnaces that keep us going. And just so long as they don't sink oil wells up and down *our* main street and build refineries all over *our* town to create the petrol that brings us our megabucks tourists in their fancy-shmancy cars and RVs and airplanes—let's keep that oil in Nigeria, thank you very much Ken Saro-Wiwa and General Abacha (RIP). And just so long as we don't have to deal with all the impoverished South African diamond miners who create the wealth that is parlayed by the entrepreneurs manipulating stocks and municipal bonds so that we can have *our* wonderful luxurious beehives of vacation-oriented condo euphorias keeping all of us (in the bracket of the 10 percent of the earth's population that controls 70 percent of the planet's wealth) happy.

We Haves on earth have always refused to recognize how wealth is created, where it comes from, who and what is exploited to create the profit that coddles us. We ignore the chain of command, we refuse to hear the initial gunshot that kills the union organizer in El Salvador so that somebody like Maxwell House—at enormous profit—can bring us our yummy cup of morning java cheap before we don our thousand-dollar polyester outfit (with gold-plated moon boots to match) and hit the slopes for a day of mogul hopping before partaking of the evening holocaust of food and booze and entertainment. A holocaust fueled, coincidentally, by rapacious bauxite mining in Puerto Rico that has displaced half a nation's population in order to make aluminum cans for Miller and Coca-Cola and—

It's an axiom that has disturbed me all my life: my fabulous wealth is always generated by somebody else's lack of wealth; my clean skies are clean because of killer smogs over China, India, and Brazil; my well-being is created by untrammeled dislocations elsewhere. There are enormous gravel pits savaging the landscape somewhere to create the lovely road I traveled on to get here today. There is a Death Alley of chemical wastes on the Mississippi River creating the chrome on the bumpers of my car, the chords of my guitars, the rubber on my bicycle tires, the insulation in my walls and roof—where does fiberglass come from, anyway? Who makes it? What happens to *them* so that *we* can be warm all winter—?

The journalist John Reed, who wrote *Ten Days That Shook the World*, put it this way:

> All I know is that my happiness is built on the misery of other people, that I eat because others go hungry, that I am clothed when other people go almost naked through the frozen cities in winter, and that fact poisons me, disturbs my serenity, makes me write propaganda when I would rather play—

Same here. But enough. Obviously these trends are not going to stop for a long time. Yet things certainly need to change. And I believe we're the guys to change it all *if* we can manage to change ourselves. The first step toward that change is realizing that our happiness and well-being are a picture of Dorian Gray.

There's no need to despair, however. Nobody ever promised us a rose garden. Humanity has been polluting the earth since time immemorial. The Anasazi rubbed themselves out by screwing up their land. Pre-Victorian London used to keep the lid on its over-population problem through the judicious deployment of cholera epidemics. For most of the 1940s and 1950s the United States pasteurized its milk naturally by radiating it with strontium 90 from atomic testing expressly designed to combat the unchecked growth of most organisms, including human beings.

Yet always the earth survived and humanity has moved forward despite itself. Why? Because a dedicated few like you kindly folks—who ill-advisedly brought me to your beautiful town, thinking I'd be a class act moderated slightly by a quirky sense of humor—see a point in the promulgation of human, animal, and plant evolution on this festering globe.

Put another way: In all the courses of human events there have always been idealists who figured it was worth the fight against impossible odds to save the earth. These people have run an interesting gamut from Harriet Tubman through Aldo Leopold to Bernadette Devlin and Rigoberta Menchú . . . and, I would like to think, all the misguided heroines and heroes around the Rocky Mountain region who believe that deep down a commitment to life, love, and a social conscience ought to be the desire of us all.

I know the planet would have been gone long ago if it wasn't for folks like you who get up each day, peek out the window, see that it's a totally messed-up, hopeless, chaotic, disintegrating, mean, evil, selfish, and self-annihilating world out there, and yet you never flinch. You confidently put your pants and bras on backward, make sure the Velcro straps on your flak jackets are mushed together tightly, pop three Thorazines, two Valiums, and a lithium capsule, then adjust the visors on your battered World War I Snoopy Fokker biplane helmets, hop into your old dilapidated Toyota Rocinantes, and zoom off looking for industrial polluters to tilt against, developers to sabotage, programs for human justice and equality to struggle for, church programs to subsidize for the elderly and the poor, and clever speakers to expand your horizons by expounding brilliantly on the nature of race in America today.

True, it's a dirty job, but somebody has to do it.

And believe me, though it may not seem so to you all on the surface, a grateful nation will always thank you for allowing gadflies like me to invade your comfortable bailiwicks with their bland, modulated comments on how free market economies should work above seven thousand feet in Shangri-la.

And even if the nation doesn't thank you for your courage and commitments, so what?

For as Woody Allen might say: "An anonymous, stress-laden, and hopeless struggle for bad pay against impossible odds needs no public accolades; it is its own best reward."

Speech in Breckenridge, Colorado, June 18, 1998. Early portions of this talk were also included in an address to the EPA in Denver, Colorado, April 19, 1995. Published in the Summit County *(Colorado)* Free Press, *August 1998.*

What Is to Be Done?

The real question is to discover what kind of economic and
social order is best adapted to serve as a partner in the alliance
with nature.—*Barry Commoner,* The Closing Circle

It is time that we seriously question our economic system, much of
which is, after all, based on greed and envy. Now, lest you think I
am unpatriotic, consider that there is a big difference between the
economic system called capitalism and the political system called
democracy.—*Wes Jackson, Altars of Unhewn Stone*

All of us agree the planet is in trouble, and we need radical solutions to problems of overpopulation, chemical agriculture, social
decay. We condemn the destruction of community, the nonsus-
tainable extraction of resources, racism and economic tyranny. We
worry about the greenhouse effect and ozone holes. And though
many of us specialize in certain areas of concern, I think we all
agree that the ultimate understanding of any individual concern
or effort depends on a macroscopic overview.

Yet whether we are biologist, novelist, or social critic, I think
we often neglect that overview. Specifically: We regularly fail to
address the problem of revolution that will be required to bring
about the sustainable and egalitarian world we desire.

Therefore, I wish more of us, in our work, would address in
general philosophical terms the overall nature of capitalism, its effect
on the planet, and the need to get rid of it.

Clearly, in a world of finite resources, an economic system based on planned obsolescence and conspicuous consumption is a formula for planetary suicide. Capitalism is based on a philosophy of terminal growth. The profit motive promotes class warfare and relegates three-fourths of humanity to humiliating living conditions while it also destroys the land, air, water, and species that sustain us. To the extent that we choose to work within, or consider ourselves bound by, the rules of this system, our efforts will be doomed to failure. And our precious islands of wilderness or rational farming or alternate schooling will eventually succumb to the juggernaut of capital development.

I am certain that the globalwide social and environmental changes we are working for will not occur unless we challenge all the broad precepts of our economic system, making that challenge a part of both our national and universal consciousness. Too often, despite the radical passion of our endeavors, we neglect to bell this cat. Yet it is obvious that our own commitments to voluntary simplicity or sustainable agriculture won't have a chance unless we articulately demand—now—this ultimate revolution.

Ergo: At some point, in all our discussions, we ought to address the general question: How can capitalism be erased, and with what shall it be replaced? For me, a logical translation of this question is: How can we create a democracy (an egalitarian sustainable system with an informed and participating electorate) capable of addressing the earth's crises?

Of course, we should also discuss the failure of Marxist material exploitation to protect both people and the environment. Still, I would equate my ideal democracy with some type of socialist organization. Barry Commoner said in *The Closing Circle,* "The theory of socialist economics does not appear to require that growth should continue indefinitely."

To reiterate: Whether we say so openly, implicit—in all the work of cogent environmentalists or progressive social scientists—is the overthrow of the capitalist system that drives the modern industrial engine. Yet too often we avoid a direct confrontation with the capitalist bogeyman, even though it impels everything we say and do. This is sort of like understanding that cigarettes kill, yet refusing to discuss the need to eliminate tobacco products and the corporations that market them, while planning for the jobs and taxes lost as a result of these actions.

At heart, we progressives are still afraid to truly change our own lives (and our messages) commensurate with the logic and passion of our beliefs.

What our struggles need today are more Che Guevaras and Carlos Fonsecas, more Lucy Parsons and Mother Joneses. We need our arguments, studies, and dreams to include the revolutionary next step. Otherwise, cries for a sustainable agriculture, for a rational forest ecology, or for justice on earth will end up as just so much ineffectual pissing into the hurricane.

Speech at The Prairie Festival, The Land Institute, Salina, Kansas, May 25, 1996. Published in the Summit County Free Press, *July 1998.*

Part Five
The Writer at Work

The author at Ranchos de Taos church, photographed by Maestri Smith.

When I was in college a bunch of us sat around the PX, drinking coffee and talking about becoming writers after we graduated. All of us had read Hemingway and Scott Fitzgerald and Thomas Wolfe and we wanted Max Perkins to be our editor. Our short stories and poems were published in the Hamilton literary magazine, The Continental. We also acted in theater productions and played Woody Guthrie songs on our guitars. After experiencing On the Waterfront everybody wanted to be in movies. Our vision of the writing life was very idealistic. Most of us never realized that dream, but I "made it." Writing is what I've done ever since I graduated from Hamilton.

The career has not been at all as I imagined it would be. The workload has been astronomical. I am not a "good" or a "natural" writer. What might in the end seem spontaneous or effortless to the reader has usually involved thousands of hours of frustrating and backbreaking labor. Even a small book of essays like this one required Herculean efforts. They included months of typing material into a computer, editing and selecting text, being rejected, trying again, undergoing relentless critiques, rewriting and more rewriting, until finally, by blind luck and perseverance, something of a book took shape and a publisher was found. By then I was exhausted. And the production stage hadn't even begun!

Still, the job has always thrilled me. Being a writer means that everything is relevant all the time. I'm always on the job, even when I'm sleeping. It doesn't get any better than that.

My Sentimental Education

Every life is a shaggy dog story.—*Pliny the Elder*

I was once a child and went to school in order to get an education in America. I attended kindergarten in Montpelier, Vermont, in 1945; first grade in St. James, New York; second and third grades in Westbury, New York; fourth and fifth grades in Berkeley, California; sixth grade in Wilton, Connecticut; seventh grade in Forestville, Virginia; eighth grade in Herndon, Virginia; and ninth grade at the Loomis School in Windsor, Connecticut, where I matriculated in the autumn of 1954.

I have delightful memories of all my schooling at these various locations. In Montpelier, I refused to learn how to tell time and drew a fabulous picture of Pinocchio. In St. James we had a carpool to a one-room schoolhouse for rich kids, and one day I used the rear door handle as a tommy gun and the door flew open and my friend Peter Sharbert fell out and split his head open. In the second grade I became a Brooklyn Dodgers baseball fan, a seminal event that gave me a social conscience for life. It happened this way. A little mensch named Emerick Tedesci came up to me and said, "Who do you like in the World Series, the Dodgers or the Yankees?" Though I had no idea what or who he was talking about, I took a wild guess, saying, "The Dodgers." The kid hauled off and punched me in the face and I fell over backward like a sack of potatoes dropped off the Empire State Building (in a vacuum). From that moment on I hated the Yankees, loved the Brooklyn Bums passionately, and *always* rooted for the underdogs.

When we moved to Berkeley in 1948 I attended Whittier Elementary School and was soon arrested for shoplifting a Hopalong Cassidy two-gun cap pistol and holster set. The cops put me on probation when they discovered I had five hundred dollars' worth of previously stolen goods stashed underneath the front porch of our house. That same year me and my buddy Dallas Texas Carsey followed a girl we were in love with home from school, grabbed her on the sidewalk, and both gave her a kiss, then fled. If it had been 1998 instead of 1949, I'm sure that we would still be doing time, having been tried as adults at the age of nine.

My family left Berkeley during the Korean War and moved to Wilton, Connecticut, where I shot bullfrogs with a bow and arrow with a friend of mine who was later killed by lightning. We sold the frogs' legs to the Village Market for a buck a pound. I played third base on a baseball team in the Westport Little League and had the distinction of never making an error and never getting a hit during an entire season. I was also starting to be a troublemaker in school; one of my teachers kept throwing erasers at my head. On report cards I received straight A's, but beside all of them were 4's for attitude. The dancing school I was forced to attend made boys wear white gloves, and I became incredibly self-conscious about girls with tits. Perhaps because of this I started many fights, winning most of them by squeezing my opponents so tightly in scissors grips they usually cried, "Uncle!" while spitting up blood. I fell in love with a girl named Louise Young but lacked the guts to tell her. And when Mother and Pop moved us to rural Virginia the day after Eisenhower's inauguration I was greatly relieved, having worn my Wilton welcome pretty thin.

Virginia was weird because it was segregated. I went to an all-white grade school and later an all-white high school. On hayrides I was the only guy who didn't burrow under the straw to make somebody—anybody!—pregnant. I became a Boy Scout but promptly got the ax for guzzling applejack at a Fort Belvoir (Va.) jamboree. I worked for a chicken farmer caponizing birds and candling eggs and continued to chalk up nothing but straight A's in school. I was always the teacher's pet because I could write poetry and wasn't missing three fingers from trying to pull weeds free of a jammed sickle bar. I earned A's in math because I *knew* I had ten toes and thirty-two teeth.

Yet it wasn't all gravy and nonstop kudos in the Old Dominion. Though I was a spirited boy, a decent marbles shooter, and something of an athlete, the vice principal at Herndon High School throughout my eighth-grade "season" constantly frisked me for water guns. A bunch of sadistic seniors ran around depantsing me during lunch hour because I was a wiseapple. A *smart* wiseapple. And believe me, *nobody* likes a smart wiseapple. My eighth-grade girlfriend tied the knot with somebody else and had a kid with him in the ninth grade while I still thought sex was a German word for the number six.

About that time my father decided I needed a better education. So we applied to the Loomis School in Windsor, Connecticut, a college preparatory institution for smart boys with money, not necessarily in that order. We didn't have money, but my dad's sister was willing to front my academic career, so I took the entrance exam. The math and social studies and history were difficult. But finally I reached a question right up my alley: *Imagine that your great-grandfather was a settler traveling west in a covered wagon in the 1870s. Give a description of his journey.*

I took off like President Clinton chasing Monica Lewinsky. Oh, to still retain a copy of that hyperbolic narration! My great-grandfather almost drowned crossing a river; sustained rattler and coral snake bites on both knees; was saved by angels that fell from heaven; battled Indians who could turn themselves into kangaroo rats, turtles, and nighthawks; and was run over by buffaloes and chased by wolves and almost eaten during hand-to-hand combat with a grizzly bear. An eagle attacked, lifting off his scalp, then he almost starved to death, nearly perished from thirst, and was finally mutilated by killer hummingbirds from Costa Rica, then kidnapped by Jesse James. But he made it to California easily enough . . . and I was accepted at Loomis. Commenting on my entrance exam, the admissions director said, "Well, your math scores stink, but you sure can sling the bull."

I presumed that was a compliment.

They incarcerated me in remedial English for two years because I did not know the difference between a semicolon and an adjective. I didn't much care, either. And for the next four years I died. They never gave me another free theme. Instead they drilled me with subjects and predicates; they told me what to write and how to write about it. They taught me expository writing because they wanted me to learn how to *think*. But they didn't want me to have any fun doing it.

Naturally, I rebelled. I grew my hair too long . . . and wound up in detention. I quit worshiping Patti Page and Eddie Fisher and started buying 45 records by Elvis Presley, Chuck Berry, and Screamin' Jay Hawkins, which I listened to much too loudly . . . and promptly wound up in detention. I wore blue jeans when they were illegal . . . and wound up in detention. When I was late for a class and the teacher gave me a demerit and I told him to go to hell . . . I wound up in detention. I dropped a water balloon on my French professor . . . and wound up in . . . *jail*. When I failed math four years in a row the petulant administrators wanted to kick me out.

But I had a pretty good time at Loomis when I wasn't in detention. They let me play football, and the newspaper—*The Loomis Log*—once credited me with making several "bone-crushing tackles" during a varsity contest. I became captain of the hockey team and had my front teeth bashed out. They gave me two hundred bucks in insurance money, all of which I spent on wanton hussies in nearby Hartford . . . ha ha, I'm kidding about that. At sixteen, in a puritanical Connecticut prep school (circa 1956), I was so innocent I thought all women were airbrushed like Barbie dolls below the waist and all babies were born of storks through immaculate conception.

The tooth insurance money went for a Gibson guitar, a Black Beauty switchblade knife, a Davy Crockett coonskin cap, a shotgun, and a .25 automatic pistol. My friends and I went over to the Connecticut River with that gun and when the school clock started loudly banging the hour, the quarter hour, or the half hour, we emptied several clips of dumdums at soda pop cans floating on the water.

My springtime sport was track—I ran the mile and the 220 low hurdles. I smoked a pack of Luckies before every meet just to prove I could be stupid and win anyway. One day I vomited from nervousness before I ran the hurdles . . . then I won and vomited afterward. Next I vomited from nervousness before the mile . . . and won that race too . . . and vomited again. Later I snuck behind the power plant building and smoked another cigarette. . . .

My girlfriend was a townie named Brenda. She had a pink-and-white Dodge that she drove to Loomis every afternoon and parked in the lot underneath my dormitory window. I'd go down and we'd make out for hours dry humping with our clothes on in the backseat while all my buddies hung out their windows goggle-eyed, spanking their monkeys. I was called before the discipline committee and chastised for committing immoral acts instead of going crazy from sexual frustration and killing my dorm adviser with an ax. Detention once again "welcomed me with open arms."

The academic side of prep school stumped me. Like I said, I flunked math four years straight, got tutored every summer, took makeup exams in the fall, and passed with a sixty every time, no more, no less. "Nichols, you're not exactly a rocket scientist," my algebra prof observed. "But you aren't really an Einstein either." I pondered those words of wisdom on my way over to the Snug for a crumb bun and an R.C. Cola.

The only way I could pass Latin exams was to memorize verbatim dozens of chapters in Caesar's invasion of Gaul and regurgitate them verbatim into blue books like a pelican feeding its young preavalated herring.

(The Loomis symbol/mascot, by the way, is a pelican. I don't know why. Can you imagine playing on a fierce football team *not* known as the Loomis Tigers, the Loomis Mustangs, the Loomis Eagles, the Loomis Lions, the Loomis Trojans, the Loomis Golden Bears, or the Loomis Fighting Dervishes, but rather as the Loomis *Pelicans?* Whenever we played in visiting stadiums the home crowd threw fish at our helmets and also barked at us like seals.)

Though English was supposed to be my strong suit, I found it flabbergastingly difficult. I never understood the difference between a dangling participle and a gerund, and I split every infinitive that meandered down the pike. In a trunk somewhere I still have stashed many long essays so marred by red marks they look like surgical operating aprons in the emergency room of a big city hospital on a turbulent Saturday night in July.

And although I loved to read, I could no more have explained the Dissonant Realism of a poem by Matthew Arnold than I could have baked a cheese soufflé. And after my French professor flunked me and I retaliated with that infamous water bomb on his head, it was finally decided to kick me out of school.

Before I could depart, however, they had a student council election and I was chosen—get this—as a write-in candidate. All the masters at Loomis probably hated my guts, but my fellow repressed peers obviously admired me in the way 1980s students would admire Johnny Rotten and Sid Vicious, Jeffrey Dahmer, the Circle Jerks, and Freddy Krueger. Happily, the Loomis oligarchs believed in "democracy," so I was invited back for my junior year, the first student councilor and dorm adviser ever to be on probation. The headmaster called me "a fox baby-sitting the chicken coop," and I was not allowed to remove my radio-monitoring ankle bracelet even when I went swimming or got a job stomping grapes in a barrel at the local winery. Thus forewarned, I cleaned up my act so well that at graduation I was awarded the Evelyn Longman Batchelder Sportsmanship Prize given annually to the boy most closely resembling a cross between Hoby Baker and Joe Namath.

I graduated from Loomis in 1958. Or to be more precise, I did not "truly" graduate. I had to be voted through by a faculty committee because I didn't have a graduating average. In fact, I was sixty-ninth in a class of seventy-two people. Of the three guys below me, one had committed suicide, one had been kicked out for urinating on the headmaster's pet monkey, and one had refused to dissect his frog in biology on religious grounds, an automatic F way back then. (Nowadays, according to most animal activists with whom I have caucused, you have the right to file a class-action suit against the biology department, the school, and God for being asked to mitigate in any way, shape, or form the internal organs of an amphibious creature protected under the laws of the state, the nation, and the EPA from wanton perturbation by sadistic anthropocentric academicians, even if for educational purposes only. We've come a long way, baby!)

I'm sure the faculty committee that voted me through was thinking: Do we really want this loose cannon back in our stately groves of academe for yet another go-round? In the Senior Superlative section of our yearbook I was adjudged Most Likely to Parachute Nude into a Christian Diocese Camp for Virgin Girls Who Just Wanna Have Fun. Obviously it was time to beam me up to the next level, Scotty, before I caused any real damage.

Loomis encouraged me to apply to any college I wanted. You pays your money (at that level), you're entitled. My basic interests in life at that point were rock 'n' roll, hockey, cartooning, Jayne Mansfield, and John Barleycorn, but I liked hockey most of all. Plus I was captain of the Loomis team; hence I applied to four hockey schools in the east: Middlebury, Hamilton, Clarkson, and St. Lawrence. And it's a mark of the integrity of our college admissions systems that I was readily accepted in the blink of a jaundiced eye at all four places, no questions asked.

The moral? The shortest distance between two points on the line between academic standards and student admissions is a good slap shot. By then I had become a fanatical jock. Hamilton's football coach invited me to school early in August to play for his team. At the start I practiced twice a day, with a chalk talk or scouting movies at night. I spent my lunch hours in downtown Clinton, New York, working out on ice with the Clinton Comets of the Eastern Hockey League. When school began I registered for a full load of classes and happily continued exercising twelve hours a day until my adviser called me in and complained, "John, what are you doing playing *football?* We accepted you to play *hockey*. Your grades at Loomis were terrible. If you don't quit football you'll flunk out of here before hockey season begins. I urge you to desist immediately."

I ignored him and played football, hockey, track. Then I quit football and ran cross-country in the autumn. I played tennis and lacrosse goalie and tried out for diver on the swimming team. I also acted in plays and wrote a humor column for the newspaper and played electric guitar at house parties and survived car wrecks on the New York Thruway on weekends, never seriously hurt because I always wrapped myself in a flak jacket cleverly constructed from empty beer cans.

How does a boy accomplish all this at an institution priding itself on the high level of education offered to its eight hundred male undergraduates? I'm not quite sure. Yes, I garnered a forty on my English final freshman year, but I also played third line on a hockey team with the second-best record in the East. Taking logic instead of math, I went into *that* final exam with a thirty-six average . . . but the test happened to fall on the same weekend that I won the low hurdles during spring house parties. And although in my history of philosophy course I couldn't really tell the difference between a Transcendentalist and Winnie the Pooh, at a party at Dean Wertimer's house one enchanted snowy evening I recited every verse nonstop not only of "The Cremation of Sam McGee," but also of "Abdullah Bulbul Amir."

Man does not live by bread alone!

I even found time to write a novel every year. This I did for fun, not credit, because there weren't any creative-writing classes. The books I wrote were horribly written, yet enthusiastic and full of mawkish bombastic emotion and really *freewheeling*. Think of a Megadeth versus Ozzie Osborn concert officiated by Ted Nugent on New Year's Eve in East St. Louis.

Nobody knew I was writing these puerile epics, so nobody told me to stop. I didn't look like a violence-prone anti-social opium-saturated space case, either. On the surface I appeared to be "normal." I had a flattop haircut, I wore tweed sports coats and black knit ties and either white bucks or suede hushpuppies that we called "brothel creepers." I bore a resemblance to a Pat Boone who, co-incidentally, had been hit in the mouth by a hockey puck.

One thing Hamilton did make me do, however, was READ

BOOKS. And God knows I loved reading books: Faulkner, Carson McCullers, George Eliot, Scott Fitzgerald, Richard Wright, Katherine Anne Porter, Joseph Conrad, Charles Dickens, Ernest Hemingway, Mickey Spillane. I'd been reading books and comics and newspapers since I was five, voraciously, nonstop. *How* to read them interested me not at all. I hated tests on themes and theses and symbolism and imagery, preferring instead to draw my own conclusions. Nobody was gonna tell *me* how to interpret or *what* to think.

(1) Jay Gatsby represents an American yearning for the original innocence of a continent commensurate with man's capacity for wonder. (2) *The Catcher in the Rye* is actually a postmodern Freudian dream about an adolescent oedipal complex as seen through the lionized id of a depressed teenybopper whose sign is on the cusp of Leo and Cancer. (3) When broken down into its individual components, *Look Homeward, Angel* is actually Ecclesiastes written backward by a tubercular genius. (4) And as for trout symbolism in *The Sun Also Rises:* Everybody knows that Hemingway, in denial, was playing with Japanese fish fertility emblems because he was impotent and a slave to the gremlinlike whims of his inner child.

Gracias, but I don't think so.

Yet I loved the storytelling; and I went positively ape over the *words*. I could relate to almost anybody. Tolstoy and Max Shulman; Wonder Woman and Jane Austen; Faulkner and Grace Metalious; Ralph Ellison and Dick Tracy.

I guess much of my adult (*sic*) critical thinking and writing developed as a reaction *against* the academy. When I graduated from college after the best private education money could buy over the past eight years, I had three career choices in mind. I wanted to be either a rock guitar player devoted to chauvinistic lyrics and S&M orgy-oriented album themes . . . or a writer of gangster epics in underworld slang . . . or a cartoonist like Al Capp, Chester Gould, and Walt Kelly morphed into a single lunatic. No desire for money or a normal place in society motivated my desires. Thanks but no thanks to a future based on society's terms. But I did have a burning desire to create . . . let my imagination wander . . . *enjoy* myself in life. And be my own boss.

Wonder of wonders, Hamilton gave me a diploma. To get it I had to take comprehensive exams. The night before the oral I read *Bleak House, Absalom, Absalom!, Jean Christophe,* and Balzac's entire *La Comédie humaine.* Next day I passed . . . out . . . with flying colors. I had a diploma; I was an "educated" man. With a mere snap of my talented fingers I could get a job anywhere in America . . . washing dishes, peeling potatoes, or serving hamburgers at a drive-in on roller skates.

Somehow, after all those years of American education, I had retained an inquiring mind. So I went to Spain and learned Spanish and French, taught English to Spaniards, and discovered calamari, octopus, and bullfighting. I lived with my French grandmother, who was six feet tall, weighed three hundred pounds, and had purple hair. I fell in love with a Parisian girl and was drafted for the Algerian War, an honor I politely declined, thus losing my rights to French citizenship. I also drank a lot of champagne at 3 A.M. in the underground garage of my grandmother's apartment building with the auto security guard while playing guitars and singing raucous songs.

One day the Spanish dictator, Francisco Franco, was driven down the Diagonal coursing past my grandmother's apartment in an open touring car and I gave him the finger. Immediately I was grabbed by the Guardia Civil and deported to New York, where I lived in a cold-water flat typing around the clock, day and night, week after week. Before long I had published two novels, gotten married, had a child, moved to New Mexico, had a second child, got divorced, started working for Hollywood, got married again and divorced again and married again ad infinitum.

During that chaotic time I somehow published twelve more books, wrote a half dozen screenplays for movies that were never made, lost my house in Upper Ranchitos right here in colorful downtown Taos, acted as a commissioner on an irrigation ditch for ten years, and decided that I understood about as much about women as Theodore Kaczynski, the Unabomber.

Currently, I am a day away from turning fifty-eight, and I must say the tussle has been interesting. By far the most interesting part has been an education that started in kindergarten in 1945 (where I drew that picture of Pinocchio) and has continued right up to the present. All along the way, despite my arrogance and blindingly vapid surface charm, I had teachers and educators and coaches at all levels of the U.S. school system who believed in me. Or even if they didn't they tried to so that I would move on to the next grade level and be out of their hair.

I responded by kicking and fussing and mocking and cursing and challenging and dropping water bombs and giving the finger, and in general acting artistic and gifted. Underneath, of course, I was happy as a pig in a pen full of mud and half-eaten corncobs.

To sum up: A lot of things happened between 1945, when I entered kindergarten, and today, July 22, 1998, when I find myself before you all slinging just about as much BS as I unloaded on my entrance exam to the Loomis School in 1954, only this time around I'm getting paid for it, thank God.

Though not hardly enough, really, if I may be candid. In fact, afterward, if any of you wish to slip me a few bob or an extra sawbuck when nobody is looking, I wouldn't mind. Truth is, if I can get out of here with an extra five hundred under the table I promise that I'll protect every donor's anonymity: I won't breathe a *word* to the IRS.

Abridged from a speech to The Rocky Mountain Association of Collegiate Registrar and Admissions Officers in Taos, New Mexico, July 22, 1998.

$E = mc^2$

Many years ago I read an autobiographical book by Erskine Caldwell; the name of the tome was *Call It Experience*. In this memoir Caldwell recounted how he'd managed to get his first piece of fiction writing into print. I'm sure I don't have all the facts straight, but as I remember the tale goes like this:

Caldwell sent a whole bunch of stories to Max Perkins at *Scribner's Magazine* and all of them were rejected. This got the writer's dander up, and he decided that what was needed was an all-out assault on the magazine. So Caldwell went up to Maine or Vermont, rented himself a cheap cabin, brought in enough wood for the winter, and then he began to type. He wrote one, two, three pieces a week, maybe more, and as soon as they were finished he sent them off to *Scribner's*. The magazine poobahs read, rejected, and sent them right back. This did not deter Caldwell one whit; he just kept writing stuff and sending it off. All through November, December, January, and February his typing never stopped. He was like a werewolf scrivener maddened by the moon, determined to succeed. Dozens, then hundreds of yarns arrived in the *Scribner's* mailbox and Caldwell never let up, never became discouraged. He just wouldn't take no for an answer. Finally, along about April or May after this relentless onslaught, he received a letter in the mail from Max Perkins, who begged, "Please, stop, no more stories! We're going to publish the last two you sent, on the condition that you never darken our door with a manuscript again." The author shrieked, "Hallelujah!" and promised never to send them another story . . . but he'd finally broken into print. Caldwell came

120

out of them thar hills, wrote *God's Little Acre* and *Tobacco Road,* made a million bucks, and lived to a ripe old age venerated by one and all.

My own writing career has been a lot like that. I've always figured bombardment is the name of the game. In college professors often accused me of employing the "shotgun method" in my exams. I had a peculiar skill, when under stress, of rendering enough orthographically reproduced knowledge during a limited time period to get a high enough grade (exactly seventy) to qualify for varsity athletics: I spewed verbiage. I regurgitated words. I set up grandiose smoke screens of *palabras*. I'm the only person in the history of Hamilton College (a small, liberal arts, all-male school in upstate New York) to turn in eleven blue books, answering just three questions, in a chemistry final exam. Too bad I got a zero on the test.

No matter: I always figured if I sprayed language and ideas in every direction, a few of them were bound to hit a target. Verbal Diarrhea was my middle name. The Erskine Caldwell theory of literary success: It's $E = mc^2$. Excess equals mass times the energy of typing, squared.

Put another way, I have written about eighty books, beginning when I was a tiny tot and continuing through to the present. Of those eighty I only published fifteen. Yet so long as I've been able to produce in the Caldwell tradition, I have been able to survive.

It hasn't always been easy, I'll admit.

Like, here's an update on my condition today after this wonderful literary career: I'm fifty-four years old, and in the last six months I almost died of a bout with endocarditis that blew out the mitral valve in my heart. I finished writing a script about Kayapo Indians in the Amazon jungle for director Ridley Scott while in the Taos hospital. Two weeks out of the hospital I married my young and very volatile girlfriend, Miel Castagna. Then I went on tour for a recently published novel called *Conjugal Bliss*. During the tour I bogged down with congestive heart failure. Soon enough the condition worsened. But I finished a short novel called *Great Feelings of Love* and sent it to my editor in New York. Next day I entered an Albuquerque hospital and had open-heart surgery to repair my destroyed mitral valve. When I toddled out, my editor told me *Great Feelings of Love* was no good and she rejected it cold turkey. So I spent a couple of months rewriting it while taking flamenco guitar lessons so I could play for my wife, who's a great flamenco dancer. I also learned how to walk again. But my heart locked into permanent atrial fibrillation, so I returned to the Albuquerque hospital two weeks ago and was cardioverted (by great bangs of electricity) back into sinus rhythm. Then last Thursday I began a screenplay of my own novel, *American Blood,* for a producer who took an option on that book last month. I'm also writing an article for *Rocky Mountain Magazine* on the forest firefighters who recently died in Glenwood Springs, Colorado. And I'm slated to do a one-week writing workshop in Santa Fe followed by a seven-day photo workshop in Taos the first two weeks in August. Then I plan to enter that Albuquerque hospital again to be *re*cardioverted.

The Ridley Scott project seems to have been shelved. My editor's probably going to reject the newly revised *Great Feelings of Love* novel again. And it's a one-in-a-million chance that *American Blood* will ever reach the silver screen or that my heart will ever be free of mitral valve prolapse and atrial fibrillation at the same time. But hey, I figure what my former football coach once told me pretty much holds true: "As long as you keep moving you're less likely to get hurt." You're also *more* likely to score. Witness *Forrest Gump.* That ludicrous movie is about a quasi–mental retard who's an actual genius, and he *runs.* This is after he's been a college football hero, won the Medal of Honor in Vietnam, and become a billionaire shrimp salesman. He runs from Maine to California and back, and then back to California again. He doesn't know where he's going or why he's doing it. But he *runs.* And that's kind of the story of my life so far.

Yup, much of the time I never knew where I was headed, but I sure was a typing fool. And sooner or later, God and the Vietnam War notwithstanding, some of it actually worked out.

My first writing teacher was named Miss Cynthia Applewaite. She taught all twelve of us in a one-room schoolhouse in my childhood hometown of Possum Trot, Georgia, population thirty-six. One day when I was in the second grade, shortly before she died of rickets and pellagra, Miss Cynthia gave me a copy of *Finnegan's Wake* to read, and that book really changed my—

Actually, I started writing in the summer of 1955 right after my parents divorced and my father and I were living in a small apartment in Chevy Chase, Maryland. Pop worked in Washington, D.C., for the CIA, and every day I was left alone in our little crib, so I wrote stories. I created them in exact imitation of Damon Runyan, who was my early and most powerful literary hero. My efforts were all about New York gangsters and they were written in the first-person present tense using very graphic Yiddish shtarker slang. For example:

> I'm sitting in Mindy's restaurant on a Saturday night when who should come through the door but Harry the Horse, and he's packing a pizzolover the size of the Empire State Building. So, before he gets the drop on me, I outs with my own John Roscoe and I proceed to practically crochet my monogram across his chest, leaving him exceptionally deceased indeed.

That was the start of my writing—I mean running—career, and I haven't quit running—I mean writing—ever since.

I wrote my first novel when I was still installed in a remedial English program at the Loomis School in Windsor, Connecticut. Then I went to college, where I churned out at least a novel a year, not for any class, nor for any grade or professor, just for myself. Writers were considered bohunks and commies back in my adolescence, and you couldn't actually take a course in creative writing because that would have been considered un-American.

Once, in college, I almost died of blood poisoning, and during the two weeks I lay flat on my back in the infirmary, I wrote a two-hundred-page novel called *Don't Be Forlorn*. It concerned racism in the South. Another novel I produced at college traced the career of a blind guitar player called Pheasant Mellow, living in the Storyville Jazz period of New Orleans. His best friend was Jelly

Roll Morton. A third book was about two kids who killed their parents and set up a commune with other sicko delinquents who'd offed their parental units: my point was to demonstrate how evil innocence can be. It was *Lord of the Flies* (long before William Golding thought of the idea) meets *Children of the Corn*. Ultimately, I only managed to prove how evil bad *writing* can be.

I never could get anyone to actually read my books. Although once an old professor at Hamilton, to whom I'd given a draft of a saga about vegetarian vampires who grow cannibal cabbages at night (using bat shit for fertilizer), showed up in back of my fraternity house on horseback to return the manuscript, unread, and as he leaned over to hand it to me, he dropped it. The wind caught all the pages and blew them across campus like leaves from the magnificent maple trees that made shady our bucolic academic haven. That, by the way, is the best distribution of one of my works that I *ever* had.

One year after my graduation I found myself living on the corner of West Broadway and Prince Street on the isle of Manhattan in New York City playing my guitar in funky coffeehouses and dives on Bleecker and MacDougal streets to earn a notoriously meager living. Simultaneously, I worked on five novels at once, hoping to strike it rich. *The Sterile Cuckoo* was about a kooky college romance. *The Wind Heart*—my Scott Fitzgerald epic—detailed the disintegration of a robber baron family on the North Shore of Long Island. *Hey and Boo and Bang* covered the last week in the life of an alcoholic bum who earned a living gathering crushed cardboard boxes in a shopping cart along the Bowery in New York City. A family saga titled *Autumn Beige* concerned a kid who kills his brother in a shooting accident while they are duck hunting. *The Wizard of Loneliness* dealt with a Vermont family torn asunder by World War II and by an evil nephew who visits them in 1944. But after witnessing the family's agony, the nephew becomes a compassionate human being.

Like I said about writing, $E = mc^2$.

The first novel I tried to sell was *The Sterile Cuckoo*. I simply took the manuscript up to the offices of Random House or Knopf or Farrar, Straus & Giroux, and I left it at the front desk with the secretary. I included a self-addressed postcard they could send me when the book was rejected, and then I went home. In those days it took about three weeks to be rejected. Then I carted the book to another secretary at another publishing house. I did this about ten times. Occasionally, somebody made a suggestion—one line, an offhand comment—and I would immediately rewrite the book according to those words of wisdom because they came from a pro. I would sometimes type twenty-four hours straight without sleep so I could rewrite the story in six days.

The eleventh house, David McKay, said they'd publish *The Sterile Cuckoo* if I could expand it from a novella into a novel. Wow! In seventy-two hours I added another one hundred pages. David McKay liked them, *Cuckoo* was published, it became a Literary Guild alternate, sold to paperbacks for $37,500, and was translated into British, Dutch, Danish, German, Italian, Portuguese, and Japanese. It triggered reviews that compared me to both F. Scott Fitzgerald and Max Shulman, and it went out on film option to Alan Pakula (who later directed *Sophie's Choice* and *All the President's Men*). Alan hired me to do a screenplay. I went from earning $500 in 1964 to earning $35,000 in 1965. I spent this money wisely by giving half to a tax lawyer (who took me for a royal ride), by putting my brother through his first year of Dartmouth, by bailing a relative out of imminent jail (by paying off their debt to the IRS), and by sending my new wife to an orthodontist.

Before I sold the novel no agent would touch me with a ten-foot bottle of Perrier. The minute I scored the money, however, agents fell out of the sky like members of the 82nd Airborne on maneuvers at Camp Lejeune. And the first one that landed at my feet got the job. Thirty years later we're still together. The agent immediately took my second novel, *The Wizard of Loneliness*, and submitted it to G. P. Putnam's, who said it would win a quarter-of-a-million-dollar prize that they were sponsoring. They wined me and dined me at the King Cole Room of the St. Regis Hotel and at the Oak Room of the Plaza Hotel in Manhattan. They also suggested I retain a big-time lawyer to invest all the money I was going to receive. So I hired the lawyer, but it turned out the Put-nam Prize was actually a ruse to lure distinguished writers from other publishers, then nobody won the prize, and that was that.

The Wizard of Loneliness was released and sank like a stone. It was translated into a single foreign language—guess which one? Polish! Meanwhile, I'd taken a bus to Guatemala to visit a friend, and there, totally blown away by the oppression of the indigenous population (thanks to U.S. imperialism), I began my metamorpho-sis from bright young talent (and heir to the F. Scott Fitzgerald mantle) to raving Marxist-Leninist, anti-Vietnam-war protester, and writer of polemical left-wing novels.

My career halted with a screech that was not exactly heard around the world. I never published *Autumn Beige, The Wind Heart,* or *Hey and Boo and Bang.* In fact, for the next seven years I did not publish a thing. I wrote five or six novels during that time, but in one way or another they all read like Dobie-Gillis-goes-to-Stalinist-Russia-and-opens-a-tractor-factory-with-Mike-Gold-and-Upton-Sinclair.

I was enmeshed—to the top of my disillusioned, culture-shocked brain—by the struggle between form and content. Fuck form, hail communist content! I mistrusted everything I'd been taught about bourgeois art. I didn't quite come to the conclusion that Chopin was a pig, but I derived a lot more from reading Malcolm X or Ida Tarbell (on the history of Standard Oil) than I did from reading *The Alexandria Quartet.* Yet I couldn't *truly* get into socialist real-ism. Whenever I started writing about a feminist factory worker in Detroit, somehow I'd wind up describing her Brazilian-cut silk panties and humongous tits.

Nevertheless, I thought it was probably more valuable to per-son the barricades than to write namby-pamby fiction that had been inspired by the likes of Truman Capote and W. H. Hudson. So I marched on the Pentagon, organized for peace candidates, read *The Guardian* and *I. F. Stone's Weekly* instead of the *Times Book Re-view,* and drew anti-Yankee cartoons for Liberation News Service in New York.

One novel I penned was about a guy who goes to Vietnam, wins the Medal of Honor, comes home, shakes the president's hand, and discovers that America is a violent, racist, crime-ridden, imperialist horror show. He winds up venting a bit of frustration by blowing away his entire family at a cocktail party, then walking down to the seashore and symbolically throwing his Medal of Honor into the ocean.

I wrote another book about a Native American victim of genocide whose sheep herd is rubbed out by nerve gas drifting over from the Dugway (Utah) Testing Grounds. I completed a third harangue about a kid like myself who goes to Nam after this brilliant college career and is instantly wasted.

In my books I'd set up scenes much as I'm sure old Scott Fitzgerald might have: a penthouse glitterati party in Manhattan, glib and witty conversation, champagne and charming Gibson girls. Then suddenly my tipsy hero would jump onto a table, wave his arms for quiet, call all the guests "running dog lackeys of warmongering capitalist pigs," and proceed to deliver a fifty-page diatribe to the assembled revelers about the history of colonialism in Indochina from the advent of the French in the early 1800s to the Tonkin Gulf Resolution in 1964.

During these tirades the narrative tended to slow down a trifle. Jack London's *Iron Heel* was alive and well and living in my Converse All-Stars. My plots could usually be summed up in a one-sentence slogan that was popular in the sixties:

"Up against the wall, honky motherfucker, or black power's gonna get your momma!"

During that time, *The Sterile Cuckoo* was made into a decent little movie starring Liza Minnelli, who earned an Academy Award nomination for her work in it. And the theme song, "Come Saturday Morning," sung by the Sandpipers, actually won an Academy Award; it was so sappy and so apolitical that I almost committed *sepuku*.

The day Neil Armstrong stepped onto the moon, I left New York City and moved to Taos, New Mexico, cursing the U.S. space program for wasting money on lunar bullshit while four-fifths of the world was starving to death. By then I was almost broke, an unknown again, and without any literary prospects to speak of.

They say the average writer's public life lasts about as long as that of a marine beachhead commander or a rookie linebacker in the NFL. I was twenty-nine years old and I'd already had my fifteen minutes of fame. One day in the library I looked up F. Scott Fitzgerald's obituary in *The New York Times* the day he died at the age of forty-four. I learned that when the author of *The Great Gatsby* kicked the bucket none of his stuff was in print. True, I was still breathing, but I felt as if the Fitzgerald Eclipse had already happened to me.

For some reason, though, I kept forging novels. I knew they were bad, but I just kept typing. Me and Forrest Gump: plod, plod, plod.

There came a day, however, when it looked like curtains for sure. The year was 1972, the month November. I hadn't earned a dime in ages. My children were gnawing on the last of the worm-infested turnips that I had carried up from our root cellar in a blizzard. My wife had left me for a successful orthodontist. We were freezing because I hadn't paid the gas bill in four months. I was finally staring into the shiny skull, grinning teeth, and sunken eye sockets of the need for a "real job." Like that of a college professor, or a landscape artist, or a gasoline profusionist.

How did I react to this crisis? I started running faster. I sat down and wrote a novel called *The Milagro Beanfield War,* using the shotgun attack, or, as my friend Mike Kimmel called it, the "blam" method of writing. In five weeks I churned out an almost plotless five hundred pages with two hundred characters. I took three weeks to correct it, three weeks to type it up on my little green Hermes Rocket (the original disposable typewriter), and I sent it to my agent in New York. He sent it to an editor at Holt, Rinehart and Winston, and she bought it for ten thousand dollars. A year later the book was published . . . and sank like a stone. But, thank God, it stayed on movie options for the next fourteen years and that saved my career. Eventually *Milagro* was made into a film that sank like a stone. It was also published in a paperback version that floated lethargically on the tides of literary reputation, becoming a sort of "cult classic" in due course.

I published twelve more books in the next twenty years, none of which earned back their advance. A few of them my publisher thought might be the "breakout book" that would justify all their heartache. But that never happened, and today, even though nine or ten of my titles are still in print, the combined royalties for any given year don't amount to more than $3,000.

Mostly, Hollywood keeps me alive. My career in movies truly started when I received a phone call at the end of 1979 from a producer asking me if I wanted to discuss rewriting a script for a Greek-French director, Costa-Gavras, the creator of *Z* and *State of Siege*. I went to L.A. and schmoozed with Costa for three days, then returned to Taos and in three frantic weeks (over the 1979–80 Christmas holidays) I rewrote a picture that ultimately was called *Missing*. It garnered four Academy Award nominations and ultimately won for Best Adapted Screenplay. But by then I'd been arbitrated out of a credit by my own union, which caused a *very* minor scandal. Sadly, I never got to clutch an Oscar in my grubby fist while shouting anti-American slogans over prime-time international TV from the podium at the awards ceremony.

Hollywood loves new meat. I speak English, French, and Spanish. Instantly I became a good guy to hire for liberal, lefty pictures saddled with foreign directors. I worked on two more pictures with Costa-Gavras, about nuclear war and science and human values in the twentieth century. With Louis Malle the topic was cultural genocide. With the Czech-British director Karel Reisz (best known in America for *The French Lieutenant's Woman*), I developed a screenplay on Haitian refugees and U.S. immigration policies under President Reagan. And I slaved away on the *Milagro* film for Robert Redford.

I also spent two years scripting a miniseries for CBS about the life of Pancho Villa and the Mexican Revolution.

Unfortunately, most movies that go through development are never made, and a majority of the projects I worked on didn't see the light of day. I published one novel during my Hollywood sojourn, *American Blood*. It's about the violence underlying our culture. Most readers throw it against the wall by page ten, rush to the bathroom, and vomit. *American Blood* sank like a stone.

In 1988, a bit weary of L.A., I went back to writing novels full-time. I decided to create an epic with two hundred bigger-than-life characters. In two years I finished a draft of this behemoth and sent it to my editor at Holt. She commonly refers to me as her "favorite four-foot-tall Stalinoid dwarf on a soapbox." Let me quote a few choice lines from her 1990 rejection letter. My book was tentatively titled *Democracy in Action.* The editor wrote, "What's wrong with *Democracy in Action?* After eight-hundred-some pages I had to conclude, just about everything. It's got no center and the result is it has no real plot. The scams don't work. The motivations are glossed over, the characters are paper-thin. The effect is part harangue, part maudlin commentary, and large-part tedium."

Then, and here's my favorite statement from her rejection letter: "This is a big monster of an oil spill flowing every which way, meaning very little." *Dulce et decorum est pro patria mori.* Undaunted, I sat down and rewrote the book three more times and it merely became worse. What's the expression—it's just as difficult to write a bad novel as it is to write a good one? You better believe it. I cut that manuscript from fifteen hundred pages to nine hundred pages. Then I threw out eight hundred pages and added two hundred fifty new ones. Then I switched it from third person to first person. But nothing worked. It was like trying to shovel shit from a septic tank with a pitchfork.

Disheartened, I finally quit that boondoggle, and, at age fifty-one, going broke yet again, I wrote two short novels very quickly. The first, *Satan Was an Angel,* was about a man and his girlfriend and the girlfriend's child, who starts in the book as a ten-year-old and grows up to be eighteen, the age at which she begins an affair with her mother's lover: bad things happen to all three of them. My editor thought it was slick, twisted, perverse, and she gave it two thumbs-down.

Promptly I whipped off another tale about a woman being tortured for smuggling a loaf of bread to a doctor in hiding because he had given medical care to local revolutionaries. In *The Holiness of Water* my brave heroine stood up under torture. My agent felt her ordeal was the most depressing thing he'd ever read.

Okay, okay. I sighed deeply and took a gig teaching at the University of New Mexico for the spring semester of 1992. It was my first straight job since college graduation in 1962 and a really weird experience, like, sort of *comfortable*. Whenever I received a paycheck at the end of the month I felt like apologizing to the people of Haiti, Rwanda, Bolivia, and Bangladesh for my secure bourgeois existence.

At semester's end I hightailed it back to Taos and wrote a novella called *An Elegy for September*. In it a writer suffering heart problems hunts grouse with an angry, female teenybopper in the Sangre de Cristo Mountains of northern New Mexico, and for some reason my editor bought that one, giving me the biggest advance I'd ever received, $40,000. *Playboy Magazine* did an excerpt, handing me a check for $6,000. Holt had high hopes, but of course *September* sank like a stone.

Back to the old drawing board.

I should mention here that twice in my busy life I have churned out batches of short stories and begged my agent to market them. But he never could sell a one, so I bagged that medium.

I have managed to survive, however, with my integrity intact. Some pundits have commented that in my case integrity translates as stupidity. Myself, I've always believed that "if you don't get caught up in the gelt, you won't be wrapped up in the guilt." To boot, you may actually live a life that somehow translates down the stretch as an endeavor that was blessed with freedom.

Very early in my career, specifically when I was offered a quarter of a million bucks and then unoffered it in the next breath, I made a decision that whether or not I earned five grand a year or a hundred Gs per annum, I'd always try to live as if I only had the five. I would get rid of the rest to good or noble causes or to destitute friends or to liquor stores. That way I could never be trapped into working at something I hated to do in order to pay for material habits. My life has worked out in a nicely bizarre balance thanks to that strategy.

Because I never wanted it much, folks in the art racket have thrown a lot of money in my direction. But I fended it off alertly and never accumulated much that could weigh me down. I find myself at fifty-four living in a little three-room house, driving a

1980 battered Dodge truck with 160,000 miles on it, and with three pairs of sneakers in my closet. Coincidentally, I'm also about $80,000 in debt from a mortgage, college loans, and recent medical fees. But I'm a happy man. Life is a bowl of cherries.

Unfortunately, my wife, Miel, is not exactly a happy camper. She thinks I probably had a lobotomy back in my youthful days. She feels I throw out too many babies with the bathwater on my maniacal quests for integrity. But I tell her, "Mellow out, relax, stick with me, kid, and even if the roof leaks and the termites undermine our foundations, it won't matter one whit, because as long as we have each other we'll just dance down a delightful yellow brick road without a care in the world into a future that is sublime."

Whereupon the charming, well-mannered and innocent tyke sums up her attitude toward *my* attitude with a succinct phrase that I suppose could stand as the epitaph on my long and distinguished career. Like, whenever I explain to Miel that the greatest adventures are in the mind, or that integrity means more than moolah, or that material goods don't matter at all compared to the satisfaction garnered from a paragraph written as if the angels of Shakespeare and the devils of Cormac McCarthy were copulating upon my scribbled page, you know what she replies?

"Fuck you, John, and the Olympia portable typewriter you rode in on."

Adapted from an address to The Pacific Northwest Writers Conference, Seattle, July 22, 1994. Reprinted in The Pursuit of Happiness. *Blue Heron Publishing, 1995.*

Night of the Living Beanfield:
How an Unsuccessful Cult Novel Became an
Unsuccessful Cult Film in Only Fourteen Years,
Eleven Nervous Breakdowns, and $20 Million

One

I've had my teeth bashed out playing hockey, and I spent nine years protesting the Vietnam War. I've been married and divorced three times, and I raised two children. I've been in a head-on collision, and I almost died of endocarditis two years ago. I then went through five months of congestive heart failure that culminated in open-heart surgery. But I can safely say that the toughest thing I ever did in my life was to have a movie made out of my third novel, *The Milagro Beanfield War.*

The story begins in 1973.

That was the year the Supreme Court issued its renowned *Roe v. Wade* decision . . . and Henry Kissinger won the Nobel Peace Prize . . . and members of the American Indian Movement occupied Wounded Knee in South Dakota . . . and John Dean blew the whistle on Richard Nixon.

1973 was also the year that I sold *Milagro.*

I was broke, *Milagro* was the first book I had sold in eight years, and the purchase price was $10,000—an incredible fortune to me in those days.

The novel was published in 1974 to a resounding shrug. *The New York Times* lambasted it, and local newspaper mogul Mark Acuff, editor of the infamous *New Mexico Independent,* called the book a "bomb" and "a shallow insult" to all of us. A Santa Fe scribe, Tom

Mayer, writing for *The Rio Grande Sun* in Española, accused me of creating a world "utterly without moral subtlety," functioning with a literary design that "is too obvious, too calculated and polemical, and not one character escapes symbolic function to achieve the status of a person you know, let alone care about."

Next day the *Los Angeles Times* called me a "second-string sports reporter" and terminated their review by saying I had written a "book that takes hours to read, a moment to forget."

Meanwhile, back at the ranch—in fact, while the book was still in manuscript form in a forlorn pile on the desk of my agent, Perry Knowlton, at Curtis Brown in New York—an actor/producer/director guy named Tony Bill happened to pick it up and read it, and he gave it to a couple of friends of his named Bob Christiansen and Rick Rosenberg, who'd recently won Emmys with a TV film called *The Autobiography of Miss Jane Pittman*. Convinced *Milagro* would make a wonderful movie, Chris/Rose promptly took out a film option on the novel.

They hired Mark Medoff (now famous for writing *Children of a Lesser God*) to do a script. He hadn't penned *Children* yet, but he had written *When You Comin' Back, Red Ryder?*, which was a popular play in New York.

Me, I figure I'm in like Flint—this movie is gonna change my desperate life.

Unfortunately, Medoff bungled the job. Then the company fronting the bread went defunct and filed for a Chapter 11. But a different outfit promptly jumped on board, so Bob and Rick started looking for another writer—at about the same time *Milagro* was finally published (in the autumn of 1974) . . . and nothing happened.

Not with the book, not with the movie.

Perhaps before I delve into the celluloid shenanigans of shallow, racist, childish, chauvinist, anti-communist, moneygrubbing, egomaniacal, fascist Hollywood, I should give you at least a basic synopsis of my profound, tolerant, adult, feminist, pro-communist, money-scorning, humble, self-effacing, compassionate novel—in case any of you have not been able to read it yet.

Milagro begins with a nineteenth-century lunatic digging a hole to China, trying to find his lost dog. It ends with a Vista volunteer getting his lights punched out after riding a vicious Shetland pony during a fiesta celebrating the fact that not all the horses in China can stop disempowered people from harvesting the fruits of their own labors if they are really hungry for a bean burrito. In between, a vast and jumbled assortment of characters catch trout illegally, fornicate in runaway VW buses, butcher mice, fire dumdum bullets at undercover police agents, kill crows with their bare hands, drive bulldozers into the Rio Grande Gorge, commit adultery, play boogie-woogie piano with just one arm, adopt orphan robins, slaughter skunks, rip up parking tickets, chuck pebbles at tourists, almost rape inquiring reporters, snowshoe around the high mountains in midwinter, and declare war against the U.S. Forest Service, the New Mexico state engineer, the governor and his lackeys, the banking system of America, all realtors and resort developers within a five-hundred-square-mile area, and the president of the United States.

In short, the novel, like anyone who has ever tried to explain New Mexico to an outsider, tends to ramble. Like our state, the novel is big, it is bold, and it is mostly empty spaces.

That tendency is not real cinematic. Basically, your average movie has two main characters, two supporting characters, and a fairly tight plot.

For example: *Rain Man* features Tom Cruise and Dustin Hoffman—period. The plot? They drive across the country from the East Coast to the West Coast.

War of the Roses? It stars Michael Douglas and Kathleen Turner, with a bit part by Danny DeVito. The plot? A couple gets married. Then they get divorced.

Bugsy? Warren Beatty, Annette Bening. The plot? He wants to build a hotel. He goes in debt to build it. So the people holding his chits kill him.

What can we learn from these brief synopses? It's simple. Movies are short stories. Usually they're about two hours' duration, max. A film script is almost always between 110 and 120 pages long, and most of that is air. You can't play too much with the structure because of the limitations. Movies are not like epic poems. They're like sonnets—same number of lines every time. The story has to be told with great economy. If the plots are too complicated the machine breaks down, the audience becomes lost. If too many characters are involved there isn't time to flesh them out, so they become very thin and the story doesn't work.

That's why *Driving Miss Daisy* is a perfect movie: him, her, and Dan Aykroyd. Its only drawback is that it hints of racism in the United States and treats a black man as a human being, almost with respect. Hollywood, a bastion of reaction, home of Rambo, is not partial to the liberal imagination. Remember: All the commies in Tinseltown went to jail or were blacklisted during the McCarthy period in the 1940s and 1950s. Ever since, Hollywood has prided itself on keeping its nose clean and its high moral banners flapping in a reactionary, violence-obsessed, misogynistic, homophobic, red-baiting amoral ambience of good clean patriotic American entertainment fun.

So *Milagro* had a couple of strikes against it when Bob Christiansen and Rick Rosenberg took out an option in 1973.

What sort of strikes—?

Let me count the ways:

Its length.

Its subject matter.

Its politics.

Its numerous characters.

Its ethnic composition.

Its lack of structure.

Its filthy language.

Its foreign setting.

Its support of Spanish culture and tradition.

(In a country where thirty-seven states have passed English-only laws, this story had a foreign—well, Spanish—word in the title. My agent wanted that word *out*. My publisher wanted that word *out*. For a long time, the film people wanted that word *out*.)

(Now, to my utter horror, the tables have been turned. In Taos there's a Milagro Bed and Breakfast, a Milagro Art Gallery, a Rancho Milagro, too. A Denver excursion outfit runs Milagro Tours to northern New Mexico. A Santa Fe gardening operation sells Milagro Organic Fertilizer! And at least twice a year in northern New Mexico, when somebody goes crazy over land or water issues, the newspapers hail the conflict as a "real-life *Milagro Beanfield War."*)

Another negative for Hollywood is that the book also respected women.

And nobody is slaughtered, mangled in a car crash, dropped out of a high-rise window, raped, sodomized, or otherwise brutalized in accordance with the high moral traditions of the entertainment industry and the motion picture rating academy.

Like: *booooring!*

But Christiansen and Rosenberg didn't think so. They felt they could have a winner. After Medoff and the first company dropped out, they found a new studio to front the bills and hired Tracy Keenan Wynn (who had written *Miss Jane Pittman*) to do the script. That script turned out to be lukewarm. When I saw it I got scared and wondered if this project was such a good idea after all. I felt the script was, among other things, patronizing—though not deliberately—and violent in a way that felt creepy. It also didn't have much humor. I took a bus out to Hollywood and, in three days, we shredded it to ribbons.

Tracy wound up rewriting *Milagro* God knows how many times. It ceased being patronizing, it ceased being violent. It also kept on not being humorous and never quite worked out. Tracy left the picture.

Then the new development company also pulled up stakes and booked. So Christiansen and Rosenberg found yet another studio with money to burn and hired a new pen pusher, Leonard Gardner (who'd written a novel called *Fat City,* which had also been made into a movie), and a director named Michael Wadleigh (who'd done the film of *Woodstock*), and they knuckled down to business.

But how to distill from such a cluttered book a simple workable screenplay? Everybody agreed that in the novel the *town*—all those people *together*—is the main character. Obviously, the film needed to be an "ensemble piece." That is, a story about a bunch of characters with *equal* billing—although not, of course, two hundred characters. Some would have to be merged, many others discarded. The producers and writers believed there had to remain at least ten or twelve principal characters for the *feel* of the novel to be retained.

But giving equal billing to that many people in a 110-page script was like trying to juggle a bowling ball, a chain saw, an apple, and six bananas while eating the apple (and then the bananas) without letting anything fall to earth.

Now about the plot: You could spend a whole growing season reading the novel. But you could spend only two hours at the movie, tops. Meaning about 90 percent of the incidents in the book had to be thrown out of the movie.

There was another problem, too.

Sometimes a film is made because a big-shot actor or actress commits to the project. Often studios spend development money if they even *think* a big shot might commit.

Translated, this usually means a *white* big shot.

In the case of *Milagro,* every time Christiansen and Rosenberg started talking money with the studios, the studios' first question was: "Who wants to see a movie about a bunch of Mexicans?"

If Christiansen and Rosenberg complained about that attitude, the money men pulled out marketing reports and demographic surveys and said, "There aren't twenty million Spanish-speaking people in this country, so where's the paying public for this movie?"

Occasionally, the weasels softened their stance a little: "If you guys can land a commitment from either Robert De Niro, Al Pacino, or Dustin Hoffman, we'll think about it."

If Christiansen and Rosenberg began talking Chicano actors, the accountants got glazed eyeballs.

But none of that really mattered yet, because the latest script was in trouble. Tracy Wynn had come and gone. Leonard Gardner and Michael Wadleigh were heading nowhere fast.

One year when the option was up for renewal, a young producer came to see me. He had access to Charles Bronson, and Bronson had committed to do the movie. This meant for sure the movie could be made. The producer asked me, "How much are you getting in option money?" I said, "Five thousand." He said,

"I'll triple it." I said, "Forget the money; let's talk about your approach to the movie." He said, "John, what's the current purchase price of the book?" I think it was around $25,000. He said, "I'll double it." I said, "Relax. You could have it for the same price as now. I'm mostly just interested in your approach to the movie." He smiled and said, "What's your participation on the back end of the picture?" I said it was 2.5 percent of the net—which, unless you're talking *Star Wars* or *Indiana Jones,* is like owning 2.5 percent of a North Pole gladiola distributorship. So he said, "I'll give you five percent of the gross"—which is an incredible offer, because it means that when *any* money comes in, I have a piece of the action.

I said, "Really, I'm serious; I'm basically just interested in your artistic approach to the movie."

He laughed and threw up his hands. "Okay, John, you drive a hard bargain, but I'm hip, so write your own ticket. Just tell me, how much will it cost me to buy you?"

I put on my wizened little self-righteous face and renewed the option for one more go-round with Christiansen and Rosenberg.

Another year went by with no success on the film, and finally Christiansen and Rosenberg gave up. They had tried hard for six years, we had become good friends, but they simply could not put together the movie.

Incredibly, however, *Milagro* was still in print. Who knows exactly why? Only one paperback company, Ballantine, had had an interest in the reprint rights, and they bought the book for $7,500. Though I had made a few hundred bucks in royalties, for the most part my literary career had continued its brilliant nosedive. I wrote several novels between 1974 and 1978, but they were rejected. Finally, however, I published *The Magic Journey* in 1978.

Just in case anybody had missed the point with *Milagro,* I made sure, in *The Magic Journey,* that cultural genocide, climax capitalist decadence, and my Marxist-Leninist politics were spelled out in spades.

Naturally, the book was a BIG hit. It was an alternate selection of the Moscow Book Club. It won the Leningrad Academy Sickle and Fountain Pen Award for 1979. Jimmy Carter invited me to the

White House to accept the American Medal of Freedom, but I tact-fully declined. I explained I was going to a reunion of the Black Panther Party, the Sparticist League, the Young Lords, and the Symbionese Liberation Army, an event being held that same week in Habana, Cuba.

But when Christiansen and Rosenberg gave up on *Milagro,* my five-Gs-a-year option payment also went down the tubes, bad news for a literary wunderkind of my increasingly limited financial prospects.

Thank God that by then Milagro had become what is commonly described in the trade as a "cult classic." Cult classic means that even though there were only six tattered copies of the book in print in America, those six copies had been passed around for the past seven years by a fanatical band of die-hard book lovers until almost three thousand hard-core *Milagro* addicts existed.

Cult classic also meant my hard-to-find book had acquired a certain cachet that was not going altogether unnoticed in Hollywood. In fact, no fewer than five different entities wanted an option on the book.

One was Robert Redford. But I figured no, he's too famous, and too blond and blue-eyed like me . . . and too much money would blow the production all out of proportion.

Cheech Marin, of Cheech and Chong fame, was also interested in an option. But I figured no, he's too famous, plus I can't stand Cheech and Chong movies . . . and too much money would blow the production all out of proportion.

A third interested party was a group of Albuquerque real estate tycoons who had money to burn and offered me the moon. I figured they wanted a tax dodge and maybe the Mafia was involved. *Very* politely I declined.

A fourth Hollywood producer with big bucks and a big reputation didn't seem right at all: same old story, too much money, not enough integrity.

The fifth person interested was a fellow named Moctesuma Esparza, a small producer in Hollywood, with little money and few credits. We met for a beer in the Albuquerque Old Town Sheraton and I liked him a lot. The one piece of his work I saw was a short documentary on a Medanales (New Mexico) weaver, Agueda Martínez, which I found quite beautiful. Plus Mocte had been arrested during the Chicano movement days of the 1960s in L.A. To my thinking, pretty good credentials.

Integrity.

So we put together a project that would be funded by the National Endowment for the Humanities, aided by the National Council of La Raza. A small film, for public TV. Eight hundred thousand dollars. I even helped write the grant proposal. I structured my contract with Moctesuma so it'd be cheap and the NEH would fund it. I agreed to write a script for Writers Guild minimum wage. In fact, over the next two and a half years I did five drafts for $25,000.

I must admit, however: As my book headed into its eighth year under option I was thinking, "I hope to God they *never* make this thing into a movie, because if they do they'll just pay me off, and I'll lose a five-grand-a-year sinecure that could probably keep me alive forever."

Unfortunately, right about then Robert Redford went to Moctesuma Esparza and they palavered and decided to sign a joint venture agreement. Because the purchase price I'd negotiated with Mocte was so modest, Redford decided to buy the book. Hence I lost my gravy train of option payments, also my "control" of the novel. And the tone of the project changed.

I was now in the employ of Robert Redford.

Two

Bob invited me to the Sundance Institute in Utah so we could begin collaborating on the script. Instantly, the Writers Guild went out on strike and I told my new boss I couldn't work on the script. He invited me to Sundance anyway, and I went, but I wouldn't even order an enchilada in the cafeteria for fear it could be construed as scabbing. Too bad, because that was the last time I ever had Robert Redford tied down in one place long enough to actually *talk* about the project.

But I fuddled along writing mostly on my own for a couple of years until, at the end of 1982, I was dropped from the project.

And I heard nothing about *Milagro, the Movie* until 1985, when a script by a fellow named David Ward arrived in the mail.

I read it with a calm heart and an objective manner. Then I sent a calm, objective, twenty-page letter to Redford, Esparza & Co. explaining in a no doubt tactful and considerate style the few little flaws I had noticed in the piece.

For example, the punch line of the movie: Joe Mondragon, who has lived and farmed in the north all his life, plants his beanfield. But when everyone goes to harvest the beans at the climax of our story, they discover that silly old Joe has made a teeny-weeny mistake. Instead of planting beans he has planted *peas!* But he does not notice this until the triumphant moment of harvest at the end of the film.

Remember when Jackie Gleason was stunned and flabbergasted on those old *Honeymooners* shows? He would stand there with his jaws bouncing up and down going *"Hamma hamma hamma . . ."*

Then I sent Bob and Mocte a letter that could have been fired from the barrel of a shotgun!

Over the next year or so they tinkered with the script. Whenever a rewrite arrived, my heart sank. I sent the screenplays back with my suggestions, praying, "Please, dear God, don't *ever* let them make a movie of my book!"

Understand, the option had been exercised long ago and there was no way I could halt the project short of donning a saffron robe, dropping into the lotus position in front of Universal Studios in Los Angeles, drenching myself in gasoline, and striking a match. But I figured, smugly, that nobody in their right mind would *ever* fund that bad script.

Then Universal funded that bad script.

It was 1986. It was May. It was crazy.

Redford called and asked me if I could do a rewrite before the cameras rolled.

I said, "Bob, I just got married and it's a real doozy, and I'm working on a six-hour miniseries for CBS about Pancho Villa and the Mexican Revolution, and I'm also completing a novel titled *American Blood,* a nonfiction book called *On the Mesa,* and a photo-essay, *A Fragile Beauty.*"

"Great," he said. "I'm so happy you can find the time to do it."

I flew back up to Sundance for a story conference.

At a round table in a barn, Redford assembled a bunch of famous actors to do a reading of the script. The actors included John Shea, Laura Dern, Lee Grant, and Alan Alda. As they read, I slouched deeper and deeper into my chair. My ears were burning. I'd *never* been so humiliated. This had to be the worst screenplay ever written. Even Alan Alda couldn't save it. I was mortified. Worse than that I kept telling myself, "John, if anybody ever again asks to take out an option on one of your novels, and you let them do it, slit your *own* throat. Use the car keys, just to make it really painful."

At the end of the reading the actors clapped politely. I wanted to jump up and apologize, but I was paralyzed by shame. Eventually, I said to Bob in a low whisper, "You couldn't make a *movie* of that script, could you?"

He said, "Sure. It's great. I figure it's about three-quarters of the way there."

My heart started fibrillating and I sat down.

But I hadn't seen nothing yet.

I went back to Taos and, in three weeks, rewrote the picture. It was June. Shooting was planned for August. I suggested to Redford that he film it on the back lot at Universal, just to avoid trouble. No, no, he wanted to be in northern New Mexico. For authenticity. I decided to visit Tahiti for six months.

Redford picked Chimayo as the perfect bucolic village for his picture. But Chimayo told him to go screw himself. So Bob decided to choose a more insane path and he made a deal with the small tough proud insular mountain town of Truchas. I couldn't believe it. I envisioned all-out race war in the boondocks, and me the guy to blame.

I delivered my script, Bob said thanks, and three weeks later a few dozen tanned, muscle-bound cocaine freaks wearing Acapulco sunglasses arrived in Santa Fe and started planning the picture.

Immediately, the attendant publicity cut out my heart and ate it while it was still beating.

Redford to Make Movie in New Mexico! Sonia Braga, Brazilian Bombshell, Bags a Role! John Nichols Sells Soul to Hollywood for Megabucks!

Every day, if Redford so much as sneezed, *The New Mexican* and the *Albuquerque Journal* gave it front-page forty-eight-point head-lines. When Chimayo said no, wiseapples on the street in Taos chortled and cackled and pointed their fingers at me, saying, "Ha ha, Chimayo said 'No!' to your stinking patronizing racist exploita-tional movie."

I thought, "God, I've never asked you for anything before in my life, and I never will again, I promise—and I don't even believe in you, either—but *please* let Robert Redford have a stroke. Not mor-tal, you understand, but just enough to get him *out* of commis-sion, *out* of New Mexico, and *out* of this movie forever."

Then, start of August, believe it or not, the cameras began rolling. In Truchas. Another writer was on the set. A third writer checked in daily from L.A. Apparently, Bob was calling a fourth literary goon back east every night for further revisions.

Not much filming could be done, however, because Redford only had one actor under contract—Ruben Blades (not a Chicano, a Panamanian). But in short order he also hired Sonia Braga (a Brazilian who couldn't speak a word of English, let alone Span-ish). Then he won a lot of points from the Chicano community by shunting aside Eddie Olmos and Cheech Marin in favor of hiring an Italian and a Puerto Rican to play the lead roles of Joe Mon-dragon and his wife, Nancy. Next, he hired a Mexican national to play Amarante Cordova.

Every day I went down to the newspaper tube at the end of my driveway, opened up to the *Milagro Daily Herald,* and promptly vomited another couple dozen cupcakes.

Racist Redford Rejects Chicano Actors in John Nichols' Movie!

Toxic Poisons Discarded by John Nichols' Movie Crew into the Truchas River Are Killing All the Trout!

Traffic between Santa Fe and Truchas, Caused by John Nichols' Movie, Is Dangerous to Local Residents, Who are Picketing Because They Are Afraid Their Children Are Going to Be Killed!

On Taos streets total strangers came up and hugged me, congratulated me for being a billionaire, then asked if I'd like to donate a few thousand dollars to the Sisters of Angelic Mercy Dyslexic Golfers' Emergency Famine Relief Fund.

One morning I saw my face, Robert Redford's picture, and Reies Tijerina's handsome mug in *The New Mexican* and the *Albuquerque Journal.* Tijerina was suing *Milagro* for stealing the story of his life. When I read the article's fine print, I saw that Robert Redford, Universal, David Ward, Moctesuma Esparza, and a couple of producers were being sued, but not me. A Universal executive was quoted asking, "Why are they suing *us?* They should be suing John Nichols. *He's* the guy who wrote the book."

Hollywood, the most compassionate shark on earth.

I sat at my desk working on my novel, my nonfiction book, my photo-essay, and my six-hour miniseries, and I said, "John, your reputation is shot. Everything you worked for the past seventeen years in New Mexico is going down the toilet. The dream is over, you have no more credibility, it's time to move to Alaska."

By then my heart was so screwy I was popping verapamil, tenormin, digitalis, Quinaglute, beta blockers, calcium blockers, and a blood thinner called Coumadin.

I couldn't *stand* the publicity. My loss of anonymity was worse than anything I could have imagined. I only went to Truchas three times during the shooting. I was terrified that that race war really *would* break out between indigenous people and the film company and somehow I'd be blamed for fomenting all the discord. My effigy would be hung upon telephone poles from Vadito to Alcalde: GRINGO GO HOME! Instead of burning Zozobra at its fiestas, Santa Fe would now incinerate a Juanito Nichols stuffed with dry pinto beans.

Naturally, the filming went smoothly. Technicians had a greenhouse full of bean sprouts in different stages of growth. The night before shooting a beanfield scene, crews planted the new shoots. It was August, but Truchas is above eight thousand feet, and the bean plants froze. So they brought in another five thousand plants, set 'em in the earth . . . and the overnight temperature dropped to *twenty*. Finally they trucked in plastic beans and stuck those in the ground. That night it snowed and all the "summer" mountains in the background turned *white*.

They were spending money like Adnan Kashoggi. My little $800,000 movie had turned into *Antonio y Cleopatra* meets *Raiders of the Lost Arco*. I was surprised they didn't hire a flotilla of Kirtland Airforce Base helicopters wielding huge hair dryers to fly over the Truchas Peaks and melt away that snow, which had blown the continuity of every location shot up until now.

The New York Times interviewed me and asked what the film was about. I said, "It's about class struggle." Then they interviewed Redford, asking him if *Milagro* was about class struggle. "God no," he exclaimed, "it's about something a lot bigger than that."

I picked up *People* magazine. They were calling the movie "Redford's Folly." I checked out the *National Enquirer*. It said Redford and Sonia Braga, during the making of "John Nichols' *Milagro Beanfield War*," were indulging in hanky-panky.

I sobbed in my beer. My name was being bandied about America between transvestite bearded dwarfs shot from cannons and a 1,140-pound baby born to a ninety-pound mentally retarded Page Three Girl from Dublin, Ireland.

I'd once had dignity, integrity, a reputation.

Now I felt that I should don a pair of pink tights, a belled stocking cap, and a spangled leather jerkin, and, playing my zither and dancing like a fool, I should wander the streets of Taos begging people to throw moose excrement at my head.

I actually became pretty sick. My shaky heart went blahooey from stress. It wasn't *all* from the movie. During the past couple of years I had gotten married, published three nonfiction books and two novels, done two book tours around the United States, toured Europe with my new wife, completed a bible for the Pancho Villa miniseries, and gone on location in Vermont to watch the filming of my second novel, *The Wizard of Loneliness,* an unpretentious little film made for $1.5 million and ultimately shown on public TV. If you're interested, you can rent it at your local video store.

Meanwhile, back in Truchas the filmmakers, running late and way over budget, finally called it a wrap. As soon as they left town, the locals torched the elaborate Milagro Plaza that had been built for the movie at great expense. Too bad, because a year later Redford had to go back and reshoot some scenes: but first he had to rebuild the entire Plaza.

Three

In March 1988, they had a benefit opening of *Milagro* in Santa Fe. I still had not seen even a rough cut of the movie. I didn't know if it was good or horrible or racist or patronizing. Would my life, my career, and my political credibility be ruined? Would I become The Land of Enchantment's number-one target for assassination?

New Mexico was taking the whole project in an absurdly personal manner. For two weeks before the benefit opening, the *Journal* and *The New Mexican* dedicated their front pages, their arts sections, and their lifestyles reports to stories about the movie.

By then, I had never hated anything more in my life than I hated *The Milagro Beanfield War.*

Talk about being blown out of proportion.

No matter: I had to pretend everything was okay. It was my book; I had launched the whole sick k-fuffle by letting it out on option.

So I had to give interviews about a film I hadn't seen that were both supportive and noncommittal. *Entertainment Tonight* babbled about the movie. Siskel and Ebert were coming to Santa Fe. Redford & Co. were still cutting the picture right up to the last minute, so nobody could give me any advance warning of what to expect.

The lady or the tiger? I figured there was doom behind *either* door.

Everyone I knew and didn't know kept coming up and congratulating me. Friends were so excited for me. They said this must be the most wonderful moment in my life. They envied me. Lucky stiff, to receive such a wonderful fifteen minutes of fame.

I was taking ten pills a day to keep my fibrillating heart in rhythm. I was so dizzy from Ménière's disease I could hardly walk, I had to *crawl* whenever it grew dark. I'd been constipated for the past year and a half. . . .

On March 19, 1988, in Santa Fe, I walked into the first benefit showing of *Milagro* sick to my stomach and scared to death. Fans were lined up watching us glitterati enter the theater. I staggered through a gauntlet of paparazzi and took a seat with 650 locals Redford had bused down from Truchas for the special showing . . . and the public lynching of yours truly afterward.

Everyone pointed at me and shook my hand and thanked me for the movie. *What* movie? None of us had even *seen* it yet.

The lights dimmed, the projectors began to roll. Every credit got a standing ovation. When the music began, *it* received a standing ovation. The first adobe house earned a standing ovation. When a corral and a horse showed up, *they* triggered a standing ovation. The audience cheered a cottonwood tree. And then the mountains. When the pig appeared—BOOM!—another standing ovation. By the time the movie was thirty seconds old it had earned fifteen Academy Award nominations from the people of Truchas!

And I understood that at least my life might be spared.

I don't remember much else about the screening. They all cheered at the end. By then I had lost ten pounds sweating.

After the final credits I went outside to face the press. That morning U.S. Marines had landed in Honduras on training missions to further help the Contras murder Nicaraguans. When reporters asked me what I had thought of the movie, I said U.S. troops should get the hell out of Honduras and Ronald Reagan was a reactionary scumbag for sending them down there in the first place.

The fourth estate backed off and left me alone.

I had to speak on three occasions that day, at different benefit events, numb from stress and fatigue and tension. I almost fainted each time from tachycardia attacks. But I let myself be puppeted around saying how wonderful it all was. At one point I tried to address the crowd holding a real live lamb in my arms. It bleated and peed on me.

I barely survived the Santa Fe benefit opening. Then I had to go through another benefit in Taos. More speeches. I *hated* the limelight. In Taos, I had to buy tickets for *all* my friends. If I forgot just one person there was hell to pay: jealousy, hurt feelings, resentment, death threats. I purchased all the food and refreshments. I think I spent $3,000 on that fucking benefit. I never asked for it, but local organizers (and the theater boss) informed me they were going to go ahead anyway. So I had to be supportive; otherwise the local press would have ripped my heart out and shoved it up my own butt while it was still beating.

I had no say in which progressive groups would share the benefit proceeds. Legal Aid, The New Mexico Community Foundation, a co-op called Tierra Wools. Immediately the two million groups who *didn't* share the loot hated the organizations who did. And guess who they took out their resentments on?

Some of my political friends blew me off. Why? Because I was exploiting New Mexico, reaming minority peoples. The movie would bring in more tourists. I was getting rich by committing CULTURAL GENOCIDE against my neighbors.

Gulp.

At night, all alone, I cried. I felt guilty. I wanted to end it all.

When the hoopla died, I was nearly broke and totally exhausted.

I quit working on *Pancho Villa* because by then I hated movies. And anyway, I had been interested in teaching prime-time America all about U.S. imperialism in Mexico during their revolution, but CBS was more enthralled by the fact that Pancho Villa had had twenty-six wives.

Then my marriage collapsed.

I lost my house.

I withdrew from the world, living in a dank basement drinking Everclear and eating moldy parsnips and Wonder bread.

The movie of *Milagro* earned mixed reviews. It received only limited release in the United States. And, like I said before, it was a financial disaster.

For all its flaws, however, *Milagro* was a gentle and loving picture. I could not for the life of me figure out how something that compassionate, humorous, good-hearted, and decent had emerged from such chaos. All along it must have been a secret inside Robert Redford's head.

But it sank like a stone in the United States—just as the book had fourteen years earlier. Later, it played in Europe and in Latin America. Friends told me *Milagro* was popular in Haiti, Nicaragua, and El Salvador—where I'm sure that most people understood it really *was* about class struggle.

Other than that, the book was written a long time ago. And our struggles for land and water rights and social justice in New Mexico haven't changed at all in the past twenty years. As for myself, I hate to be remembered for just one book, simply because it was made into a movie. I've spent a lifetime struggling to do good work. And I hope one day I'll write something that supersedes *The Milagro Beanfield War*.

Epilogue

Actually, I'm working on that new book right now. And despite the traumatic experience of having *Milagro* made into a film, I am a glutton for punishment, already eager to transform my current novel-in-progress into a movie of dramatic and powerful social commentary. Though the story is a long way from being published, I think it has all the elements for a successful film.

The novel is called *The Voice of the Butterfly*. My first draft was over twelve hundred pages long, but I've pared that down to only 1,157 pages. Yes, the novel has about two hundred characters, but only forty are crucial to the story.

The tale focuses on a group of developers in a small town who band together to lay a highway bypass through the last bit of unspoiled agricultural land in the valley. The highway will enable these gangsters to build a large industrial park, shopping center, new airport, massive water transfer plant, low-income housing development, time-share condo heaven for the rich, and other assorted emoluments. To pay for the bypass with taxpayer dollars, the developers must get passed a mil levy called Proposition X. So the book also deals with democratic politics, the electoral system, political corruption, underhanded payoffs, gerrymandering and grandfathering election districts, kickback scandals, suppression of the free press, money-laundering schemes to back scum-sucking political candidates involved in lucrative drug smuggling, and other scandalous intrigues pertinent to the American electoral process, including the collapse of the savings and loan industry from upstreaming loans based on nonexistent collateral and letters of credit that aren't worth the paper they're printed on.

The book details *all* the skullduggery and peculations involved as various banks and holding companies and sicko entrepreneurs become involved in countless Ponzi schemes and the creation of collateral based on future production that has been overappraised in order to generate greatly inflated origination fees on loans made to dummy corporations that exist only as a figment of the imagination of some joyboy selling Jumbo (junk bond) CDs through offshore brokers (in the Cayman Islands) whose real and spendable loot actually exists only in numbered Swiss banking accounts, which actually belong to the chief executive officers of institutions like Citicorp and Morgan Guaranty Trust, also Continental of Chicago and Seafirst of Seattle, who wind up in deep shit for taking overextended participations in upstreamed loans, that, in the final analysis, lead to Fizzlick coming in and slapping down dozens of classifications and cease and desist orders that almost wind up toppling the banking system of the United States, largely because all the banks involved in this development have been buying their audits from crooked CPAs who are receiving kickbacks in the form of loans, given at twice the value for half the price, at least two or three points above par, so that the free vigorish above the line can be reinvested in Eurodollars for not a single out-of-pocket expense by the investors involved.

Then some ecologists in my fictional town discover that a tiny butterfly called the Rocky Mountain Phistic Copper lies in the path of the proposed bypass, and it is a very rare bug. If they can secure an endangered species classification for this insect they can stop the bypass dead in its tracks. So the book also talks about eco-guerilla warfare, both legal and extralegal, as a method for building public awareness of the gathering global catastrophe in such a way that local voters will rise up in a bloc and vote down Proposition X. In their battle to stem the tide of rapacious development, my quirky eco-saboteurs cut down billboards, blow up fast-food Burger Boy franchises, broadcast pirated tapes of secret Mafia meetings over the radio, conduct platoon-level armed attacks against the evil developers' mad-dog surveyors, foment riots in ritzy restaurants, trick-or-treat on Halloween disguised as punk rock Eco-Terminators, infiltrate the legal apparatus of the opposing side, kidnap the corpses of dead octogenarians and parade them around town disguised as monkeys in electric wheelchairs, and perform other acts of rational campaigning in hopes of persuading people to vote against Proposition X.

Just to add flavor, I describe gang-bangs in executive jets flying between dog and pony shows in Cut 'n' Shoot, Texas, and Weevil Harbor, Mississippi. There's an all-out brawl in a high-tone restaurant. One character, a ninety-two-year-old devil woman with a mind like William Buckley's, Norman Mailer's, and Morton Downey Jr.'s all rolled into one, chain-smokes cigarettes and drinks a bottle of bourbon a day. A major shopping-cart demolition derby occurs in an enormous supermarket. There are many gory scenes of cruelty to bulldozers, cruelty to the armed policing agents of our democratic state, and cruelty to butterflies on a level heretofore unimaginable in a society as civilized as ours. Lest all that seem too crude,

I have balanced the violence against some whimsical journeys into codependency, inner-child release weekends, crystaldigitation, etheric manipulation, and aura adjusting, also tacky sexual deviation, alcoholism, Al Anon's twelve-point Get Right with God follies, and modern interpretations of the *Bhagavad Gita* and Kahlil Gibran's *The Prophet*.

I don't want to give away the ending, but the good guys win.

How come?

Because that's the way Hollywood likes it.

And in the film version, which I've already sketched out in some detail, my story boils down to this:

Joe, a developer, falls in love with Mary, an environmentalist. As soon as they get into bed they forget their differences and have sex like crazed rabbits for 119 minutes. Each time they kiss, another butterfly—trailing a tiny banner that proclaims Save the Rain Forests—is set free.

Mickey Rourke and Kim Basinger have already signed to play in the movie. Paul Simon and Sting have agreed to compose the sound track, which will also incorporate original songs from Madonna, Bruce Springsteen, and R.E.M.

The option on my as yet unfinished novel is held by a consortium of environmentalists whose spokespersons are Barry Commoner, Gretel Ehrlich, and Wendell Berry. After months of negotiating the purchase price, I finally convinced them to pay me nothing over a period of fourteen years, so it's my kind of contract—it has unlimited integrity.

We're planning to pass out free, biodegradable condoms made of recycled latex at every screening.

And I've already been assured that *this* movie will be a real hit—

From a speech in the University of New Mexico Centennial Speakers Series, March 1992. Adapted for Albuquerque Monthly, *March 1994. Also given as a talk to Santa Fe Cardiology Symposium '96 at Rancho Encantado on August 2, 1996 and to a gathering in Breckenridge, Colorado, in the Father Dyer Methodist Church on May 3, 1997.*

A Labor of Love

It's going to be a long, cold, December night in Bristol, Vermont. Jenny Bowen, the director, can hardly talk, her throat is so sore. She's sucking on local herbal lozenges that have come to be known as "duckballs." And she looks like Roy Scheider in the last reel of *All That Jazz,* moments before his big heart attack.

The scene that cameraman Dick Bowen, Jenny's husband, is supposed to get perfectly on film (sometime before 3 A.M.) calls for the eleven-year-old star, Lukas Haas (playing a kid named Wendall Oler), to carry a .410 shotgun. But his social worker won't let him be on set with a weapon even if it's unloaded. "Another film assassin!" groans Dick, pulling his earflaps down lower. The upshot is that Lukas's dad, Bertold, has to be called from home, where he and his wife Emily are apprehensively watching over one of their three-year-old twins, who's coughing and turning blue. Later tonight they'll drive the child to Middlebury Hospital ten miles down the road. Emily herself, once an opera singer, now a successful television writer who's currently developing a feature film for Ed Pressman, just got over five days of serious strep throat.

While Jenny slouches half catatonic in a blue canvas igloo, seeming to shrivel ever deeper into her puffy snowsuit with every degree that the temperature falls, Bertold Haas arrives on the set and gives the okay for Lukas to work with a gun. But Jenny asks Bertold to look into the .410 barrel anyway, just to "verify its emptiness."

By now it's 8 P.M. Dampness and wind chill factors make it feel like thirty below zero. The only footage Dick has gotten so far today, after seven hours of preparation, is of a shotgun being fired into the turf. Yet they're not even sure of that one. Perhaps the wires to a charge that blew up the earth (you can't fire a real gun on a movie set) were exposed in the shot.

Another major problem, at this late date in the filming of *The Wizard of Loneliness,* is that there should be snow on the Bristol Green. But God didn't provide it, so Wizard Productions had to find it. Unfortunately, the dump trucks did not arrive in time for this afternoon's daylight shooting. Producer Thom Tyson, who's terrified the production will now go over a day or more, at a cost of twenty-five Gs a day (there's insurance, but it's $10,000 deductible, for starters), wanted Jenny to shoot without snow, but she adamantly refused to budge. She's fought too long and too hard to give this picture the authentic look she feels it deserves.

Close to dark, the dump trucks did arrive. But their snow had been through hell and looked real dirty. "So paint the snow," some glib kibitzer suggested. To the AD, Chuck Myers, who can barely function himself after two days in bed with the flu, the comment isn't even half funny.

Reeking of bourbon, a local, sixtyish Bristolite good-naturedly wanders about taking pictures of "famous" people with his little camera. It's devoid of film, but the flash attachment functions at every *click!* Meanwhile, actors portraying the Oler family patiently rehearse the upcoming shot. Adjustments have to be made in the dolly track. Wedges are inserted under the rails, which are then checked by a level. Sandbags are piled on the south end of the track to weigh it down. Camera operator Mitch Cheselka and his assistants, John Allen and Murray Van Dyke, keep fiddling with the camera, peering into the eyepiece, conferring with Dick.

Veteran actor John Randolph (who played Jack Nicholson's father in *Prizzi's Honor*) and his film wife, Anne Pitoniak, are bundled up in a dozen blankets each: they look like Pueblo Indians from my hometown of Taos, New Mexico. John is getting antsy about the delays. He's been invited to meet with Mikhail Gorbachev in Washington D.C. tomorrow and is terrified he won't be released in time to get down *there* on time.

To me, he shouts, "I once voted for Eugene Debs!" In reply, I holler back that I once blew a VW bus engine in Terre Haute, Indiana, and spent three days (while they repaired my car) going through Debs's scrapbooks with an old journalist named Ned Bush, in the basement of the Debs House Museum in Terre Haute.

So we kill time while more bad news rolls in. A small ice pond, necessary for the next few scenes, isn't frozen yet. Located halfway across the Green in front of the First Baptist Church, the pond was fabricated only yesterday out of sand, several backhoes working for hours to level it, a lot of ten-mil plastic, and water conjured up by the local volunteer fire department. So another problem for Thom Tyson is: How can he dig up some plywood and roller skates in order to fake the ice skating if necessary?

Too, Thom is trying to calculate what and who the insurance covers, what and who it doesn't. Already today he's dismissed a lawsuit by a former participant in the film as a "nuisance" . . . and he's also arguing desperately with the Oler house owner, who's balking about the late-night scenes slated to take place shortly at his home. The house has been featured throughout the film, so losing it now would be a disaster.

On the brighter side, this freezing night, I'm told by Lance Guest (who plays John T. Oler in the film) that at least all the principal actors are wearing electric socks. For a person like me, however, and my wife, Juanita, who are just frozen onlookers (wondering why these insanely dedicated folks, under such adverse conditions, are making a movie of a novel I published twenty-one years ago), the good news is that Cubber's Café, on Main Street in Bristol (fifty yards from the present set), is still open. They serve tall cups of very hot coffee and chocolate chip cookies the size of small pizzas. The sign over the door proclaims, "Famous since 1975."

Whenever Juanita and I feel that either gangrene, rigor mortis, or frostbite is setting in, it's to Cubber's that we scramble for heat and rejuvenation.

Finally, everything is ready for the shot. Jenny turns off her reading specs, they kill the noisy propane heaters, and an assistant AD, Bryan Curry, tells everyone to be "very still." Over the walkie-talkies it's verified all the streets are locked, so nobody will drive through the shot. The youngest actor, an irrepressibly charming and mischievous four-year-old named Jeremiah Parker, who hails from nearby Ripton (Robert Frost's old stomping grounds), pulls his woolen cap down over his eyes. Someone says, "Rolling . . . ," and Jenny rises to croak, "Ready . . . and . . ."

And Jeremiah flips up his cap and hollers, "ACTION!"

At which point the town hall clock starts bonging out the hour, and another take is sabotaged by the film assassins.

Jenny throws up her hands and gives in to fatigue, fever, being frozen. They cart her off, sick as a dog. With that, the film is certain to go over schedule (and budget) by at least a day or two. The good news here is that John Randolph will be able to meet Gorbachev. The bad news is you can't leave all this equipment strewn around the Green overnight. So the scissor lifts supporting the bright arc lamps high in the air start cranking down . . . the lamps are extinguished. The crew dismantles the dolly track, which took hours to lay. They put things away in boxes, lug off cameras and sound equipment, store 12-By reflector frames in waiting trucks.

Yesterday they shot seven pages, twenty-four setups, an incredible amount of film. Jenny called it "a hell day." Today, if they were lucky, was going to be worse. They only got about thirty seconds of footage. The shoot was supposed to end tomorrow: now the agony will be prolonged a few more days.

I conclude that making movies, even small ones like this, with a limited crew working in a low-key and amiable little town like Bristol (population *maybe* two thousand), is like trying to crawl through an acre of peanut butter with a serious head wound, wearing mukluks and a straitjacket, dragging a wheelchair behind you—

In July.

Almost exactly a year ago, on Thanksgiving 1986, I was present in Santa Fe, New Mexico, 2,500 miles west of Bristol, when Robert Redford wrapped another film made from one of my novels, *The Milagro Beanfield War*. That day he shot a "summer" scene in eighteen inches of snow. He had a hard time of it, but still, that was a "big" production, fraught with public controversy, featuring fifty-two speaking roles, extras by the hundreds, and a budget of between $14 million and $20 million (depending on which source or gossip columnist you believed). When *Milagro* needed a desert, they bulldozed the land and painted it brown. When they needed lush summertime vegetation, they bulldozed off the brown, spray-painted the remains green, and planted a plastic garden. I suppose if they had needed snow, they would have made it from scratch on the set, using machines manufactured expressly for that purpose. *Milagro* went on location in a northern New Mexico town probably even smaller than Bristol, Vermont . . . and then they built another town right beside it!

But I knew from the start *Wizard* would be very different. They had barely $2 million with which to pay everybody, buy film, re-create 1945. Before production began, Thom Tyson begged me to defer my $40,000 payoff up front when principal photography commenced . . . otherwise, he claimed, principal photography could never start. And I had agreed to that.

Thus, before arriving in Bristol, I pictured a production crew of maybe eight to ten people all walking around with handheld 16-millimeter cameras, filming actors working for no pay simply because *Wizard* was "a labor of love."

Well, I was shocked by the size, complexity, and difficulty of making even a low-budget labor of love.

In fact, I was astounded that anybody had managed to put this film together in the first place.

That any movie ever gets made is, of course, a miracle. In this case, *The Wizard of Loneliness* was a novel that was published to hardback silence, then it had a brief, unsuccessful run (one year) in Signet paperback. After that it went out of print. Norman Lear once held an option, but nothing happened. Producers-writers Alan and Judy Seegar developed a script, but then lost heart. And out in America, after 1966, the only place I ever encountered a copy of the book was on a paperback rack in the Greyhound bus depot in Winnemucca, Nevada.

For about a decade *Wizard* lay (very) dormant. Then, toward the end of the seventies, a Boston photographer, Phil Porcella, took an option and asked me to write a script. I complied while the screenplay contract was being "negotiated." In the end, Porcella wouldn't sign the contract, so I had written a script in vain. Later, I told Phil in advance I wasn't going to renew the option with him when it lapsed . . . and he promptly exercised the option, much to my surprise and chagrin. About that time Pocket Books reissued the novel and it stayed in print a couple of years, then disappeared again.

No need to graphically describe the twisted path of the *Wizard* toward filmdom after that. Suffice to say that for another decade, *Wizard* (The Movie) floundered up a dozen dead ends, got lost on a hundred back roads leading nowhere, and circled a thousand cloverleafs without exit.

Maybe it always happens like that. Hollywood is a lot like Beirut: all life seems to emerge from ashes.

In fact, somebody once told me that perhaps 60 percent of the films that eventually do get made are realized in turnaround.

Be that as it may, I figure it took great courage for Jenny Bowen to get involved in this movie. How she put it together I'll never know. But suddenly, one crisp autumn day, a small, very sweet person showed up in Taos carrying a Nancy Larson script that she (Jenny) had rewritten extensively. The screenplay was loving, awkward in places, compassionate. Sundance and American Playhouse had somehow become involved in the project. Money was coming from a New England developer. The only catch was that at least some of the movie had to be shot on Martha's Vineyard. "No problem," said Jenny. For the financing she could fake *anything*.

Next I heard the money was coming out of New Orleans. Every couple of months Jenny called to say, "We're almost there. I just have to fly back to the south one more time. . . ."

And of course, in the end that deal also collapsed.

But all movies are about snatching Victory from the jaws of Defeat. So suddenly here came Skouras Pictures to spring for a large chunk of the limited chunk that was needed to make the picture, and everybody ran to Vermont.

Weather is always a nuisance on location. The *Wizard* production, which began in September with the intent to film four seasons in three months, had its share of meteorological frustrations. First they enjoyed a warm, colorful autumn . . . for about three days. Then it rained, froze, hailed, killed the foliage. They shot a Fourth of July baseball game in T-shirts while temperatures hovered around freezing. Dylan Baker, who plays a war casualty gone mad (named Duffy Kahler), spent half a day standing in a shallow pond whose water was one degree shy of freezing. His love interest, Sybil Oler (Lea Thompson), repeatedly splashed the water on her neck and bosom just to emphasize the "summer" season.

The only place most crew members and actors could be housed together was on the other side of the Appalachian Gap, about twenty miles east of Bristol, in the Sugarbush ski resort. A narrow, twisting mountain road is the only way to get there and back. Thanks to the early snows and icy rains, a slew of crew car accidents occurred. "Eight so far," I was told on my arrival. Each accident threatened to sabotage some important part of production. Three weeks after her mishap, Lea Thompson was still sporting a bandage on her forehead.

And when they really needed snow, they couldn't get it. Such capricious weather plays havoc with continuity. Now, in December, rolled-up snow blankets lay everywhere within reach, awaiting orders. On film, this white carpeting actually "reads" like snow . . . *if* you don't know it's white carpeting. Especially if, as happened in one tense, solemn scene, an actor, in tearfully exiting stage right, trips over it.

Of course, when they didn't want snow, it fell in droves. Take the day they shot a scene where Wendall Oler arrives in Stebbinsville, Vermont, and is greeted by his new family. Thom Tyson lobbied to use a bus; Jenny insisted Wendall arrive on a train. So the entire crew moved fifty miles north to Greensboro, where a picturesque little station still abides. And Jenny got her train. In return she also got rain, snow, sleet, and hail. And that was just during the first *hour* of the shoot.

Yet the dailies came out looking great.

Bottom line is this: almost all the footage shot so far is beautiful. For me it's hard to understand how, especially after hanging around on the set in the cold, the slush, the dirt . . . with all the film technology (wires, cameras, tracks, lights, etc.) so haphazardly slobbered about. In daily production the *Wizard* film can seem terribly disjointed. It's a cacophony of folks babbling into walkie-talkies. Crises galore. Ice on a tiny skating pond still won't freeze. Backhoes aimlessly push snow around. Actors' trailers ringing the Green are idling, humming, chugging day and night. Church bells play "O Little Town of Bethlehem." Baffles go up. Sound technicians fiddle. The cream in a coffee cup on a table in the gazebo on the Green freezes. Wardrobe people replace wet clothes with dry clothes—it's called "wardrobe doubling." They take Polaroid snapshots before every scene to ensure that each actor wears the proper clothing in the proper way, every day. Did Wendall have a scarf at the start of this scene, filmed two days ago? Better check. Was he wearing his reflective wire-rim glasses or his nonreflective wire-rim glasses? Well, it depends on the angle of the shot . . . the lighting . . . the mood Jenny wants to create . . . the film in the camera . . . the lens . . . the babble, babble, babble, babble. . . .

A wind suddenly springs up, slamming around all the 12-By reflectors. Grips grab them and holler for more sandbags. The guy who wrangles old cars drives up in a '39 Chevy. Somebody immediately sets to work frosting the car windows. Stand-ins take direction from Dick and Jenny, Mitch and John and Murray, as they choreograph the next shot—

Fat black electrical cords lie everywhere, snakes in the snow . . . or snakes in the *lack* of snow. In the *slush*. In the *frozen* slush. It's impossible to visualize what's really being recorded onto those little strips of celluloid. One day, when they opened a magazine, the film leaped out all over the place, like black spaghetti shot from a cannon.

A day before the operation moved to the Green, Dick had a shot in a store in New Haven, five miles west of Bristol, that he just couldn't get right. Duffy Kahler mounts porch steps to his mother's store at midnight—he finds a key, opens the door, slips inside. Shooting from inside the store, Dick wanted Duffy's shadow to grow against the frosted front windows as he climbed the porch stairs. But the lighting was never quite right. Finally Dick figured the light behind Duffy would have to rise up the stairs with him. But that would have meant halting for forty-five minutes in order to set it up. And it was night, very cold . . . and they just didn't have the budget to indulge in that kind of perfection.

"I hate this shot," Dick groaned. "It's the first one in the movie I really hate. . . ."

But in the dailies it seemed quite powerful.

Is it worth all the effort to make this movie? Everyone I speak to seems enthusiastic. Emily Haas calls the role for her son Lukas "the role of a lifetime." Even Thom Tyson seems cheerful and philosophical despite the endless crises. But when I ask what he's going to do after the *Wizard,* he grins, grimaces, and sighs: "Now I've got to figure out how to make some money."

Jenny Bowen's first film was *Street Music.* It starred Elizabeth Daily. Her second movie, *Animal Behavior,* features Armand Assante and Karen Allen. So *Wizard* is her third picture. Husband Dick brings home much of their bacon by making commercials. He was the cameraman on one film I've seen, *Belizaire, the Cajun,* another low-budget effort, with Armand Assante, that doesn't quite succeed. But the camera work is wonderful.

Judging from the *Wizard* footage I saw in Vermont, this film may be, for them both, a breakthrough. And Lukas Haas, and Lea, and John Randolph . . . all the actors are going to be wonderful. Clearly the film is a labor of love. *Wizard* is likely to be an earnest, funny, dignified little movie, gentle and compassionate. The whole production, at some level, seems to have discovered a kind of innocence in experience, and in filmmaking, that is rarely encountered these days.

Perhaps it's also Vermont, and the town of Bristol . . . and the dated material. One character in the film is a girl, Ercel Perry, who won't surrender her virginity despite her boyfriend's urgent pleadings. The role is played by Andrea Matheson, an undergraduate at the University of Vermont in Burlington. Late on the next-to-last night of filming, watching yet another take on the Bristol Green's tiny skating pond (which finally froze solid just moments before shooting started!), Andrea tells me that she must now drive home to Burlington, an hour away, because she has classes at 9 A.M. tomorrow. When I then ask her to sign my copy of the *Wizard* before she leaves, she writes:

> I can't tell you how glad I am you wrote a book that could be made
> into a movie my grandparents could see.

Would you believe a Tender Mercies meets Heartland during The Trip to Bountiful—?
That's certainly a nice dream.

From Film Comment, *published by the Film Society of Lincoln Center, October 1988.*

Part Six
To Be of Use

John T. and Cornelia Floyd Nichols at Mastic, N.Y.

These are "eulogies" for people I have loved, family members and friends who shaped my soul. Their lives speak in universal ways to the critical values that ought to shape human experience. Each person gave me a world I can feel at the center of my being every minute that I'm alive.

What Is a Naturalist, Anyway?

One of my earliest wonderful memories is of riding a Long Island Railroad train in the late 1940s. I am seated beside either my dad, David Nichols, or my grandfather, after whom I am named, John T. Nichols. We are going to spend a day at the Museum of Natural History in Manhattan. My excitement and anticipation are boundless.

As I recall it through a small child's eyes, my grandfather's office at the museum was a magical and chaotic place featuring stacks of books and papers, messy ashtrays full of burnt pipe tobacco, and countless bottles and jars of pickled fishes. I don't recall any of my conversations with the old guy on those occasions—in fact, I recollect that he was a fairly taciturn bloke when it came to small, hyperactive children. Yet he allowed me free rein to poke about and gawk and to ask endless questions, like: "What is this?" and: "Wow, what is *that* funny-looking thing?"

Granted, I have no tape recordings of his replies, but I suspect they were more or less like the answers my father, who was inspired to become a naturalist by his father, often gave to similar queries. Namely, "That's a *Rana grylio,* John." And, "That's a *Storeria occipitomaculata.*" And, of course, "We call that *Lucanus elephus.*" My father had an erudite habit of also adding a comment on the subject in either Russian, French, or rather elemental Chinese.

Hence at an early age I was forced to learn how to translate Latin into real language, such as, "That is a big green frog," and "That's a little snake," and "That is a fat black beetle with very BIG pincers." In this manner I first became enamored of, and privy to, the incredible secrets of the natural world.

When I think back to who first inspired me to delve into that world, it's hard to differentiate between my tall, skinny grandfather and my tall, skinny dad. The genetic, spiritual, and intellectual lines of connection pass directly from my grandfather through my dad to myself, and I have since bequeathed the passion to my own children.

In my early childhood, the best thing about being a budding naturalist was that I got to kill things and inspect them close up. I know that the indiscriminate application of this practice is frowned upon today, since the rare snaffular grosbeak that one shoots and prepares for a museum collection is liable to be the last of its species. But back in those profligate days, when nature was still in flower, if one wished to understand better the marvels of life on earth, one went out and harvested living things by abrogating their life expectancies with an abrupt application of extreme prejudice.

A person could also mix epicurean delights with scientific research. For example, here's one of my favorite passages from my grandfather's journals, dated Saturday, August 21, 1915:

> We got up before dawn and crossed the bay to Little Beach Point for snipe. It was a bad morning, nothing doing. After a time a single large bird, which might have been a Greater Yellowleg, came in with steady flight, high up. I pronounced it a Willet, and although marvelling somewhat at its long, slightly bent bill, and different color from fall Willet with which I was familiar, I did not until late in the evening of the following day, after having gone through the painful process of making a skin of it, and having eaten my share of the succulent bird, realize my mistake. Then, starting to measure the skin for eastern or western race of Willet, I immediately became suspicious of its identity and promptly determined it as Ring-tailed Marlin.

I would suppose that after making a number of observations in this manner, my grandfather eventually was able to distinguish between a marbled godwit and an igneous avocet by using his educated palate rather than a field guide, provided that he had not ladled on too much garlic during the preparation of the specimen.

Only a week later, that same August of 1915, my grandfather

was again out observing nature, this time accompanied by his good friend, noted ornithologist Ludlow Griscomb (who was also a prominent member of the Linnaean Society). To quote JTN's notebook verbatim:

> In the afternoon with an easterly coming on we found two Northern Phalarope on the weed in Beach Point Cove. In the early morning of the 30th, after the storm, presumably the same two birds were still there. They were very tame and when flushed flew only a short distance before alighting again. L.G. tried unsuccessfully to "harpoon" one with a paddle of the canoe.

Now, I myself was never prone to harpooning phalaropes with canoe paddles in the name of science; I much preferred to attack them with a slingshot, at least until I was old enough for BB guns. Eventually I outgrew my lust for death, however, and many a tiny bird or scurrying little mammal breathed easier at my conversion.

Nevertheless, I shall always be very grateful that as a child I had access to the close-up study of those moribund critters. My proximity to countless organisms pickled in jars or stretched out on mounting boards created in me a fascination with nature that has led me to spend much of my adult life agitating on behalf of animals.

In my grandparents' Garden City (Long Island) attic, there was a treasure trove of specimens that I always inspected first thing whenever we went to visit. These were mostly oceanic birds that my grandfather had collected in his younger days during his two voyages around Cape Horn. But it was at my grandparents' summer home in Mastic on the south shore of Long Island, about sixty miles east of New York City, that I really went to town. In that old house was a fantastic collection of stuffed birds, including a stately great blue heron, which in memory looms taller than myself. Beside it were all sorts of ducks, a ring-necked pheasant, and numerous shorebirds in the sanderling/sandpiper/plover category. Also a rare and imposing snowy owl. And there was a large butterfly and insect case, which I guarantee still has my greasy childhood fingerprints pressed indelibly into the glass.

I spent all my days at Mastic avidly collecting things. There was a colony of native box turtles whose survivors roam the grounds to this day. For decades my grandfather had marked the shells of individuals with identifying codes and dates, and he actually paid for turtles that I and other family members brought in. As any naturalist knows, a love of the natural world is always enhanced when there's a bit of filthy lucre at the end of a day spent in the field.

I also caught butterflies at the butterfly bushes planted around the old house. I gathered thousands of tiny hop toads in cardboard boxes and watched them for hours as they scriggled about. I climbed down into the icehouse to retrieve rabbits that had fallen in. And, using a flashlight and a gob of peanut butter in a mayonnaise jar, I snagged mice alive in one of the barns, earning a dollar a mouse from my dad until he realized I had enough skill to catch thousands and he canceled the reward.

A principal activity of naturalists at the Mastic place was simply walking and observing. Myself, I followed and I listened. Whenever a bird went "tweet," my dad or grandfather said, "Hmm, there's an ovenbird," or, "Yup, a red-eyed vireo," or, "Hear that hermit thrush?" Naturally, they usually added absentmindedly, *"Seiurus aurocapillus"* or *"Vireo olivaceus"* or *"Catharus guttatus."* If I picked up a feather, they almost immediately gave it an identification: "towhee," "blue jay," "osprey." Almost anything I stumbled upon they could identify, quantify, or categorize, be it animal, vegetable, or mineral.

Another endeavor at Mastic was collecting animal tracks. We poured melted paraffin into a fox's or a raccoon's footprint, encircling the casting with a tin can from which both ends had been cut. Then we pressed the wax form into a dish of plaster of Paris, and—voilà!—the tracks were transformed from soft mud originals into hard copies. I also became a fan of animal scat because my father and grandfather saw nothing wrong with squatting and intimately inspecting fox shit or an owl casting and commenting at length on the dietary habits and intestinal fortitude of the excretor involved.

So one of the traits that marked my grandfather and that he

passed on to my dad, who passed it on to me, was his curiosity about almost everything in the natural world. Grandpa was an eclectic man of science. To earn a living, he wound up specializing in fishes. But he was also an avid and respected ornithologist, a fan of weasels, a good man with a bat (the flying kind), a turtle junkie—and he was intrigued by almost everything else. In a 1916 article, "On Primarily Unadaptive Variants," he ran through a wide gamut of discussion, including observations on black-backed gulls and Spanish mackerels, tree squirrels and bay-breasted warblers, black bears and wild guinea pigs.

To boot, the man was a philosopher and a poet. And he also had a sometimes wacky sense of humor. Talking about the nature of matter and energy, he once wrote (in an unpublished essay titled "The Rhythm of Life"): "For philosophical purposes we have at least one rational explanatory hypothesis of straight lines of primal energy running in every direction through ubiquitous undifferentiated matter, forming the reservoir of more complicated energy of solid substances, which in turn and for that reason throw an energy shadow into which other solid substances are driven by impact from without. If matter is universal, a single substance, differentiated only by localized forms of motion or energy into everything from solid substances which gave rise to the original matter concept, to the nothingness of interstellar space, why bother with the matter concept at all?"

The same mind that was capable of producing that mind-blowing philosophical doggerel also conjured my favorite poem of childhood:

I had a niece
Who ate a piece
Of candle grease.

For goodness sake,
How it did make
Her stomach ache.

Run, run, anyone
Get a gun

Because we love her
We can't let her suffer,
We'll shoot her and stuff her.

But a passage from an article he wrote for *Marine Life* in 1958, dealing with his observations at sea over fifty years earlier, seems to frame most truly the soul of the man I admire:

> From my seat under the bowsprit, I could glance back from the surface of the water ahead, and see the ship behind me with all sail set, from her fore royal, filled by the light air aloft, to and aft along the decks, as comprehensive a view as I ever had of her under sail, when I was always aboard. And she was beautiful. I had no control of her, nor had I over the sea stretching to the horizon, the sun, the winds, my own youth, for that matter, but for the moment all belonged to me and were serving my purpose. My spirit drank them in, to remember when time had robbed me of them, for I knew they could not last.

I like that passage, corny as it might seem, because in it my grandfather wasn't afraid to wear his heart on his sleeve, speaking with passion and sentimentality about the natural world and the mystery, beauty, and sadness of life on earth. I think his statement that he had no control over any of it shows a humility rare to find in twentieth-century men and women of science.

And that brings me to the central query of this rambling discourse: "What is a naturalist, anyway?" The question was asked by my grandfather in a short autobiography he wrote in 1923. He answered his own query in this manner, and it is the way he defined himself:

> A naturalist, it would seem, is one interested in natural phenomena. The term may be further limited, however. All persons working in

the broad field of science deal with natural phenomena, but modern tendency to specialization has carried the majority of scientists into fields of thought far removed from those of the old-fashioned naturalist; and in the study of animals, for instance, there are anatomists, cytologists, physiologists, geneticists, etc., so numerous, that in its narrower sense it is convenient to reserve the term naturalist for those investigating life from an older, different viewpoint. A naturalist takes the most obvious first phenomenon, the individual animal, for the basic unit of his science, and instead of cataloguing its parts investigates its place in nature, and that of the larger units, such as the species, of which it is an integral part.

My grandfather's definition of a naturalist reminds me of a statement by John Muir, which I feel best describes the situation of all life on earth. Muir said, "Whenever we try to pick out anything by itself, we find it hitched to everything else in the universe."

Of course, that's obvious, and it should be the first building block of all knowledge. Yet in a world that has reached its current technological ascendancy largely through specialization, we have all but forgotten that nothing exists apart from everything else. And so we find ourselves in a major-league pickle that features a diminishing ozone layer, the greenhouse effect, and, coincidentally, perhaps ultimately the premature end of most evolution on earth.

The responsibility of science in this dilemma was emphatically driven home to me some years back when I spent a while working with the European film director Costa-Gavras on a movie that dealt with problems of science and human values in the twentieth century. We developed a film (never produced) about the daily lives of some nuclear physicists. All of them were brilliant, dedicated, and compassionate people, but their dependency on government money for perpetuation of their scientific specialties ultimately led them to create a technology of megadeath. While researching this film, I came across quotations like this one by the noted biologist Jacques Monod, who proclaimed, "Any mingling of knowledge with values is unlawful, forbidden."

Sociologist Max Weber put it this way: "Whoever lacks the capacity to put on blinders, so to speak . . . may as well stay away from science."

And Steve J. Heims, author of a joint biography of John von Neumann and Norbert Weiner, had this to say about the rise of modern science: "After sciences became professionalized in the nineteenth century, any consideration of social responsibility in connection with scientific research became a direct violation of the standards and values of the profession. Thus, falling into a false innocence was the price paid for 'benefits' of scientific progress."

Two of the more interesting thinkers I met in my reading were the astrophysicist Freeman Dyson and the physicist Max Born. In his book *Disturbing the Universe,* Dyson speaks of how some modern molecular biologists have adopted a terribly narrow definition of scientific knowledge. He notes that they have achieved tremendous success "by reducing the complex behavior of living creatures to the simpler behavior of the molecules out of which the creatures are built. Their whole field of science is based on the reduction of the complex to the simple, reduction of the apparently purposeful movements of an organism to purely mechanical movements of its constituent parts."

In his autobiography, *My Life and My Views,* Max Born elaborates on this tendency and blames it on "the length and complication of the path between a human action and its final effect." For example, "Most workmen know only their special tiny manipulation in a special section of the production process and hardly ever see the complete product. Naturally, they do not feel responsible for this product or for its use."

He goes on to explain that "the most horrid result of this separation of action and effect was the annihilation of millions of human beings during the Nazi regime in Germany: the Eichmann-type of killers pleaded not guilty because they 'did their job' and had nothing to do with its ultimate purpose."

Born felt that scientific research "had led to an enormous widening of the horizon of knowledge, in the macrocosmos as well as in the microcosmos, and to a stupendous increase of power over the forces of nature. But this gain is paid for by bitter loss. The sci-

entific attitude is apt to create doubt and skepticism toward tradi-
tional, unscientific knowledge and even toward natural, unsophis-
ticated actions on which human society depends."

Born concludes, "I am haunted by the idea that this break in
human civilization, caused by the discovery of the scientific method,
may be irreparable. Though I love science I have the feeling that
it is so greatly opposed to history and tradition that it cannot be
absorbed by our civilization. The political and military horrors and
complete breakdown of ethics which I have witnessed in my lifetime may be not a symptom of social weakness, but a necessary
consequence of the rise of science—which in itself is among the
highest intellectual achievements of man."

Now, it may seem that I have strayed a bit far afield from my tall,
lanky grandfather dressed in a rumpled blue suit and a tattered old
fedora, with a pipe hanging out of his mouth, squinting as he
notched yet another box turtle and then leaned over slowly to set
it free in the grass. Yet I have always felt that in that man, and in
the legacy he passed on to my father and thus to me, there was an
important lesson to be learned. It was evident in his strength of
character, in his personality and his view of the world, in the dis-
ciplines he chose to follow, in the curiosity he had for many things,
and in the humility that typified his way of doing science. But most
important, my grandfather saw the natural world as an intercon-
nected whole: he understood and sympathized with "the complete
product."

Today science is much more sophisticated than ever he could
have imagined. Yet in this world of vast complexity, instant communication, and technological sophistication, we seem to have completely lost track of the overall scheme of things, which has led to
a building ecological catastrophe of perhaps insurmountable pro-
portions. And interestingly, it seems as if my grandfather's per-
ception of the world, placing value on biodiversity, is increasingly
one that the environmental movements of today are adapting in
order to save the globe.

At a recent meeting of the American Society of Ichthyologists
and Herpetologists (an organization founded by my grandfather)

between a fourth and a third of the presentations dealt with conservation, endangered species, environmental damage, biodiversity, species protection, and the relationship of "anthropogenic perturbation to the extirpation of species." I find that both sad and hopeful. Sad because, obviously, each day there are many fewer snakes and fish and salamanders out there to learn about. (Approximately three thousand species became extinct in the United States alone last year.) But I also feel hopeful because obviously the conscience of science today is struggling to learn how to rectify the situation.

In a book called *The Tangled Wing,* the biological anthropologist Melvin Konner writes: "It seems to me that we are losing the sense of wonder, the hallmark of our species and the central feature of the human spirit." And Konner calls for a reinstatement of amazement and fascination. "At the conclusion of all our studies we must try once again to experience the human soul as soul, and not just as a buzz of bioelectricity; the human will as will, and not just a surge of hormones; the human heart not as a fibrous, sticky pump, but as the metaphoric organ of understanding."

I think my grandfather probably always operated on those presumptions. He was awed by the mystery of things. He never wished to dominate the natural world. And he was as moved by the emotional content of beauty as he was by the factual components that made it beautiful.

So, "What is a naturalist, anyway?"

Well, I would propose that a naturalist is a person whose curiosity is boundless. He or she is interested in kinkajous and sticklebacks, in astronomy, French wine, magpies, baseball, prairie rattlesnakes, quantum mechanics, corn on the cob, great sperm whales, and even Bolsheviks and hummingbirds. A naturalist is a person who tries to delight in everything, is in love with the whole of life, and hopes to walk in harmony across this earth. A naturalist might also be a lunatic like myself who would like to overthrow a capitalist system based on planned obsolescence and conspicuous consumption because he believes that is a formula for planetary suicide. Put another way, a naturalist probably understands that human growth for the sake of growth is the ideology of the cancer cell. So a naturalist most likely gets a vasectomy or a tubal ligation after 1.8 children and sends money to Planned Parenthood and Zero Population Growth. Naturalists also try to consume a lot less in their lives so that all the other critters they love can use that unexploited biological capital for their own benefit and survival.

In short, a naturalist chooses not to be anthropocentric, believing, rather, that every thing has an equal right to life on earth—whether it's an elephant, a peasant from El Salvador, an African cichlid, or a tiny bacterium. A naturalist understands, and defends, the product as a whole. I feel certain that the answer to our future lies in this worldview. And I am grateful I learned it as a child, because it has immeasurably enriched my life.

Keynote address at the seventy-fifth annual meeting of the American Society of Ichthyologists and Herpetologists, Museum of Natural History, New York, June 1991. Reprinted in Natural History Magazine, *November 1992. Also in* Copeia, *journal of ASIH (Dec. 1991), founded by my grandfather, John T. Nichols, in 1913.*

To Be of Use

I met Rini Templeton in 1970, when both of us were working on *The New Mexico Review*. She was a very intense person and somewhat removed. I did not have an easy time talking with her. Perhaps shyness made her seem aloof. The *Review*'s lack of discipline bothered her. Later, when we became closer, she revealed what a deep frustration it was to her that so many different groups lacked the discipline or dedication that could really make them *work*.

Rini always tended to business, or brought us back to business when we strayed too far from the agenda. She believed in using time wisely and resented it when others wasted hers. There were so few hours for so much that had to be done.

Rini contributed many lovely drawings to the *Review*. I also bumped into her off and on in Española at the *El Grito del Norte* office. I helped get out mailings of that paper. Rini was more comfortable at *El Grito* because its politics were closer to her heart.

Nevertheless, when I took over as volunteer editor of the *Review* in 1972 Rini offered to help me publish the paper. I lived in Taos; she lived on Pilar Hill, ten miles to the south. Together, for about four months, we *were* the *Review*.

It was an exhausting, exhilarating time. We slaved away without any pay. Because Rini had most of the newspaper tools at her house, I spent much time there, working all day and far into the nights. We broke for beer, long talks, or walks with her dog Fea across the mesa to the Rio Grande Gorge a mile from the house. During that time we maintained a polite distance from each other.

Rini taught me a lot about the aesthetics of layout and production. I learned the *emotional* difference between a dignified Times-Roman type and a sans-serif boldface. She had a great love of design and repeatedly explained how material should (or could) be presented to a reader.

Her deep concern for such things fascinated me. I was intimidated by her intensity and unselfishness. I liked her rawboned house with all the drawings, political posters, animal bones, spiderwebs on the walls. Steller's jays gathered on a feeding table outside the big west window of her living room; large sculpture pieces were scattered in the sage. It was all earthen—earthy—and close to the natural world, wildlife, the weather.

I never met anyone who worked such long hours. Just by dint of her effort and discipline she wholly commanded my respect. She wanted her art to move people, but seemed indifferent to acclaim. "It is the work that counts," she once wrote, "not any secondary results of it, however noble those may be."

I was a trifle awed by the woman. Sometimes I felt guilty for my less exemplary life. She was horrified if I expressed that feeling to her. Later in our friendship she described herself to me as "a drunken, battered & crazed old wreck. If life is good enough and strong enough that I can give you some things, take them, take them with all my love. Only don't for godsake envy or admire me—I'm too wrecked, too far gone. In spite of which, I love life very much—!"

Rini had no illusions about success or failure, but operated on faith that the struggle was valuable:

> It is not a matter of any one particular time being a million-to-one
> Now, but of doing what best we can with our own particular bit of
> time. . . . And yes, there is mostly defeat and frustration. In the head,
> that's bearable because that necessarily implies struggle and purpose.
> In the heart, it's bearable because of those we love, and greet, and
> share with . . . and in the soul, because of the sheer wonder of the
> world we live in, halfway between electrons and quasars, fucked
> over, enduring, the indescribably beautiful world.

Rini could certainly despair. But if she caught *me* in a despondent mood, she'd land like a ton of bricks. I once made the statement to her in a letter that "Wounded Knee was over." [The occupation of 1973.] Her reply—?

> Wounded Knee is NOT over. Wounded Knee touched, united,
> the quiet Always center of the earth and the urgency of Battle Now.
> The future of the continent will be reached by that beat. Wounded
> Knee has hardly begun.

She had an old guitar and told me stories of being a street musician in England when she was a youngster, "busking" for money. I played the guitar often and she loved to listen. She would heat up tortillas at midnight in her oily frying pan, make burritos or tacos, and we'd sit and talk, eat, drink wine. She joked about being an alcoholic, but I never saw alcohol have an effect on her. She was big, she smoked way too much and coughed a lot. Once I teased her about smoking and she told me in no uncertain terms to fuck off; I never mentioned it again.

Her personal life remained a mystery to me. Odd, all those days we spent together, how formal we remained.

In November 1972 we decided to kill the *Review*. And after we quit working together our relationship changed. We became close and for a year saw each other often. Still, if I inquired too deeply about her private self she would scotch the subject, as in this letter of 1972:

> You wanted to know more of me, of my heart? What to say? What
> to tell you? All these years, so many people . . . I guess I have been
> intimate with multitudes of people, in talk, in bodies, working
> closely on things, sharing the really moving things of life and art.
> But what can I say? It has never seemed to me that the point was to
> add it all up or articulate it. It's just all there, you know, and you
> just keep going. (And I'm not advocating irrationality—obviously
> there are continual choices to be made with as much reason and
> intelligence as one can muster. But that isn't what you were asking.

And I don't have much of an answer, anyhow.) In Breugel's *Icarus,*
for instance, everything leads to the sun.

Rini was awkward physically, yet very strong. When we hiked
across the mesa she always strode ahead of me, carrying a walking stick. On New Mexico's higher mountains she moved up the
slopes way ahead of me; Rini *never* trailed behind. I saw her march
into an alpine lake at eleven thousand feet and dive beneath water
so cold it made my ankles numb in half a second.

She liked living in the cold; her house was always chilly. She
used an outhouse at twenty below on January nights, illuminated
by the piercing icy stars while spooky coyotes howled. To hell with
creature comforts. I see her at dawn standing in the alcove between
her kitchen and bedroom, taking an icy sponge bath. Afterward
her skin prickled as cold as snow.

Rini was always off somewhere attending meetings—in Tierra
Amarilla, Las Vegas, Albuquerque. Her letters about the journeys
to and fro were delightful. Here's an excerpt from February 1973:

Blizzards, stuck trucks, guys getting busted Wed. afternoon for
accomplices to speeding Saturday night, & meetings, meetings, add,
subtract & draw plans . . . too much of all of this to get to the P.O.
and say—There was an eagle, a golden eagle, rose up from a rabbit
carcass as I topped the hill by Canjilon. . . .

Or again:

The ponderosa and spruce were washing in the strong gusts of wind,
snow blowing over the road in the bright sun as I drove here. By
Mora there were six roan horses running in a snow field; there were
crows wheeling, having at each other; there was a fat middle-aged
man playing tag with his kids in front of an adobe gas station.
Enough to break your heart six times in an eighty-mile drive.
So precious, then, to touch another heart, so good.

She sculpted a lot that year. I had no car. I would hitchhike to
her house on Pilar Hill and walk down the driveway to her small

work shack surrounded by high sage, a few junipers, piñon. When I shouted, "Hello!" she came to the window, her hair always under a bandanna. She grinned and pushed goggles up on her forehead. Rini wore dungarees and work boots and thick leather gloves when she used an acetylene torch, and she was usually sweaty and filthy. Her greeting was often uncertain, a bit haunted. I never understood that brief anxiety. Perhaps, after a long life in the Movement, she always half expected bad news, another defeat, somebody jailed. . . .

When she called on the phone her voice was breathless, as if terrified of interrupting me. Rini had an almost pathological fear of being an imposition.

Her sculpture pieces were raw, jagged, blunt. She cudgeled metal, cut it, cut herself—her hands were calloused and half ripped to shreds. Though constantly with other people on political matters, she cherished her hours and days alone. Some of her happiest experiences occurred while "snowed in." She puttered about talking to herself and to the dogs in the vein of this passage from another letter:

> Fea runs in circles, Bouncer rolls his degenerate eyes, one of the neighbors' cows got through the fence, the sun is soggy smogging across the mesa. I set the peanut butter traps every night. During the time I was so down, they sat there. These past nights, one mouse, *un ratoncito muerto, cada mañana*. Do mice hear dreams? How much do we do that we don't know we do—quite aside from what we know & don't acknowledge?

I never took her picture, I wonder why? She joked once about not wanting her soul to be captured on film. A photograph might have been too self-conscious. If I said, "You are beautiful," she was embarrassed and liable to make a crack about being old and ugly. She'd laugh, scornfully putting herself down as a *"coja, manca, tuerta. . . ."* Lame, one armed, half blind. She implied I didn't know the darkness in her, but then refused to discuss it. In 1973 she denigrated herself often for being almost forty; to me her kvetching seemed incongruous.

Up the little rivers we went fishing. She stumbled over rocks and got snagged in underbrush. You needed a guerrilla's stealth to catch the trout, but Rini was clumsy and never succeeded. That did not stop her from trying. She was exasperated by her weaknesses. I never saw her crying.

When she drove in her VW hatchback at night, middle of winter, the sunroof remained open. I froze to death beside her but rarely had the guts to ask her to close it.

Rini introduced me to Walter Lowenfels, who wrote one of my favorite books, *The Revolution Is to Be Human*. Through her I became acquainted with Eduardo Galeano and the art of Rockwell Kent. Also Inti-Illimani and Victor Jara. We listened to Radio Habana on her shortwave radio.

She was a Marxist, albeit an eclectic one. She believed in and loved so many things. Ghosts were not outside her purview, nor magic. She had her deeply tender sides, also moments of dark holiness that were impenetrable. Though I had an intense curiosity to learn much more about her, I never pushed it: she forced me to respect her privacy. Rini emphasized to me that much personal angst in this country is truly a bourgeois affectation. Her focus seemed uniquely on things and people out *there:*

> 35 years today since Vallejo's death: they kept talking about him
> reading poems, on Radio Habana, so I had to go & get my Vallejo
> off the shelf, and sit there. . . . Funny poet. Funny how so much
> despair, put rightly, put well, grows flowers.

During 1973 I worked on my novel *The Milagro Beanfield War*. With the manuscript in a backpack I hitchhiked to Rini's place on Pilar Hill. She would sculpt or draw or correspond while I labored on the book at her living room table. What a quiet and industrious atmosphere! She never interrupted me . . . nor would I have dared to interrupt her. She read the *Milagro* manuscript, critiqued it, and did illustrations that made the book beautiful when it was produced. Her graphics work is out there in a thousand places. I can see it on the front cover of a 1971 *Motive* magazine . . . on the jacket of an Inti-Illimani record . . . and in the pages of newspapers, magazines, greeting cards, calendars, and countless radical publications.

For a couple of years after she left Taos for Mexico we had little contact. Then I began to see her again once or twice a year, never for very long. An afternoon together, drinking coffee or wine, and talking, talking, talking. Or maybe we had dinner, then an all-night rap session. Rini was a pipeline to a fascinating outside world of struggle and culture. In between our infrequent get-togethers she sent books, newspaper clippings, and magazine articles about poets and revolutionaries. Her letters were always rich:

> The sun is setting on the last of '80, Radio Educación is pouring
> out *palikari*, I am finishing up the Big Mountain drawings and
> thinking of beloved *compas*—up and down the continent, up &
> down in our national & personal lives, but strong little fibres of love
> & commitment that hold us together, not unlike whatever it is keeps
> geese on millenary courses . . . (Not that we're silly. But not that we
> ain't part of nature, either.)

On a bus in California, May 1983, heading home to Mexico, she wrote the following:

> Maybe the best I carry back from this trip, a phrase of [Blase]
> Bonpane: "They are old men, they are dead men, sitting on top of
> this country, running this country, and this country has so much life
> in it, life that must prevail. . . ." He's good. Lotsa folks doing good
> work, from down-in-Guatemala, down-in-El Salvador. . . . There is
> understanding, there is good, good commonsensical, fighting
> spirit. . . .

Do I romanticize her?—perhaps. I always felt that with Rini out there, wherever she might be, *somebody*—at least—was taking care of business. I regretted that I was not as strong and unselfish as she seemed to be.

In the autumn of 1984 Rini returned to Taos for a typically brief visit. It surprised me how run-down she appeared. She had lost several teeth, but seemed indifferent; her clothes were worn, almost those of a lady bum. I visited her in the work shack below her house. It was *cold* in that shed. Her bed was a skinny wooden pallet. I wrapped up in a coat, she snuggled in her shabby sleeping bag, and, by candlelight, teeth chattering, we talked until dawn. As always Rini smoked incessantly and coughed a lot, sometimes almost choking. When I left I seriously worried she could freeze to death. But that was her tough style and she let nobody mess with it.

One day, a year before she died, we took a long walk across a wide expanse of sagebrush and snow. Though only fifty, she tired easily. I had not seen that degree of fatigue in her before. For once Rini dawdled behind me. That caught me by surprise and made me feel awkward. It would have been a breech to act solicitous, however, stopping to let her catch up. She brooked no mollycoddling. That was a bravura front she must have carried to the end.

I last saw Rini in March 1986 on the Taos Plaza. We went into the drugstore for coffee and a sandwich. She was busy doing a million things, and I was busy, so we didn't have a long visit. With much energy and animation she talked about Mexico, Nicaragua, and the Big Mountain movement in New Mexico. I brought her up-to-date on my current project, a film script about Pancho Villa. Immediately Rini suggested books I should read about Villa and the Mexican revolution: she scribbled their titles for me. Then we hugged good-bye and she strode off in her work boots and dungarees, smoke wafting from her mouth, and I never saw her again.

Within a few weeks a package arrived from Mexico. In it were two books, in Spanish, about Pancho Villa and the Mexican revolution. Rini had followed up: she *always* followed up.

From the memorial for her a few months later in Pilar, I recall two comments. A dear friend said: "Looking at you all, I realize how extraordinarily complicated a well-lived life can be." And someone else declared: "I would like to die as Rini died, of exhaustion from helping other people."

I have a letter from Rini, going back many years, in which she tried to answer my questions about life and death:

> It was so hard to try, even, to answer the kind of questions you were asking. They are Always questions, and the answers are just in somehow living them out, living them out *well*. Like with music, catching the beat, the tone, and going with it. So much that you *know*, you just *know*, and I don't mean to be obscurantist, it's just that words won't quite keep up. . . .

> Death, too, defines a lot. I mean, I feel this isn't half of what there could be, this isn't half of what should, this isn't 50 percent of what I could . . . and then catch a glimpse of La Muerte, sniffing at the chicken bones, rattling the chess pieces, *y bueno, pues, me lo llevo en cincuenta*. . . .

Rini and I laughed at the daily holocaust: I don't know if this is how she was with other people. Although we shared similar connections to many aspects of the Movement, what we shared together was private and quite apart from our respective lives.

Rini had a great anger against the Reagans and the Pinochets of this planet. And on occasion she criticized the politics of other people in the Movement. But I never heard her *personally* attack another human being. She had more tolerance for human foibles than most anyone I've known.

She was not a saint, nor a genius. She made her share of inappropriate or disastrous choices and decisions. Part of her nature was self-destructive, a serious contradiction in one so concerned with a better life. But she chose the correct historical side and refused to become cynical. She had faith in a better world, and all her energy went to bring it about. The triumph of her life may be this simple: "She was a tireless worker."

At the Pilar memorial for Rini, I read this poem by Marge Piercy. It is called, "To Be of Use:"

The people I love the best
jump into work head first
without dallying in the shallows
and swim off with sure strokes almost out of sight.
They seem to become natives of that element,
the black sleek heads of seals
bouncing like half-submerged balls.

I love people who harness themselves, an ox to a heavy cart,
who pull like water buffalo, with massive patience,
who strain in the mud and the muck to move things forward,
who do what has to be done, again and again.

I want to be with people who submerge
in the task, who go into the fields to harvest
and work in a row and pass the bags along,
who stand in the line and haul in their places,
who are not parlor generals and field deserters
but move in a common rhythm
when the food must come in or the fire be put out.

The work of the world is common as mud.
Botched, it smears the hands, crumbles to dust.
But the thing worth doing well done
has a shape that satisfies, clean and evident.
Greek amphoras for wine or oil,
Hopi vases that held corn, are put in museums
but you know they were made to be used.
The pitcher cries for water to carry
and a person for work that is real.

Published in abridged form as a forward to The Art of Rini
Templeton. *Seattle: Real Comet Press, February 1987.*

A Man for All Seasons

I live in a small house in Taos, New Mexico. From my kitchen door-way I look across a narrow strip of garden to a storage shed where I keep many books and file cabinets. Nailed high on the far edge of this prosaic structure is a nesting box for starlings. It's two feet tall, six inches wide, eight inches deep. The entrance hole up top has a two-and-a-half-inch diameter. The roof boasts a three-inch overhang. The box was once painted light umber but is now simple weathered wood covered in front by bird droppings. My dad built it for me twenty-six years ago, and birds have nested in it every year since.

The box has been through my three marriages and three different locations. It has been nailed to silver-tip poplars, Chinese elms, and my storage shed. Cats, ravens, and magpies have attacked it to no avail. It is a professional starling box made by a professional birder (who's also a good carpenter). My dad knew what he was doing.

His name is David G. Nichols. He is eighty-one years old and lives in Smithville, Texas, a small town forty-two miles southeast of Austin. As long as I have known him he has taught me about wildlife, especially birds. His father, my namesake, John T. Nichols, was a distinguished naturalist and for many years curator of fishes at the American Museum of Natural History in New York City. From him my father learned much about tanagers, sharks, and spiders—the fantastic web of life. To me he passed on a natural-ist's awe and curiosity.

When my mother died shortly after my second birthday, Pop
went off to World War II. I lived with cousins in Smithtown, New

York, on Long Island. From the Solomon Islands, Dad sent letters in which he drew me pictures of frigate birds, butterflies, wild pigs, bats, lizards, cardinal lorys, monkeys, and "white pigeons with green backs and red knobs on their bills" sitting in banyan trees. Perhaps that is when I became irrevocably hooked on nature.

I did not truly "meet" my dad until after the war in 1945. My fondest early memories are of being with him at his family's summer home in Mastic on the south shore of Long Island, the old William Floyd estate. His mother, Cornelia Floyd, was descended directly from William Floyd, who signed the Declaration of Independence for New York State. The house was a simple white colonial structure surrounded by 613 acres of fields and forest and salt meadows leading to Moriches Bay. In 1965 the family gave the whole place to the U.S. government. It is currently a museum and wildlife refuge, part of the Fire Island National Seashore.

We found box turtles at Mastic and marked them, keeping a record for decades. Dad gathered mice and other animals for the Natural History Museum's small mammal collection. I followed him on his morning rounds checking the traps and watched as he prepared museum specimens on the kitchen table. He explained their habits and told me their Latin names. It excited me enormously to see those critters up close.

From behind the Mastic shutters my father plucked little brown bats, unafraid to handle them with his bare hands. He called my attention to woodcocks towering at dusk above the front field. He could identify any bird nest, whether it belonged to a flycatcher, a phoebe, or a sparrow. If a thing warbled or chirped or cried out of sight, Dad knew whether it was a red-eyed vireo, a green heron, or a herring gull. His veneration of those beings gave them great status in my eyes, and even before I could read, I was an environmentalist.

Dad encouraged me to have leaf collections, to learn the names of butterflies, to be fascinated by praying mantis eggs. I kept frogs in terrariums and an occasional painted turtle in the bathtub. We observed dragonflies and darning needles and paddled over sunfish nests. He lifted a snapping turtle by the tail. With bamboo poles we fished for flounder and snapper blues while gulls and dozens of other birds flapped overhead. He gave names to all things that crawled or swam or soared, telling me where they wintered and how they raised their young. Even ticks and sand fleas and deer mice belonged to a priceless habitat.

All his life my father observed birds, from primitive blinds, through one-way windows in his houses, and from cabins and mountain perches and boats and cruising automobiles. He took thousands of bird photographs that today are kept neatly, carefully annotated, in dozens of loose-leaf albums. Though a number of blinds were lost as he moved around, that never slowed him down: new camouflage boxes and bunkers and cabanas instantly arose in fresh territories.

When I was seven he tried to carry a large flimsy blind on a canoe from Indian Point at Mastic over to an island in Moriches Bay. He dumped the box in five feet of water but eventually lugged it to a beach. I have snapshots of him setting decoys in the sand. Using a Graflex camera, he photographed the birds attracted by the decoys. I crouched in the blind with him as he took pictures of sanderlings, plovers, dowitchers, and perhaps a laughing gull.

We often walked along the beach at Fire Island. There was wind in the dune grasses and least terns darting about our heads and sandpipers skittering alongside the foamy ocean wavelets. We inspected horseshoe crabs lolling in the surf. I collected crinkly black skates' eggs, hoarding them like priceless treasures. *Everything* was presented to me as an important part of the universe.

In later years we went out with a sensitive Uher 4000 recorder, capturing birdsongs on tape. Afterward Pop slowed down the tape so I could hear the higher-frequency notes, which were inaudible to us until they were altered in this manner. At reduced speed, the melodious complexity of a meadowlark's song was compounded, outdoing anything invented by Mozart or Beethoven. I was mesmerized by the intricate tonalities of bird language.

My father is a big tall man who has always worn a crew cut. He's a serious intellectual and a professional scientist. He has a lusty sense of humor and laughs a lot about sex, human folly, and

the cathecting difficulties inherent in *Homo sapiens'* titillating attempts at the "transduction of affect." He has run traplines in Nevada
and observed the behavior of pelicans at Port Aransas, Texas (1997),
and in Miami, Florida (1942). A crab spider he discovered in
Cantwell, Alaska, on August 15, 1937, was named after him: *Xys-
ticus nicholsi*. He earned a Ph.D. in psycholinguistics at age fifty at
the University of California, Berkeley, and taught for twenty years
at the University of Colorado in Colorado Springs: comparative
animal behavior, communication of emotion, human survival, and
even some courses in statistics. He speaks fluent Russian and French
and enough Chinese to raise a couple of guffaws at a good party.
Nobody can play the guitar and sing "Little Joe the Wrangler" better than David Gelston Nichols. A risqué limerick pops out of his
mouth for virtually any occasion. And he once told me this: "John,
the trouble with empirical science today is that scientists pretend
make-believe is unreal."

Pop grew up hunting and had a true aim—he liked the taste of
squirrel. But in his early twenties he abruptly quit blood sports
and then wrote a poem about his change of heart. Here are the last
three verses:

The light of day is fading
And far out on the lake
The hen duck glides as yesterday
Alongside of the drake.

They float there close together
Safe and free as air.
I held my trigger finger.
I could have had the pair.

When they move on tomorrow
Those birds belong to me.
I had a chance . . . to hold . . . or kill,
And chose to set them free.

My grandfather gave my dad his first pair of field glasses in 1925, when Pop was nine. He used the glasses in the Solomons and in China. He used them on flamingos in Florida, on pipits and grizzlies in Alaska, on avocets in Berkeley's Aquatic Park. He also trained his binoculars on crows attacking a great horned owl in Rock Creek Park in Washington, D.C. I know, because I was there.

It happened in 1956. The old man has always talked with crows. He caws to them and listens to their answers and makes a passel of notes. In Rock Creek Park he had a pole with a stuffed owl affixed to a crossbar on top. He stuck the pole in the ground, marshaled me under a tree, and cawed up a storm. Inside ten minutes two dozen birds were noisily mobbing that owl. I was properly astounded.

Pop's curiosity extends to most anything in life. He's interested in religions and has long been involved with Psychologists for Social Responsibility. He is active in the Bastrop County Environmental Network. His concern for the environment runs deep. He writes a column called Nichols' Niche for the weekly *Smithville Times*. Topics for the Niche have ranged from the proper disposal of roadkill to his thoughts on worldwide conflict resolution. In print he has pondered computer languages, biofeedback, ring-billed gulls, the endangered Houston toad, censorship and pornography, mourning dove threat posturing, the psychology of cults, and the meaning of good luck pennies found on the ground. (In pocket-size notebooks he has kept a record of every penny that he's picked up since 1960. He faithfully records his thoughts at the moment of discovery. Whenever I find a penny on the ground, I think of my father.)

Twice we drove across the United States together. In the winter of 1950 we traveled from Berkeley to Washington, D.C., in an old Studebaker loaded with suitcases, a parakeet, and a Siamese cat named Boris Caleb Cadwallader. He gambled for me in Reno; we slid off the road on ice in Colorado, almost tipping over. The old man kept a record of bird life along the way. In Kansas we clobbered a ring-necked pheasant. Pop slammed on the brakes, went into reverse, and threw that pheasant in the trunk, where it promptly froze. We ate it on our second night back east.

In 1978 we hit the road again, from Colorado Springs to Long Island to bury my grandmother. By now my father had a tape recorder on the front seat of his Chevy Impala, and he kept interrupting our conversations to remark on the bird life en route. "Two grackles at one o'clock . . ." "One kestrel on a telephone wire . . ." "Three turkey vultures feeding on a mound of bloody fur, probably a skunk." He did that all the way across.

Pop tells me he became a serious birder as a small child, participating in Christmas bird counts with his father. Ever since, any person who travels by foot or by canoe or in an automobile with my old man can't help observing whatever moves in the sky or flits across a soybean field or flutters through the pines. Why? Because in my dad's presence all that swoops, perches, or dives has a name, a profile, a history, a personality, a distinguished place on earth.

Last February my two brothers and I flew to Smithville for a family reunion. Pop's wife, Jackie, was on an archeological dig in Belize. Not for thirty-five years had we three sons been concurrently in the same room with our maker. We spent a memorable week together taking walks and reminiscing, catching up on things.

The old guy moves a trifle slowly of late: the usual infirmities of age are exacting a toll. Still, he goes for a promenade daily over in Buescher State Park with his dog, Scholar, by his side and my grandfather's old binoculars around his neck. Meticulously, he records the bird activity driving to and fro. His hope is that the years of data he has kept and computerized will help protect migratory-bird habitat and breeding areas in the future.

My heart still leaps up when I start walking with the old man. The same goes for my brothers, Tim and Dave. At Buescher Lake he pointed out to us a solitary sandpiper, then turned the glasses on two red-shouldered hawks screeching and circling high above. A great blue heron flying by suddenly swerved, dived, and grabbed a tiny carp. There was a great egret across the water, looking stately in some reeds.

At another point in our visit he stopped the car abruptly to watch a pair of Mexican eagles (caracaras) trying to wrestle a dead pond slider turtle off across a field. Later he mentioned how eagerly he was anticipating the April return of chimney swifts migrating north from South America. For years he has counted the number of them that dive into the post office chimney near his house in Smithville. On certain nights there are more than a thousand.

From his freezer Dad took a yellow-shafted flicker that he'd picked up off the road. He posed for pictures with the handsome bird, and we boys did also, proud to display our affection for the natural world: like father, like sons. All of us were touched by the mystifying architecture of feather, beak, and claw, the impressive palette of color, the beauty of living things that fly.

Whenever I walk outdoors with the old man, my eye is on the planet. We observe chipping sparrows, cliff swallows, the weather, foliage, beetles, and crossbills. At age fifty-seven I am always asking him questions, same as when I was ten: "What kind of moth is that?" "Where do cattle egrets roost at night?" "Is there really such a thing as a black-bellied tree duck?" I am eager to share with him by picking out, with my sharp eyes, a bluebird feather or a tiny warbler. It's my way of saying, "Thanks," I guess, and also, "I love you."

Yesterday I took a break from work and sat on my kitchen stoop, eating a grapefruit while starlings moved in and out of their nesting box, feeding the young. An almost grown fledgling poked its head clear when the parents were gone, waiting for more food. My cats, Cookie and Carlos, sat underneath the box, staring upward, plotting murder and mayhem.

The starling is a common bird, but I am fascinated by its rites of passage, which have entertained me all my life. That nesting box is a gift that keeps on giving. Each spring it reaffirms the curiosity and sense of wonder (and commitment) passed on to me by my father. Every time the birds arrive, I bless Pop for his life.

Audubon Magazine, *Nov./Dec. 1997. My father died on April 13, 1998.*

Earl the Pearl Meets Rikki-tikki-tavi

I met Mike Kimmel in Guatemala in the spring of 1964. I'd never run into anybody beside myself who was so loud and arrogant. He's five-foot four and he acts like an intellectual gangster. He told me immediately that he'd been tops in his field of journalism at Temple and could also run fifty balls in straight pool. I figured he was full of shit and challenged him to a game. We went to a pool hall. Mike spotted me twenty-five balls and then beat me, fifty to twenty-seven. I said, "Oh."

After Guatemala he would come up to New York from Philly on his motorcycle to visit Alan Howard in my old apartment on West Broadway. Him and his bomber jacket and thirteen-inch pegged dungarees and spit-polished Wellington boots with two-inch Cuban heels. What marvelous talks we had. I never met a guy who cared about literature as much as Mike: he had such a respect for, and belief in, the value of art. We'd walk around the city afternoons or late at night, talking, arguing, buying Italian sausages, a pretzel, maybe a handful of chestnuts. At first it scared me to death, traipsing along with my belligerent pal. There'd be fifteen high school corner boys six feet, five inches tall in their Afros, standing on a sidewalk, eating taco chips and drinking Pepsi, and Mike never walked around them, he always marched straight *through,* arrogantly elbowing aside kids twice his size: "'Scuse me, babe. Yo, how you doin'?" If we stopped in a deli for a pastrami sandwich, Mike would start screaming at the counterman: "Gimme that cut, not *that* one—and put *more* on it, what are you, a cheapskate?" I was always terrified we were going to get in a fight. On Canal Street, 195 buying a fish or a bag of squid, he'd snarl at the Vietnamese vender, telling him, "These better be good; you sell me a rotten one like last time and I'll break your legs." Pretty quickly I understood it was a street style, inner city, with a twinkle in the eye.

The first great influence on my life and writing was Damon Runyon. The second was Michael. He knew everybody on the street in Philadelphia and New York: Benny the doorman, Gil the short-order cook, Joey the bartender, Tommy the ward heeler, Moishe the crook, Brenda the hooker, Jimmy the journalist. He knew the museums. He fed me a Pat's cheese steak in South Philly and then took us to the Rodin museum and made me *look* at things. He introduced me to my favorite sculpture piece of all time, a Rodin called *I Am Beautiful*. It is small and passionate and arrogant, just like Mike.

Later we stopped at the Schuylkill River. Mike actually caught fish in that sewer. Next he showed me a famous brick shot tower and explained how they made lead bullets during the revolution. He had a bottomless pit of information. You took a drive on the Pulaski Skyway with Mike, he'd give you a two-hour dissertation on Pulaski himself, his entire life, the wars he fought in, the history of Poland. He made me listen to classical music, actually *listen* to it. "Nichols, only a very ignorant goy would treat Mozart and Debussy as background noise." He once gave me a tour of his childhood home, Strawberry Mansion, a ghetto in North Philly that looked like an H-bomb had smacked it. Stories of his childhood were tough and bigger than life. He ordered me to read *Bridge on the Drina* and *The Brothers Ashkenazi* and the Studs Lonigan trilogy and Nelson Algren. Years later, in a tent at twelve thousand feet in the Sangre de Cristo Mountains during a snowstorm, we read passages to each other from *The Sun Also Rises* about trout fishing on the Irati River near Pamplona. Mike complained, "What kind of phony baloney is it that Hemingway doesn't say how long the trout were in inches or how much they weighed?"

Mike's left-wing politics helped forge my social conscience; he was on the correct historical side. He grew up in a working-class family that carried cards, and he fought for civil rights and against the Vietnam War, and he supported the Young Lords. He had an informed political and economic analysis that was sophisticated and impeccable. In a restaurant once some yahoo at the next table started tossing around racial epithets, so Mike grabbed a ketchup bottle and jumped him. In Guatemala for the Quakers he learned Spanish fluently, hated the dictatorship, assisted the Quiche Maya, and wrote an angry novel about their oppression.

Nobody had more gusto. I venerated his attitude, his lingo, his intelligence, his accent. I copied him; I mimicked. We hit the Palestra for a Big Five contest; he insisted we catch the Sixers and Dr. J and bought us folding chair seats right under a basket. We attended Mets games together in the Apple. Life was good, drinking beer and eating garbage with Mike while screaming at umpires and the players and talking sports statistics, boxing, Muhammad Ali, the death of Benny "Kid" Peret at the hands of Emile Griffith, and the great year Robin Roberts had with the Phillies "Whiz Kids."

I couldn't believe Mike was as good at basketball as he said he was. Talk about ferocious competitors. I remember at the Thompson Street playground watching him go bananas. He led me over to Sixth Avenue and Fourth Street to see those intense games with the big boys from up in Harlem. When he came out west to visit me in Taos we used to shoot free throws in my driveway. Mike buried me, sinking fifty shots in a row.

One day we went to Kit Carson Park for some lazy one-on-one on a concrete surface. Two enormous Chicano dudes showed up and challenged us to a game. They had beards and Jesus hairdos down to their shoulders. Mike said, "Whatta Chicanos know about basketball? Who've you got in the NBA? Gimme a break—you don't belong on a court with us!" I thought he was going to start a race war. I also can't dribble worth squat. "Don't worry about it," Mike said. "Just feed me the ball." So we played those two guys and killed them. I fed Mike the ball. He was like Earl "the Pearl" Monroe meets Rikki-tikki-tavi. Absolutely indefatigable.

Mike had more information about life on earth than the *Encyclopaedia Britannica*. He actually read his way through most of Western philosophy from Pythagoras to Sartre and Kierkegaard.

In Taos he always got up early, made coffee, lit a pipe or cigar, camped on the portal, and started reading. He was a *serious* reader, a *serious* writer. He believed in doing things *well;* he *hated* mediocrity. I've read most of the articles, stories, columns, and novels he wrote. Flawed or wonderful, it is all original work, tough and combative. Yes, I wish he had sold *The Master Weaver*. And *On Belay*. And *Tin Blades*. And *Banished*. And *Thanks for the Memories*. He made it really hard on himself, but he had that tortured style and stuck to it all his life without getting the recognition he desperately wanted for his literature.

I admired his pursuit. How did he maintain that discipline and the courage of his convictions?

We sat at tables drinking Wild Turkey 101 and cleaning equipment. He took great care of reels and rods and shoes and clothing, sewing up tears, applying oil, lubricating gears—the man refused to be careless. He enjoyed demonstrating knots. While I sharpened my knife he'd give me a complete history of the quarry in Arkansas that produced the special whetstone that I was using that he had given me. Mike took everything seriously except his own teeth. When they got rotten or abscessed he just let them fall out; he didn't give a damn.

"I'm beautiful no matter what," he said with a snort, those big lips grinning snaggletoothed and imperiously.

My God, we laughed a lot. One autumn he came to Taos and we played Ping-Pong for a month in the rain. He was good. My kids, Tania and Luke, called him their favorite uncle. He teased them and pinched their cheeks until they squirmed and he had faith in them when they went ballistic in their adolescent monster phase. He told me my children were real good eggs.

Here's a snapshot: Mike and I are climbing over a steep mountain saddle after a fishing expedition to Bear Lake. As we go down a shale slide he puts his rod case over his shoulders and starts doing a mummer's strut in the scree.

And another picture I cherish: The first big trout he nailed in the Rio Grande he yanks out of the water, it flops off the hook, he tackles it on the sand, rolls over, lifts the lunker rainbow to his lips, and, in paroxysms of laughter, he *kisses* it like Bjorn Borg bussing the Wimbledon trophy.

A couple of years ago Mike and Alan Howard took me fishing in Barnegat Light on the Jersey shore and we stood on the beach all night baiting with eels and waiting. Early in the morning Alan tied into a large bass, twenty-four pounds, thirty-nine inches long. Mike went off the charts in a rage while Alan played it, and when the enormous creature emerged from the surf I thought Mike was going to kill Alan in a jealous rage. He actually spit in Alan's direction and threw a knife at him. But fifteen minutes later Mike snagged a twenty-seven-pound bass (forty-two inches long!) and suddenly all was for the best in the best of all possible worlds. Mike forgave Alan for catching that fish, and we pardoned the half-pint martinet for his temper tantrum.

Michael and his wife Karen amazed me. I don't know how Karen put up with him for so long. I loved Mike, and he's a huge part of my own soul, but a little Mike in the flesh always went a long ways with me. He was exhausting. I had a two-month limit on his visits, then I needed relief big time. I mean, when Mike asked if you wanted coffee in the morning, he *screamed* the question at you. Often I wondered: How can I just shut him up for a single minute?

For Karen life with Mike must have been a battle royale. I'm amazed at all the work they accomplished together in the wilderness country they visited. How did they dump all their equipment from a canoe into the Green River in Utah on their initial day out and still produce a first class photo-essay for *Sports Afield* on the expedition? In the last few years Mike touched me, talking about his love for Karen and his desire to work hard on their marriage. It seemed he grew a lot more mature and compassionate in their relationship than I have ever been in any of mine.

Everyone who met Mike during his many sojourns in Taos never forgot him. They always asked me about that unique, noisy son of a bitch. Soge Track at the Taos Pueblo. Taylor Streit, a fishing guide friend of ours. Michael Martin Murphey, a famous country-and-western singer Mike almost punched out on his last visit to my hometown in an argument over scabbing during a union strike.

Dori Vinella, who ran a café Mike and I frequented together for twenty-five years. People always asked me, "When is that obnoxious shrimp from Philadelphia coming back?" He gave them a kick in the pants. He startled folks. He offended people. He made an indelible impression. Mike regularly bragged to me, "I got a lot of nice friends. I got a *lot* of nice friends."

The novel he was working on when he dropped dead on his fire escape is flawed but filled with spectacular writing. Many beautiful passages are full of his trademark abrupt shorthand, his knowledge of minutiae, his hatred of schmaltz. He would go ten pages out of his way to spit on a cliché before he avoided it. He tormented a sentence to death before moving on to the next one. He was befuddled by plots. He refused to be facile. Like most of us, he shot himself in the foot repeatedly. But he kept on working at it, which has to be the ultimate accolade.

How did he maintain that manic energy through all his disappointments? Maybe it was the vitamins Karen pumped into him. Despite all the dismay, Mike erupted each day with a fresh garble of anger, humor, and information. He could be incredibly patient or way too easily insulted. He never quit yelling. He was infallible. "Shut up, Nichols," he hollered, "I KNOW WHAT I'M DOING!" Of course he felt defeated half the time, but that only made him twice as insolent. He kept telling Karen, "Get out there and work hard and earn more money so I can buy you things."

Each time we met after a long absence Mike grabbed my cheeks and kissed me on the mouth so hard he almost ripped my lips apart. I loved him for that.

Two nights ago Ruby and I sat together telling stories about Mike. Doug Terry and I spent an hour on the phone, laughing and crying and recounting stories about Mike. Andy Lenderman called me up three times the day Mike died with more event-filled tales about our buddy, whom he revered next only to William Faulkner. And Ron Kalom and I sat for an hour reminiscing about Mike. Ronnie is in a Taos minyan; he said Mike will be remembered this sabbath and for thirty days after and every year henceforth on the day of his death. Ron said, "He was important to Taos."

Mike came to New Mexico last year for three weeks. We talked. We hunted and fished. We had a fabulous time. Mike climbed up the mountains. He scrambled over boulders in the gorge. One day we got stopped by the cops for no taillights. Cherry tops flashing behind me, beer cans on the dashboard, I'm petrified. Before I know what is happening, Mike is out the door, walking back toward a couple of trigger-happy state *chotas* who I am sure must think he's crazy. "Hey, how you doin'?" Mike says. The cops' loudspeaker replies, "Sir, get back in the vehicle." I'm hissing at Mike, "Please, for chrissakes get back in or they'll kill both of us." Mike addresses the fuzz, "Hey, we were only fishin', we just came out of the gorge. You guys are great. You do a good job. . . ." "SIR, GET BACK INTO THE VEHICLE." By then I'm almost in tears, begging him to return. At the third warning Mike finally tips, retreats, doesn't try to punch out the fuzz, and hops into the truck, and we survived.

A couple of days later a friend of mine named Gene Berry died of a brain tumor at fifty-three. There was a memorial service at the Sagebrush Inn. It was a beautiful bluebird October day in New Mexico, perfect fishing weather. Mike and I went to the funeral. Mike was also a pal of Gene, an expert angler who got us started on fishing when Mike first arrived in Taos in 1971. So we went to the Sagebrush and listened to the homilies. Taylor Streit, the fishing guide, asked me to read one of Gene's poems. I did that, sat down, and inclined toward Mike just as he turned to me—and we had the same brilliant thought simultaneously: "Let's go wet a fly."

We sneaked from the service on tiptoes and raced up to the Wild River section of the Rio Grande and scrambled down Bear Crossing Trail. We had the river to ourselves on that pristine afternoon. I caught a few, Mike bagged a couple. At dusk we retreated to the last pool at the base of the trail. Mike commandeered the choice riffle at the bottom. I went to the head of the pool, flicked in my fly, and latched onto an enormous fish. I couldn't even muscle it out of the current. Mike screamed at me, "That's *my* fish, Nichols, you stole *my* pool, you preppy bastard, you blue-blood scum-sucking et cetera—you stole my *fish!*" He threw a rock at me, he went postal, he pitched another stone, his voice grew even more

strident. I needed five minutes to work my noble adversary over
to the net, enduring Mike's abuse all the while. The rainbow trout
was huge by our standards, maybe three pounds, twenty inches
plus, by far the biggest I had ever landed on the river, the kind you
take home and show everybody in town and brag about for a year.
I held it up. Mike battered me with vile invective. So I said, "Hey,
Mike—watch." And I tossed Moby Dick back into the river at his
feet: "This one's for Gene."

That did it. He attacked like Pancho Villa, whipping me with
his fishing rod. He actually fell upon me in the rocks. Then we
both started laughing. We couldn't stop. Later we hiked out of the
gorge in the dark, Mike cursing me, chortling, halting to gaze at
the sparkling sky—thank God he never seriously studied astronomy so I didn't have to listen to him name all the constellations
and their individual stars. And we remembered Gene. Up top at
the rim we sat on the tailgate of my truck, drinking beer, eating
sandwiches, gawking tiredly at the moon. And that was certainly
a fine day when we played hooky from Gene Berry's funeral.

Last story—even though I feel that to really honor Mike I
shouldn't quit for another two hours. This one happened last year
also. Mike and I went grouse hunting. It was a horrible, windy,
rainy, dark, foreboding day. We drove ten miles along the Rio
Grande del Rancho and then walked for fifty minutes up Saloz
Canyon and climbed old logging roads and game trails to an altitude of nine thousand feet. There we separated, Mike on one side
of the mountain, me on the other. The aspens were radiant but it
kept growing colder and wetter. No matter, we tramped and bush-
whacked and traversed for about five hours. Neither of us saw a
grouse. We got wet. We froze. We suffered, we became bored, we
complained. We finally met up again on the main trail at six-thirty,
almost dark, and started trudging three miles downhill in driving
rain, kvetching about our discomfort, tripping over blowdown,
slapped at by waist-high soaking grasses or mammoth cow parsnip
leaves or alder foliage. His legs ached so much he could hardly
navigate. He was huffing and puffing. My rotten heart bounced in
and out of atrial fibrillation. But pretty soon Mike started giggling.

He said, "Shoot, Nichols, of all the places I go, hunting or fishing or hiking or whatever I do to earn a living, the stuff we do together has gotta be the toughest, the most sadistic and masochistic and difficult." And he added, "Jesus, this is fun. *Don't we have good times together?*" And we exalted in our misery the entire way to the truck.

Well, yes, we adventured together. And we reveled in the difficulty. We shared a fair amount of agony, from the day his dog Bashion ate a meat loaf (when Mike broke his first wife's jaw) to this morning in New York City when all that remains are his ashes. I incorporated Mike deep into my life and work—the noise, the strut, the chutzpah: Little Big Man. He always quoted Willard Motley, from *Knock on Any Door:* "Live fast, die young, have a good-looking corpse." Yesterday Alan told me, "Mike was right—he always said there was no point in taking care of his teeth."

He was five-foot four . . . he was arrogant . . . and I loved him with all my heart.

Eulogy for Mike Kimmel (three days after his death from a heart attack). At 8 Beach Street, New York City, September 25, 1997. Abridged version in Fly Rod & Reel Magazine, *July/August 1998.*

Part Seven
September Songs

The Taos Valley, by Rini Templeton, 1971.

Living takes a toll. You get older and a bit tired. Maybe you quiet down, also. I know in a way I sure have. Though I'm not exactly a recluse, I do live close to my own mortality. But I have made my separate peace.

Don't get me wrong. This book, front to back, is a statement of how I think and feel and live at the millennium, year 2000. The angry young man of twenty-five still burns in the writer at sixty. And the laughter is as strong as ever. Most important, every day I keep learning new stuff. Last week I cried all the way through the movie Shakespeare in Love. *Tonight I'll work on a screenplay about Che and Fidel. And tomorrow—?*

Ah, tomorrow.

Tomorrow is another page . . . or maybe three . . . or possibly five . . . or do I dare to dream of ten . . . ?

A Habit of Seeing

Once I was virtually obsessed by panorama. Of course, I have long resided in The Land of Enchantment, which readily lends itself to wraparound landscapes and skies unbearably bloated with an infinite profusion of clouds, weather, and wanton mood changes. Anyone who lives here must thrive on this maudlin glut. I for one readily confess that I used to crave the vast emotional hit of every upchuck-beautiful sunset. And I must admit that in my speed-freak days I loved to cruise our typical endless ribbons of highway in my old '73 Chevy Impala, zooming along at ninety across shining mesas and diamond deserts whose horizons always gave credence to concepts like "eternal" and "infinity."

Then one day an ant fell into my bathwater as I was lounging in the steamy drink perusing the *Catholic Worker*. I lifted the little tyke out on my index finger and placed it on the edge of the tub. Next I watched as the ant came to life slowly, cleaning its legs and feelers, wiping moisture from little crevices with its quirky forepaws, working its minuscule mandibles overtime en route to revivification. I was captivated by the intensity of this creature's smallness and by the convoluted process of its self-restoration.

In due course, perky as a speckled pup, my resurrected *hormiga* proceeded jauntily across the white ceramic ledge, fell into the hot water again, and drowned.

Now: I'm not saying that right then a sort of grody New Age epiphany related to a fascination with simplicity transformed my wide-angled soul. But when I focused on that poor ant I was entering a truly different world, one antithetical to panorama, and a world that nowadays I find myself increasingly drawn to. In its space I tend to ignore the forest while studying the veins and coloration of a single leaf. Or I might be blind to an entire fecund orchard while doting on one yellow jacket busily excavating a rotten apple atilt in the dewy grass.

When I am tottering about in my micro mode, a delicate strand of wheat is likely to satisfy my jones for immortality in a molecule. Or my own queer shadow cast against the dusty terrain of an empty stock pond might capture my more singular fancies, imparting a transient—but nonetheless highly intriguing—delight positively redolent with fulfillment.

If I pay close enough attention, there's always an extensive landscape to be discovered in a flower, an apple, or a trout; in a culvert, or in the shadows on a church wall. I once spent almost an hour ogling the iridescent barbs of a magpie feather. On another occasion I became mesmerized watching a dragonfly lay her eggs against stalks of vegetation in a small pond. My pièce de résistance in this line of work occurred on a lazy afternoon in early May when I actually fell asleep while observing a very drowsy rattlesnake sunning itself. When I awoke, the snake was nowhere to be seen. I presume it was off somewhere swallowing a silky pocket mouse. Hard luck for the plump rodent, of course, but better a mouse than my big toe, I always say.

Sometimes I deliberately simplify my world down to this habit of seeing. No doubt, such a form of concentration goes directly against the grain of our modern frenetic world. Willfully I bypass the information highway; with calculated indifference, I sidestep all virtual realities and auto mechanics; and as premeditated as Machiavelli, I choose not to dwell on the cultural cacophonies created by those thirteen million inhabitants of New York City. In the process I adopt—for my slogan—the admonition: Think of many things, but do one. And I honestly believe this is the best way—short of senility—to forge a quality existence.

When I take the time to focus my eye, the world begins to explain its composition—and magic—to my budding awareness. A single cloud defines the entire sky, one well-executed double play (in an otherwise clunky ball game) sends me home ecstatic, and a solitary hummingbird busy at a pink hollyhock can thrill my entire afternoon. Every act of aliveness becomes a gem worth its weight in gold; every small gesture made by bug, wind, or gamboling child elucidates all creation.

Too often our imaginations are squashed by an overabundance of information and impressions. Myself, I feel better when the music begins on a single note that I can nurture with care along a path leading eventually to the blossoming of a sonata. The trick is to create a step-by-step evolution toward some distant maturity, and not be in a hurry to get there. The tragedy is to embrace the typical bombardment of daily information in an attempt to resolve the chaos of life by incorporating a million random sound bites at the speed of light and calling it wisdom. In truth, at the end of this frantic process we have absorbed a great deal of busy (and for the most part useless) knowledge, but are the proud owners of very little comprehension.

I have a friend who is a Zen master and also a saltwater fly fisherman of advanced skill whose passion is the shallow flats around Key West. Once in his life he caught a permit on a fly. I believe it took him twenty years to accomplish this feat. I had the good luck to be in his skiff as he cast to another one of these elusive fish, which was tailing in about a foot of water near Cottrell Key just north of Key West. We were afloat in the widest of panoramas, but our concentration was entirely fixed on a single fish. It spooked, of course, but the thrill stayed behind and buoyed us for days.

For me, understanding begins with that single fish, or with lichens on a rock, or with an ant cleaning its tiny feelers: these are *components* of panorama, if you will, not the end result. Bottom line?—the complexity of our universe is composed of an intricate and holy simplicity. To wit: Always stop and smell the flowers. Then, and only then, will you see the eye of your personal god or goddess winking in true admiration.

New Mexico Magazine, *September 1994.*

The Day Lee Brodsky Died

I was sitting in the café having breakfast when Barbara arrived and sat down at the table across from me. She was flushed, and her hair was a bit more tangled than usual.

"Did you hear who died last night?" she said, and I shook my head, No, I had not.

"Lee Brodsky," she said. "He just died in his sleep. Isn't that sad?"

What I usually wind up saying when somebody gives me that kind of news is, "I just saw him in the post office yesterday, or maybe a couple of days ago."

Barbara got up and went over to the counter to order. She said, "So we all better be nice to each other, because you just never know."

I recalled, "He was always smoking cigarettes. He never took much care of himself, did he?"

Lee Brodsky ran one of the bookstores in town. It was a nice little shop. I didn't go in there too often, but I patronized it enough. I liked chatting with Lee, a big guy who wore thick glasses. Though physically clumsy, he had an acerbic wit. I remembered his ex-wife, but after the divorce she and the children left town. That was a while ago.

Barbara returned to her table. "He'd just had a pacemaker installed," she remarked glumly.

I smiled and said, "I guess it didn't work so hot, did it?"

Barbara shook her head and gave me a rueful grin. She looked melancholy and rather beautiful. I folded my newspaper and put it in my knapsack, added the mail I had finished reading, and paid at the counter. Outside, I got on my bicycle and pedaled home, thinking about Lee Brodsky all the way. Already I had decided to take the day off. Put simply, I guess my reasoning was: Life's too short.

I continued thinking about Lee as I made sandwiches and put a few lite beers and some ice cubes in my cooler. I remembered his computer, which had never functioned properly at the store. It took forever to buy a book because Lee was always futzing with inventory stats that rarely came up correctly on the screen. I teased him about it, and he took my ribbing in stride.

I carried a shotgun and the edibles out to my truck, then returned for the canteen, a box of 16-gauge shells, and a couple of topo maps that were folded up and pretty worn. A few minutes later I was headed south on the main highway to Ranchos, where I turned east toward the mountains, my excitement growing, feeling free.

I don't get very emotional when friends or acquaintances die. I expect it. To me, death has become an intimate and normal part of life, and I don't consider it a tragedy. I've had a bad heart for a long time, and over the years I have learned to respect my own mortality. But I like the natural cycles. I think we often cling to life in an unseemly manner. Perhaps when I'm up against the wall I'll go down on my knees, begging for another month, more years, a few added decades. And maybe I'll finagle expert medical care to prolong my days; nobody knows the future. But for the moment I regard death as an honorable conclusion, and I don't fear it much.

The day was sunny, bland, with vibrant blue skies but no wind—not my favorite mood. I like real raggedy-ass weather rife with ominous clouds, rain, wind, hail, and snowflakes. The autumn world, radiant in dampness, makes me gloat.

Leaving the highway, I rattled up a dirt road alongside the Little Rio Grande. An old green truck approaching from the other direction slowed down and stopped. Behind the wheel was my old friend Joey. Beside him sat his buddy Raul, sucking on a Bud. Their truck was loaded with vigas. Joey is a stone alcoholic, but I like him a lot. He once stabbed a guy in a bar fight and I gave the judge a character reference letter. Joey is killing himself, but he sure works hard. He has a wonderful garden—corn, squash, cucumbers, and *habas* galore. He can wield a shovel all day in the hot sun, cleaning our irrigation ditch. Long ago he smacked his wife around, so she left him and took the kid. His face is puffy and sour from booze; his eyes are bloodshot. But he is usually chipper and always kidding around. His energy is skewed, outlaw, intriguing.

We chatted a couple of minutes, half English, half Spanish. They had cut their logs up at Cerro Vista and didn't see any grouse. Joey offered a beer, but I declined. I had my own, and anyway, I never drink before hunting.

He reached out the window, gave me the bro handshake, and we both moved on.

I miss Joey. Before I got divorced and moved out of the old neighborhood, our paths crossed from time to time. We traded gossip. A couple of winters ago I bought wood from him. His mom and dad are my good friends.

I shifted into first for the climb up to the meadows at Turkey Park. Off to the left at the summit sat a truck, an Airstream trailer, a couple of canvas tents, two visible ATVs, and a half-dozen blue-tick hounds milling around. One of the chunky visitors waved and I guess I waved back. Bear hunters. I don't much like them. Not for moral reasons, understand—I just don't cotton to their style, I dislike their attitude, I'm appalled by their methods. Yes, I hunt too, though I'd never touch a bear—or any big animal, for that matter. I go after grouse and, occasionally, doves. Also I fish. That's the extent of it. For the most part I do these things alone. To me, hunting is a private affair.

Five miles beyond Turkey Park, I pulled over at the mouth of Saloz Canyon. Down by the creek stood another trailer with nobody around. I started walking at 1 P.M., climbed over a couple of bulldozed humps blocking the road, and proceeded a ways above the creek. A dozen grasshoppers jumped up and hovered, crackling in the air. I marched right through them, smiling. Truth to tell, my feet felt weightless—I was almost dancing.

The instant I begin leaving civilization, my mood changes. Call it corny, but I'm happy. I travel light. I carry the shotgun and a canteen, ten extra shells, and a sweatshirt in my backpack, that's all. I feel lithe and secretive and expert at my trade, almost a professional.

I crossed the river by hopping gracefully from stone to stone—me and Edward Villella! I could smell mint and paused to pluck a couple of leaves. I sniffed deeply, popped them into my mouth, and chewed. Two trout scooted under a rotten log. Blue darning needles were everywhere.

A quarter mile south my curiosity really kicked in; time to investigate a new place. I stopped at a patch of raspberries intermingled with tall elephant weeds smashed askew. Few ripe berries remained on the bushes. Something had stripped off the fruit—my friend, the bear.

Proximity to wildness always makes me tingle. I could imagine that big brown hulk scraping its claws through those succulent brambles.

The slope down to the river was pretty steep, so I traversed it with care, then jumped across the water and climbed the opposite hill along a feeder creek. On the map this trickle had no name, so I gave it one: Ursus Creek. The altitude lines were real tight, a steep climb. I figured that up a ways I would bump into old logging roads, I always do. Usually I don't have to bushwhack very far.

Game trails take you anywhere. Yours truly (aka Natty Bumppo) found a good one and followed the cookie crumbs (an endless supply of fresh elk droppings). Every now and then I halted and listened. Maybe I would hear an elk bugle. But it was too early for the rut, I guess. I know next to nothing about elk even though I bump into them on almost every outing.

Again I opened the map and studied the lines. I love doing that, transposing from the printed page to a three-dimensional forest around me. I adjusted my angle of ascent. My heart was pounding. I had been off the pills for almost a year but felt pretty confident. Still, the ticker was really chugging along at a hyper pace. An aspirin a day keeps my blood thin and is all that stands between me and a stroke.

When I spotted a faded red ribbon tied to a branch in the middle of nowhere, I flinched. Man, I hate those ribbons. I don't know the codes, but some of them are tied by archeological survey teams who go through prior to a timber sale. There are yellow ribbons, blue ones, pink and red. Occasionally they are put there by guys who tramp about searching for goshawk nests or spotted owls. But usually what those tags mean is logging and the disruption left in its wake.

But not here. Moss lay underfoot, also kinnikinnick rich with red berries, scrub oak leaves, ponderosa cones, holly. Or maybe it wasn't holly, but rather barberry. I'm no expert, and even though I have traveled this country with guidebooks in hand, I often forget.

I veered up a steep rise on top of which, according to the map, was a plateau. And sure enough, the ground leveled off. As it did, directly in front of me lay a bear cave. A big hole was tunneled out underneath a mammoth slab of rock. I leaned over and peered inside the den. There wasn't much sign around the entrance. Apparently nothing had used it during the summer.

The area was scuffed from elk passing through. I found a bright blue Steller's jay feather and stuck it under the strap at the back of my cap. My pounding heart took a long while to quiet down, but it stayed in rhythm, which is all I can ask. Impatiently I took a sip of water. I don't like to drink in the mountains, but I'm told you are supposed to. It seems you can get seriously dehydrated without ever feeling it.

Once in motion I don't like to stop until dark. Usually I have to walk a ton of miles to find grouse. I like that. And the motion alone— always moving—translates into an almost trancelike endeavor.

Another steep incline began west of the cave. But the forest floor wasn't too cluttered. I move slowly over good terrain or bad, marching through the woods like a tired old man. Once I am warmed up, however, I can hike for hours. Today I had started around eighty-five-hundred feet; by now I was up to ten thousand.

Finally I reached an old logging road, probably dating back to the 1920s. For decades, most roads like it in the high country have been closed off to vehicles. And what do you know—ho!—directly in front of me stood a huge pile of fresh bear shit. I let out a whoop

for one of my favorite rituals. The moon was reflected, still rising. Some bird clucked. I killed the engine and listened to the tranquility. Concentric circles appeared on the water whenever a trout touched the surface. Gratefully, I let the scene play out for about ten minutes, then moved on.

When I reached the highway I clicked on the radio and tuned it to an Albuquerque Dukes baseball game and opened another beer. Top of the fifth, the Dukes were ahead, but then the Las Vegas Stars scored a run. "C'mon, Dukes!" The play-by-play was almost drowned out by static.

At home, exquisitely pooped, I sat in front of the TV, plucking the grouse while John McEnroe won a tennis match. I stripped the feathers into a shopping bag and found one hippoboscid fly, an odd, flat, green parasite that zips about with an oily silverfish motion. After the bird was cleaned, wrapped, and stashed in the freezer, I went outside and sat on my rear stoop and thought about things, feeling dreamy and lazy and content. The moon was up there, high above my woodpile. I listened to all the usual serene village noises: a dog barking, a far siren, a door closing. A faint wind rustled in elm leaves.

Well, it is true: I rarely weep for the dead. Instead I bless them for how intrinsically they focus in my heart all life, urging me to rejoice.

From Sacred Trusts: Essays on Stewardship and Responsibility. *Edited by Michael Katakis. Mercury House, 1993.*

Down on the Rio Grande

I have long held a passion for the Rio Grande. Fishing the deep river gorge near my home has always been a joy, a challenge, a tribulation. Where it is difficult I go the most. Narrow trails winding down steep inclines carry me to water that roars between countless slippery boulders. When I leap across those rocks I feel more alive than at any other time.

Though I have shared the river with good friends, I prefer to tackle it solo. Folks regularly warn me that it's dangerous to climb by myself into such a bold and deserted place. But I like being isolated without a safety net in that narrow kingdom.

I catch fish hand over fist. My success involves no great skill at matching the hatch or laying down a delicate line. I need only a few fly patterns, a cheap vest, a simple rod and reel, and a pair of good sneakers. Expensive equipment is wasted on the Rio Grande. A dozen times I have bashed my rod and reel while taking a pratfall among the boulders.

Tonight I get goose pimples remembering with what passionate greed and lust I always approach the river. From the moment I park my old truck at the rim and hit the trail I can barely restrain myself. If the water below is clear I suffer an agonizing anticipation: *This is going to be my lucky day.*

But usually the world caves in. If I descend in glorious sunshine . . . I'll take my initial cast in a hailstorm. Or I will have neglected to bring a reel. Or the first lunker to strike will break my rod tippet—

I court adversity, though. The Rio Grande is no namby-pamby little chalk stream, nor is it a big fat Montana mythmaker habituated by ersatz cowboys and fabled thespians. "The mighty Rio ain't for amateurs. . . ." It's a rough-and-tumble river that scorns finesse. You don't play the fish through all that aquatic thunder, you try to horse 'em out . . . and break your six-pound test in the process.

Mostly I lose the big ones. How often have I screamed as another Moby Cutbow did tarpon leaps to escape over a waterfall? My heart snaps into atrial fibrillation as I clamber over the wild terrain, chasing a fish. Too often I have plummeted into white water as yet another two-pound monster skedaddled.

"You bastard!" I cry, my entire body aquiver with trout loss dismay syndrome—the worst (and most wonderful) pain on earth. And as I sit there gasping, laughing, and cursing my flawed technique, I feel so high on the intensity of the low that anything else is an anticlimax. Meaning this game should go on forever.

Yet I'm not so sure anymore. Late at night I hold my wife and think about things. Life is complicated. Last December, I fell sick with what seemed to be the flu, but it was actually endocarditis—a strep infection inside my heart. That further weakened an already defective valve and cost me a royal fortune. Now I can hardly walk ten steps without triggering atrial fib. I feel sick all the time.

When we go to bed, my wife easily falls asleep. Her name is Miel Athena Castagna. We have been married for three months. I hold her gently and in a moment she begins to twitch. She rubs her feet along my shin and soon commences snoring. Her flesh is ample against me. She is just over five feet tall and oozes affection even while she dreams. I feel her breath against my cheek.

Miel can fall asleep with her lips touched against mine in a drowsy kiss. I try not to move, thrilled by that peaceable sensation. She's only twenty-three and I'll be fifty-four this summer. She is a great skier and a flamenco dancer. I admire her abundant energy and supple body. She can do back flips on a trampoline. We used to Rollerblade together, but for now I can't even cut that small caper. Heart specialists want to repair my valve or perhaps insert a new one.

I have trouble sleeping. Miel logs eight hours every night; I'm lucky to get four. A doctor gave me Valium and a knockout pill called Ambien, but I hate taking the medicines. Already I'm on a blood thinner—Coumadin—and Lanoxin for my heart. The side effects are creepy.

When I open my mouth I can listen to the murmur of the bad valve, a squishy noise pounding up my throat. Often our lovemaking triggers my arrhythmia. We'd like a baby, but Miel takes birth control pills. We have admitted that this relationship is not forever.

So I lie in the darkness with Miel in my arms, remembering the gorge. I cavorted across the rocks as casual as you please. I had good balance and rarely made mistakes, gamboling obnoxiously through bursts of icy spindrift. I caught a lot of trout. And climbed out on a difficult path in pale moonlight as happy as a lark.

Miel has long black hair that she braids before bed. She cuddles snugly against me, giving warmth and absorbing reassurance in return. How nice that I can solace her. She can't see what is wrong inside of me but has witnessed the effects and is afraid. I get dizzy and sick from even small exertions. But I smile because I'm an optimist and a high-energy person, even on death's doorstep. Miel says my eyes sparkle. Appearances are deceiving.

Will I ever climb into the gorge again? If not, I'll miss it profoundly. I'll miss the deer who descend from the mesa to drink. I'll miss the downpours and the icy winds and the activity of swallows. Most of all I'll mourn the sensation of being in sync when the fishing is good and I'm so in tune that I can't even hear the river or smell the pines or notice the sky. At moments like that I knew I was infallible, indomitable, immortal. Man, that sensation was *fun*.

I angled only in the late afternoon when water lay in shadows. For three hours I gave it all I had, aware of nothing else. At twilight I cleaned my fish on a sandbar and drank from an arsenic spring. Then wearily I trudged out of the gorge, pausing often to count my blessings. In the truck going home I ate baloney and Swiss cheese sandwiches lathered in lite mayonnaise and I guzzled beer, feeling battered, satiated, plumb tuckered . . . and ecstatic.

Life is a process of accommodation and bodies wear out. Bitterly, Miel complains that I gave all my energy away to others and didn't save enough for us. Intimidated by her unblemished features, I don't know how to answer. Except this: Our lives create the beings we become. Our present selves are the sum of our treasured aliveness. If we have been awake during the journey our best should be *today*.

Miel can recite by heart the Robert Frost poem "Nothing Gold Can Stay." When she does, I feel sad. Why we are together is a mystery. It's my most radical adventure ever, with an exciting luster to the daring illogic of "breaking all the rules." We love each other with passion, anger, and enormous feelings of connection that render us defensive and insecure. We laugh, play, and procrastinate in bed. It's dangerous to be so attached.

I watch her sleep in the dim light. Her skin gleams with heat. She often mutters or cries out from anxiety dreams. We've been through difficult times. In the old days I dreamed of a less volatile future.

Now, when my thoughts turn to the Rio Grande, I feel an ache that isn't nostalgia. I'm apprehensive that I may never again know the sweet danger of motoring over the boulders with a fly rod in hand. So I'll fasten the experience in memory. Water ouzels . . . and beavers . . . and those miraculous days when the river was low and clear and the trout took any imitation—

Miel has never been down there with me. I hope someday we go. Maybe I won't be able to navigate with much aplomb, but I'm sure I'll catch a trout. While Miel dreams and I am awake, I think: *What a kick, all her youthful ballyhoo and her faith in my survival.* For my part I can touch her in ways that she'll only understand after I am history. We have joked that she'll dance flamenco on my grave— and I certainly hope so.

I enjoy lying beside my drowsy erotic imp: life is rich indeed. On such banal homilies I stake my claim. So Miel gets security for another night . . . as I glide over boulders with my magic wand and it all takes place in slow motion. My green line settles on the water . . . and three ducks go flying by in that world of rough and tumble edges—

Time to steal a kiss in the dark.

Written for (but never published by) Buzzworm Magazine in April 1994, four weeks before I had open-heart surgery to repair a mitral valve damaged by endocarditis.

The Longest Night of My Life

After the operation I lay in a basement recovery room unable to move or speak. A ventilator tube down my throat did all the breathing. My wrists were strapped to the gurney, but not my ankles. I lay absolutely flat, in great pain, and tried to be aware of my surroundings. The room had no windows, but I could tell it was night. Other patients lay nearby, four or five of them. I could hear machines humming, gurgling, and beeping. The nurses gathered over in a corner were making a lot of noise, telling jokes and laughing. My body was logy from drugs, but I was awake and almost alert. The loud gabbing nurses irritated me.

My throat hurt. It felt as if the respirator tube had been jammed too deeply into my lungs. The machine breathed slowly and I waited for it either to speed up or for the tube to be removed. But nothing happened. Nobody was paying any attention. I tried to move my hands, but the restraints held me firmly. So I tried to breathe more slowly, in time with the apparatus. I dimly realized: *This is going to be a long night.*

Never had I been more uncomfortable or thirsty. *Oh God, please give me a drink of water.* That's all I could think about. My lips were brutally parched. I tried to lick my bottom lip with my dry tongue. A nurse over there laughed uproariously. I could not understand their words even though I heard the voices distinctly.

I concentrated on the rhythm of my breathing, keeping it in time with the respirator. My thirst intensified. Also the discomfort in my lungs. I looked around, trying to assess the room and focus on things. I felt a desperate need to remain awake. Time passed slowly, torturing me. *I'll go crazy if it doesn't speed up.*   225

I squirmed a little, feeling my bones and muscles against the hard, uncomfortable bed. My body felt completely broken. I wriggled my toes. On the periphery of my vision I saw a nurse move away from the corner group, responding to a series of urgent beeps at another patient. I observed, but could not really think. I was cold almost to the point of shivering. Another blanket would have been heavenly. But I couldn't speak or lift my head or make a hand signal, so I let it ride.

Gradually I grew drowsy. Finally I drifted into sleep . . . and awakened instantly unable to catch a breath.

My eyes bugged out and I arched up, smothering, desperate from air hunger, and then I pounded my heels at the foot of the bed. I strained to rip my hands from the restraints. *I was suffocating dammit help me!* I tried to call for help but no sound could emerge. My throat was blocked by the breathing tube. A huge balloon of airlessness bulged inside my lungs. Frantically I banged my heels and arched my chest as high as I could, wriggling and twisting violently to gain attention while drowning in front of all those health professionals.

A young dark-haired woman wearing glasses ran over and snapped at me, "Stop it!" Her hands fumbled at my chest and mouth. Miraculously, a hole was punched through the smothering and I gasped in air. Jesus. I sucked it in, stunned, inhaling up the tube, and caught another breath. Tentatively, my bones and muscles settled back down, but not in relief. I was scared.

"Stop thrashing!" my nurse commanded. "You're fine. You're getting plenty of oxygen. Just relax."

I rolled my eyes and shook my head, terrified. Oh, how my chest was hurting. I bent my right wrist up and shaped my fingers as if they were holding a pen and made a scribbling motion. *Bring me a pad and pencil.* She ignored me. I clutched my fingers out and they touched her uniform at the waist. Then I really made a herky-jerky writing motion. She noticed and ordered me, "Calm down, you're okay, you don't need anything."

Furiously, I kept up the writing motion and banged my heels petulantly, demanding that she acknowledge my request. Finally she went away and returned with a pad and pencil. She held the pad as, blindly, unable to see down there, I wrote: *I can't breathe. The tube hurts.*

She frowned at my scrawl, then glared at me. "I told you to just relax," she said curtly. "Let the machine do all the work. You're fine. Your heart is okay. You have plenty of oxygen. Now go to sleep."

She went away, but returned to give me some morphine. "This'll calm you down."

I wanted to write more about the grating in my lungs, but I was embarrassed. I tried to let the machine do all the breathing, but when I relaxed I began to suffocate again. I caught it in time. If I breathed faster than the machine I began to choke. So I concentrated wholly on sucking in and expelling air *exactly* in sync with the slow rhythm of the ventilator. I felt I was all alone and fighting for my life.

The morphine went to work, but I fought it, terrified of passing out. The trick was to stay awake in order to stay alive. My chest throbbed as if it had been pounded black and blue by sledgehammers. Prior to this morning's operation I had spent months in congestive heart failure, going downhill each day. Before yesterday I had barely been able to walk. The slightest exertion had left me breathless. In fact, they had advanced surgery by several days in order to save my life. My defective and flabby mitral valve, weakened by endocarditis, had been almost totally unable to pump blood.

Now I lay very still, exhausted, breathing with deliberate calm, trying to stay awake. It was important not to panic. My concentration was total. The minutes ticked by slower than snails. Every second took forever.

Thirst continued driving me wild. I gestured with my right hand again, then banged my feet once more. A spoiled brat, a troublemaker. The nursed arrived, obviously pissed off. I nodded and gestured for the writing materials. When she produced them I wrote, *I need water.*

"You can't have any. It's not allowed."

I shook my head, wanting to cry. I implored with my eyes. I thrust my mouth stuffed full of modern technology up at her, begging mutely like a baby bird for water.

"Oh, all right," she relented, thoroughly irritated. She fetched a cup with ice slivers and chips in it and rubbed a small piece against my bottom lip. *Oh God, it felt so wonderful.* But melted quickly, teasing without giving any relief. I couldn't swallow because of the damn tube in my throat.

"That's enough," she said, and went away, leaving me alone again. I thought: *She's my enemy. She is going to kill me.*

For the next half hour I timed every one of my own breaths to the respirator's beat. In . . . hold it . . . exhale slowly. If this torture endured much longer, I would go insane. The nurses had quieted down a little. My eyelids drooped and finally I could fight it no longer—

The same thing happened. Like a pillow being held over my face. My eyes flew open. I arched hard and strained to free my wrists and banged my heels and fought fought *fought* for a breath and couldn't get one until a split instant before the angry nurse arrived and cried, "Stop it, you idiot! What's the *matter* with you, anyway?"

Air whooshed in. I was crying and really terrified. I wanted that fucking tube out of my lungs so I could *breathe.* I demanded the pad and wrote, *The tube hurts. Please clear it.* What was the proper word: *suction?* She had a hard time reading my scrawl, but after I wrote it again she fiddled at my mouth and I heard a liquid gurgling sucking sound and felt a small relief.

"There's nothing wrong," she insisted, pointing to the machine to my left and above that I couldn't see. "Everything is perfect. Now go to sleep."

I demanded the pencil and wrote, *More ice.* I even remembered to add, *Please.*

"I'm not allowed," she said, and gave me another dose of morphine. I tried to indicate *No, no* with my bound hands and my eyes and my body writhing but she zapped me anyway.

"It'll calm you down. Stop fighting this stuff."

I fought it. I breathed in rhythm. I listened to their nonsensical talking. As much as possible I glanced around, inspecting the ceiling, the dim lights, the checkerboard baffles, whatever, just to keep occupied. It was impossible to comprehend the noisy patter at the nurses' station. They were speaking German or Portuguese or Rumanian or maybe Martian.

Straining hard to stay awake, I fell asleep again . . .

. . . and woke up choking, suffocating, air deprived, wildly thrashing about in a death struggle. I almost broke open my own aching chest while frantically sucking for air. The nurse shouted at me, *"Quit it, right now!"* And she reiterated that I was fine; she knew her job, the machines never lied, I had *plenty* of oxygen in my blood.

I wrote, *I can't breathe. Get the doctor.*

"The doctors are sleeping. And anyway, you don't need one."

I wrote: *Something's wrong. Take out the tube. Please.*

The nurse said, "You're just a troublemaker, a hypochondriac. Relax. It's all right. Just go to *sleep.*"

And she went away.

I had never been so frightened of sleep in my life. I thought, *All right, I'm going to die.* It would take all my willpower to elude sleep and breathe with the machine until help arrived. When would that be? Probably dawn . . . daylight . . . a rotation of nurses.

My poor heart began to flutter. The atrial fib was coming on; how could I stop it? I strained to perform a Valsalva, but when I strained down, my chest screamed in pain and I quit immediately.

I passed out from exhaustion and morphine and it happened again. I woke up instantly, choking, lurching for air, hideously smothering, banging my feet for help: *rat-a-tat-tat! Rat-a-tat-tat!*

This time my nurse noticed the afib on my monitor and called a doctor, who arrived and stood with the nurse at the foot of my bed, reading information on sheets of paper and scrutinizing the monitor screen. The doctor said, "It's definitely atrial fib." Then he agreed to remove the ventilator tube. When it was out, I felt a wonderful rush of air into my aching lungs, incredible relief. And gratitude. I could not talk, but the doctor untied my wrists. Then he listened to the heart and muttered, "Shit." But he didn't explain. I wrote, *Water, please!* The doctor said, "Not yet," and disappeared.

Then the nurse and a young man in dull green scrubs began to wash me. It was impossible for me to believe how such a simple procedure could hurt *so much*. The water was cold. They scrubbed me fast and indifferently and manhandled my aching body. They lifted my legs and dropped them. They tipped me to one side, then to the other. Each time they brusquely moved me the pain in my smashed chest almost caused me to faint. I twisted my face grotesquely and opened my mouth to protest but no sound came out. If I could have screamed at the top of my lungs I would have: *Stop these brutal humiliations!*

With my eyes I begged them to be *gentle*. I whispered silently, *Don't hurt me anymore*. But they ignored me. They pushed and tugged and lifted and heaved and the pain stabbed inside my body, withering, crunching, malicious—I don't know how to explain. Whether it was indicated in their orders or not, *how could they be so cruel to such a helpless person?*

After they finished I lay there whimpering, amazed that a human being could withstand this torture.

Time dragged along, not even moving. If death could be conscious, this would be it. I lay there engulfed by suffering. Pain enveloped me as if I were lying on stones and had been pounded all over—tenderized—by other cold stones. I could think of nothing except the hurting and my excruciating thirst.

The nurses at their station finally shut up completely. Everything in recovery was still and gloomy and humming along peacefully. All the discomfort in we patients was so astoundingly *quiet*.

If you wait long enough the sun rises. At dawn another shift arrived. My new nurse introduced herself: "Hi, my name is Carla." She held my hand soothingly for a moment. She brushed hair off my forehead with a casual yet compassionate touch. When I wrote, *I am thirsty*, she brought a styrofoam cup of ice and let me suck on one sliver, then another. *Oh, I cannot explain the beautiful and thrilling pleasure of that treat.* My hands fumbled up to take more from the cup and she let me do it.

Carla was a plump, friendly, cheerful angel. She tried to make me comfortable. I had a slim oxygen tube clipped to my nose. Two fat rubber tubes came out of my stomach. My penis was catheterized. I was so fucking miserable in a world composed solely of waiting and hurting.

But Carla tendered more slivers of ice and cool water drops trickled down my aching throat. Tiny blessings, as meaningful as life itself. Carla smiled and gave my right hand a commiserating pat. I lay there greedily savoring one ice chip after another, desperate to slake my thirst. She dealt them to me carefully, watching cautiously, yet incredibly generous to me.

Carla was like a saint, conjured by magical forces beyond my personal understanding. Perhaps I was going to live after all. Pretty soon I relaxed, closed my eyes, and finally went to sleep.

Description of the night after my open heart surgery on May 6, 1994. Written in April 1996.

A September Song

In September my joy and sorrow begin. It is the month when I feel most alive, both fragile and indestructible. It also creates in me a discomforting nostalgia, a yearning for *more* that makes me a trifle queasy. What's precious is heightened by the changing season.

The time is so beautiful, I wish it could last forever. That is also why I go out of my way to salute the ephemeral. After all, who could sustain my blissful ache for much longer than a fortnight?

And anyway, all love is ambiguous.

Come September, awake at last, I cast off my summer lethargy. Thank goodness July and August are over. I love chill nights, the first frost, and the *cosecha* in our valley. A final alfalfa cutting . . . hay bales in satisfied rows . . . magpies and dusty ravens.

For weeks I have eagerly anticipated the end of green. Summer fecundity always made me nervous. Frankly, I detest heat and cannot bear the bustle of warm weather.

Why? Well, for starters climax tourism in New Mexico makes me want to commit suicide. Beer, shorts, sunglasses; barbecues, fireworks, fiestas. In Taos, after the June solstice, everybody's so busy gardening, making money, guzzling Budweiser, fishing, procreating. Jeepers, will it never cease? By August I'm down on my knees *begging* for Labor Day.

One minute after that weekend I'm so happy, I could expire. Just feel that edgy zip in the air! Taos does not exactly empty out, but things calm down a little. There's a new murderer in our valley, contemplating the scene. Sinister scouts dispatched by winter hover on the drowsy ridgelines, planning November campaigns. Snow powders our mountaintops.

And when zucchini leaves turn black I shout out, "Hallelujah!"

My neighbors gallop around frantically gathering wood, mulching strawberries, draping dark plastic over their fat tomatoes. But not me; I'm a grasshopper. I wave good-bye and head for the hills to hunt the not-so-wily (but always delicious) grouse.

Alpine meadows start glowing with a yellow tinge, soft purple bruises, a hint of radiant beige. Aspen leaves get golden as night approaches. High country rivulets are so low and clear it's difficult to catch trout. Geese fly by just under the stars, clarion and sad, their calls a gentle warning.

By mid-September the urgency is killing me. Slow *down,* earth, take it easy, what's your hurry? Chickadees and juncos flit about the spruce branches as I wander old logging roads. Wild geranium leaves turn crimson beneath my feet. In only a week thimbleberry evolves through a dozen amber hues.

Early snows up high are thrilling. Rainy days trigger my laughter. I study bear sign; I listen to squirrels chattering; I stop to gawk at a hawk.

The harvest moon and kinnikinnick . . .

. . . and mint and little apples.

Out on the mesa sage has a poignant gleam in cooler weather. At tiny stock ponds I admire avocets, ibises, and ruddy ducks. Nighthawks and Mexican bats feed lavishly on the plentiful insects.

Each day I wander through intimate country. September is my only true "vacation," a marvelous turning point. The autumn mood causes me to woo my own vitality.

Still, death is what gives meaning to life, and September is the first shadow of a wondrous scythe. The bridge here is between Where I Came From and Where I'm Going, a most intriguing journey. I once had lust for spring, but that was at another age and place.

I'm lucky; I've had a bum heart for twenty years. And I made my separate peace. Ever since, I've been walking through an extended September. Familiarity has bred a lack of contempt. Not being afraid of dying is paramount to human liberation.

September is a dish I gobble ravenously. Or sometimes I drink it like good clean bourbon. By the end of thirty days the high ground is layered with aspen leaves. Canyon wrens will presently quit singing in the gorge. October follows, but it's for killing deer, which I find too noisy and rather fretful.

So: Each year I reaffirm my vows in September. To life, to the mysteries, to the love of growing older. The whole kit and kaboodle comes into focus. Whoever accepts their own mortality travels with a lighter heart.

It is very simple, a truth to count on: September proclaims eternity.

For New Mexico Magazine, *September 1996.*

Epilogue

Andrés Martínez in the Valle Escondido, 1972.

Everything I Always Wanted to Know about the West, I Learned in New York City

I was born in Berkeley, California, in 1940, so I guess that made me a westerner. Golden Gate Bridge, Alcatraz, Gold Rush Days. I was baptized Catholic. When I was one year old we moved to Miami, Florida, so that made me a southerner. Alligators and palm trees. My mother was French, or actually from Brittany, but she had been raised in Barcelona, Spain, making her quite Spanish, though also Catalan, I suppose. I was just learning to speak French in Miami when she died. My dad joined the marines and went to war in the Pacific and I lived with cousins outside of New York City in a town called Smithtown, on Long Island. So that made me an easterner and a Yankee. I learned English, which I spoke with French intonations for a while. My aunt and uncle had a farm, a lake, swans and ducks. I loved Bambi and Dumbo.

When I was five my father remarried. My new mom was from Montpelier, Vermont, and I moved up there for a year with her and attended kindergarten. We were Episcopalian. That's when I became a New Englander, or maybe a Vermonter—but our stay lasted only a year. I loved Hopalong Cassidy and fishing in granite quarries. When Pop came back from the war we lived on Long Island again, where I saw my first movie, Roy Rogers in *Bells of San Angelo*. I got my first cap guns on Easter, 1947. My first record, Christmas 1947, was by Tex Ritter: I can still sing "Old Shep," "Oklahoma Hills Where I Was Born," and "Roly-poly." I became a hockey fanatic; my hero was Maurice Richard of the Montreal Canadiens. I was also a baseball freak, enamoured of the Brooklyn Dodgers: Jackie Robinson, Preacher Roe, Roy Campanella. 237

My dad played the guitar, Russian folk songs, French and Elizabethan ballads, and cowboy tunes. At my grandparents' summer house out on Long Island, Abbey, their cook, was a Poospattuck Indian. Often I went in the car to take Abbey home. I believe there were eighty people of some Poospattuck blood living on a reservation of about twelve acres ninety minutes east of Manhattan.

In the fourth grade we moved back to Berkeley, California, and I became a westerner again. I was a football groupie of the California Golden Bears: Les Richter, Pappy Waldorf, Johnny Olszewski. My favorite comics were Casey Ruggles, Dick Tracy, Pogo, and Ozark Ike. Then we decided to move back east to Wilton, Connecticut.

So I was a Yankee and an easterner once more. But only for a year, during which Mother introduced me to the works of L. Frank Baum, all those wonderful Oz stories. I loved country music, Hank Williams and Patsy Cline.

But when I was twelve we moved south again, to Colvin Run, Virginia, a tiny town with only a general store and a grange hall, period. Dairy country, farm country. Lots of Confederate flags. Civil War battlefields nearby at Manassas and Bull Run. I went to all-white schools and received segregation pamphlets like Green Stamps in my grocery bags. The day after *Brown v. Board of Education* went down my classmates showed up at Herndon High toting chains, switchblade knives, brass knuckles, and baseball bats, fully prepared for a war to keep the Negroes out. I was shocked and confused.

At fourteen I was sent to a prep school in Connecticut. A Yankee again, but with a southern accent. Got an electric guitar and worshiped Fats Domino, Teresa Brewer, Little Richard, and Johnny Cash. My blues heroes were Huddie Ledbetter and Josh White. I went apeshit when the Brooklyn Dodgers finally won the World Series in 1955; then I died when they moved to L.A. soon thereafter. But kept on rooting because by then none of my emotions were bound by geography. I read Ernest Hemingway and Joseph Conrad and Carson McCullers. Instinctively I hated John Wayne and admired Joaquín Murieta.

After my junior year I went out west to New Mexico, spending a week in Taos and the rest of the summer in Portal, Arizona, at a scientific research station where Vladimir Nabokov, an inveterate lepidopterist, had written part of *Lolita*. I collected lizards, snakes, butterflies, and beetles for the scientists. I also fought forest fires in the Chiricahua Mountains with local Chicanos and Mexican nationals. Sometimes the government that hired us called La Migra to deport the *mejicanos* before they could be paid.

That autumn, back east, age seventeen, I wrote my first novel, set in a sort of mythical West, about a mestizo kid who leads his blind Indian grandfather into the mountains to die. The story was full of forests, wildlife, coyotes, bears, mountain lions, and plenty of snow. I loved Tom Lea's novel *The Wonderful Country*. By then I was an atheist.

I attended college in upstate New York, heart of the beautiful Mohawk Valley. After my sophomore year I spent the summer with my French grandmother in Barcelona. Went to bullfighting school. Ran in front of the bulls at Pamplona. Stayed with gypsy flamenco dancers in Madrid. I discovered *Platero y Yo,* by Juan Ramón Jiménez, and *Romancero Gitano,* by Garcia Lorca, a poet murdered by Franco's Falange.

Next summer, in New York City, I hung out in Greenwich Village and learned a lot of guitar from a blind evangelical blues singer named Reverend Gary Davis. When I graduated college I went back to Spain for a year, practiced my French and Spanish, and had a girlfriend in Paris. Our car was stopped often by cops seeking terrorists supporting Algerian independence. I read *The Plague,* by Camus.

In June 1963 I sailed to New York City and lived in a South Village neighborhood that was mostly working-class Italian and some Puerto Rican. After I sold my first novel in January of 1964 I took a bus to Guatemala City, where my eyes were opened by Émile Zola's *Germinal.*

Back in New York after a month I *really* started to learn about . . . the West. I read about Guatemala . . . the CIA coup in 1954 . . . the United Fruit Company. People told me about the United States in Nicaragua . . . the Somoza dictatorship. I became aware of our Caribbean record, supporting Papa Doc Duvalier in Haiti . . . and

Trujillo in the Dominican Republic . . . and Batista in Cuba. I became sympathetic to Fidel Castro and read José Martí.

Once I started down that path I couldn't stop. Bertold Brecht said: "Young man, reach for a book; it is a weapon." My friend Alan Howard gave me Charles and Mary Beard's *The Rise of American Civilization*. I read Ida Tarbell's *The History of Standard Oil*. And Carey McWilliams's *North from Mexico*. Plus Upton Sinclair, *The Jungle*. I pored over photographs of New York immigrants taken by Jacob Riis.

I grabbed *The Autobiography of Malcolm X* as soon as it was published. And *Black Elk Speaks*. Suddenly I was confronting "genocide." Westward expansion began at Plymouth Rock and didn't waver all the way to that day in 1853 when Admiral Perry sailed into Tokyo Harbor and threatened to level the city if Japan didn't open its doors to favorable trade agreements with the United States.

And we kept on truckin' thereafter.

J. P. Morgan . . . and Wounded Knee. Our presence in Vietnam was a logical extension of the Trail of Tears . . . Manifest Destiny . . . the Mexican-American War. By the end of 1965 I was protesting Vietnam and I hated Lyndon Johnson.

Our Asian war evolved for me into a logical extension of the Sand Creek Massacre or the hunting of the buffalo. Colonel Chivington, meet William Westmoreland. Kit Carson, meet Lieutenant Calley of My Lai. It all went hand in hand with our great robber barons like Rockefeller and Carnegie, Stanford and Harriman. My mind was cluttering up with Boss Tweed, Teapot Dome, the betrayal of Geronimo, Henry Ford and the auto industry, and James B. Conant's marvelous history of Detroit, *American Odyssey*. I read John Hersey's book *The Algiers Motel Incident*. Also Seymour Hersh and the revelations at My Lai.

Ray Ginger, Dee Brown, Piri Thomas, and Rachel Carson became my heroes. I did not see America as a country of different geographic locations and peoples, but rather as a unified nation with a history of growth and expansion inevitable from the start and everywhere the same. I learned that to understand any part of the whole you must develop a macroscopic overview. My child-hood had set me up for this.

In America, I reminded myself, buffalo were slaughtered as far east as Pennsylvania (where millions of carrier pigeons in the late 1700s were similarly exterminated), and forests were brutally lev-eled as far west as the Olympic Peninsula. The man who wrote *The Outcasts of Poker Flat* had been raised in Albany, New York. And my favorite book of the "western writer" Wallace Stegner, *Crossing to Safety,* is set largely in upstate Vermont.

During the 1960s, civil rights struggles in the South were simi-lar to Native and Chicano struggles out west. Two radical news-papers I read at that time were *El Grito Del Norte* and *Akwesasne Notes.* One was published in Española, New Mexico; the other in upstate New York. *El Grito* chronicled the Chicano movement, and in particular Reies Tijerina's land grant Alianza in New Mexico; *Akwesasne* dealt with Indian peoples around the country, Mohawks in New York and Canada, Sioux in South Dakota, Pima in Arizona. At one point *El Grito* did reports from Cuba and North Vietnam because they were relevant to northern New Mexico.

What difference was there between the dreams of Martin Luther King in Alabama and those of Corky Gonzales in Colorado? King's "I have a dream" speech jibed with Gonzales's epic poem "Yo Soy Joaquín." Jay Gould and Marriner Eccles were cut from a similar cloth. Immigrants to New York and Pittsburgh were like the pio-neers to Utah and Idaho. And how to distinguish between labor strife in Michigan, Massachusetts, Mississippi, or Colorado? What Rockefeller could do in Titusville he could also do in Ludlow.

For six years in New York City I went to demonstrations and study groups. I worked for peace candidates, for the Moratorium, for SANE; I marched on Washington; I watched television news and documentaries; and I read books about history, economics, culture, America, the world. I developed a socialist idealism that I felt was embodied by the words of our own Declaration of Inde-pendence: All men (women, children, races, creeds, colors) are (or at least should be) created equal.

In New York we tried to form coalitions between liberal whites, radical black groups like the Panthers, and Puerto Rican nationalists. Democrats, socialists, Trotskyists, communists, nationalists, liberals. I kept up with the labor movement in Massachusetts, New York, Indiana, Montana, California. And studied histories of people like Walter Reuther, Eugene Debs, A. Phillip Randolph, Mother Jones, Lucy Parsons, Emma Goldman, Helen Gurley Flynn. I delved into the Pullman and Homestead strikes, the Wobblies and Joe Hill. I saw the wonderful New Mexico film *Salt of the Earth*. I read Paulo Freire, Frantz Fanon, Thorstein Veblen. My worldview kept expanding. It included Sacco and Vanzetti, Chief Crazy Horse, the Palmer Raids, Bisbee (Arizona), Haymarket Square (Chicago).

My barrio in New York, the South Village, was quiet and stable and largely working-class Italian. There was a street festival each year, St. Anthony's. Some of my best friends in those early Manhattan years were also Argentinians; we made up a raucous *pandilla*.

In the midsixties, however, my home began to change. Pressure was on for Greenwich Village, a highly commercial area, to expand south. I watched in amazement as the gentrification went down. Landlords revised their renting patterns; they encouraged transients, longhairs, drug users. The high turnover rates enabled them to jack up the rent-control prices with every new tenant. A sudden instability was created in the community. I had not locked my door during my first three years in the city, and I was never ripped off. Then suddenly, lots of crime. Higher prices. More Anglos. Fancy stores. An upscale restaurant. Anger on the streets. Resentment. People tried to resist. A war went down. Puerto Ricans against Italians against some working-class whites. Divide and conquer. The indigenous population never had a chance. The money moved in, took over, opened the chic restaurants and art galleries, and by the time I departed New York City for Taos, New Mexico, in 1969, SoHo was almost a fait accompli.

When I left I was not trying to escape to a land of enchantment . . . or to some trout-fishing paradise . . . or to a thinly populated area where I could avoid the real world. I was drawn to New Mexico for political reasons. It was almost the poorest state in America. Socioeconomic statistics were as harsh as those of inner-city New

York. I expected to continue being involved in the important issues of our time.

Taos was much smaller than Manhattan, but to me it was a microcosm of the same USA. It was multicultural, just like New York, Miami, New Orleans, Tucson. It was under the gun, just like my old neighborhood in the South Village, and for exactly similar reasons.

Many New Mexico groups were involved in the same struggles that had moved me in New York. Taos Pueblo was fighting for a return of their Blue Lake land just as Puerto Rican nationalists were demanding the return of their country. The Chicano movement was in full sway in New Mexico, same as the Black Panther efforts in New York. A Black Beret friend of mine was killed by the cops in Albuquerque just as Fred Hampton, a Panther leader, was murdered by the police in Chicago. The anti-war movement was strong in New Mexico, particularly since so many Chicanos were winding up on the line, dying disproportionately in Southeast Asia. Hippies with money were moving into the area, stepping all over indigenous culture, so naturally there was a hippie-Chicano war reminiscent of the Italian-tourism-art-world war in my old Manhattan neighborhood. The stakes for all parties concerned were survival.

In Taos, local farmers were organizing against developers trying to impose a conservancy district on the valley. A document most helpful to the protestors was called "Downhill in Warren." It had been written by The Vermont Public Interest Group in Montpelier, Vermont, and detailed the development of a Vermont ski area that had disenfranchised local residents. The situation in upstate Vermont was almost exactly the same as in Taos. That document described our future in a nutshell.

My dear friend and political cohort for twenty years was an elderly Republican and devout Mormon named Andrés Martínez. I was an Anglo atheist communist. He venerated Ronald Reagan *and* Reies Tijerina, helped found a bank, had once been a dairy farmer, and was as radical as Che Guevara when it came to land and water conflicts in the Taos Valley. I hated banks and Ronald Reagan, but Andrés and I got along famously.

There was as much racial tension in Taos as in New York or

rural Virginia. A U.S.-China People's Friendship Committee in Taos was sending local residents to China so they could see how other societies handled cultural autonomy and revolution. There were nuclear freeze and environmental organizations. Tourism was changing Taos just as it was changing the South Village in New York. Mexican and Chicano migrant workers were suffering exactly the same abuses in New Mexico that migrants suffered in New Jersey, on Long Island, in Connecticut. Back there they worked potato fields, strawberries, tobacco farms, and truck vegetables; in New Mexico and Colorado it was lettuce, potatoes, chile, cotton, pecans. The welfare situation in northern New Mexico mirrored that of Brooklyn and the Bronx.

When I published *The Milagro Beanfield War* in 1974 I assumed it would be relevant to anybody anywhere. I was disappointed when critics called it a "regional novel." I thought my characters and my community and my plot were as universal as anything written by Faulkner or Carson McCullers or Émile Zola.

Local Taoseños asked me how I could know so much about their culture after living in New Mexico only a short while. I replied that ninety percent of it was universal. I knew about it long before I reached New Mexico. Maya Angelou said: "We are more alike, my friends, than we are unalike."

After *Milagro,* I spent five years working on a novel called *The Magic Journey*. It details forty years in the development of a small town like Taos. I put everything I understood about the history of my country and its economic system and its social structures into that book. During the research phase I clipped Taos and other New Mexico newspapers and developed extensive files. I talked to my neighbors and read labor histories and tales about New Mexico, Colorado, and Wyoming. But probably the most helpful book I read was called *The Power Broker,* by Robert Caro. It chronicles the rise and fall of Robert Moses, a longtime parks commissioner and city planner for New York City, whose ideas shaped the Big Apple. In the process Moses changed the nature of urban America as we know it today.

I was fascinated by the scope of that enormous book. The life of Robert Moses embodied the energy of our country. Every deed in *The Power Broker* had an echo in Taos, New Mexico . . . or in Leadville or Butte or Boston. *The Power Broker* was connected with Huey Long in Louisiana (read *All the King's Men*). Or to Roman Polanski's film *Chinatown,* which deals with water shenanigans in Los Angeles that exactly reflect the convoluted water histories of New Mexico (Colorado, Wyoming, Arizona, Idaho).

I saw *The Magic Journey* as a logical extension of *Germinal, All the King's Men, The Jungle, American Odyssey, A History of Standard Oil,* "Yo Soy Joaquín," and *The Power Broker.* Though my novel was set in northern New Mexico, I meant for it to incorporate a lifetime of reading and writing and study and experience: in Berkeley, Miami, Long Island, Montpelier, Connecticut, Virginia, New York. My topic was North America, not the West. My topic was decades of development, not some isolated caper. I was drawing on a mythology of nation, not of specific community. I aspired to strike a *universal* soul.

It all becomes entwined for me. Our West is so vast I shudder when it is saddled with regional definitions. My gut feeling has always been: You can't separate any part of the United States from the nation as a whole. We all belong to each other—history, landscape, people. You can't define some of us without defining *all* of us.

Our nation has always been a series of frontiers continuously changing: in race relations, agriculture, community survival or breakdown, environmental collapse or survival. The gangsters and angels who did it—or are doing it—come from every ethnic group and every religion, from every type of corporation and government entity, and from every type of citizen, including myself—from all of us.

The spirit of the West is the same as the spirit of the South, the East, the North, New England, the corn belt, the bread basket, the bayou, the pine barrens. . . . America is ubiquitous, relentless, untiring. Writers like John Updike and Leslie Marmon Silko speak of a similar chaos. As do Toni Morrison, William Faulkner, and Demetria Martínez . . .

What am I driving at? A fairly simple thesis. I have a tough time separating this "region" from the national whole. Our history, whether pre-Columbian, Anasazi, or with Coronado, or after Lewis and Clark or Sitting Bull, is American to the bone. It is hitched to everything else in the history of this nation's universe. And I am too.

The West has much more in common with the United States than it has ever had with the myth of itself. And I think of myself as an American writer concerned with the history and body politic of my nation . . . and hemisphere. Eduardo Galeano's *Memory of Fire* captures my West more profoundly than Frederick Turner. The eyes with which I record the world around me were forged by Tex Ritter, Albert Camus, Pablo Neruda, an Episcopalian childhood, upstate Vermont, and Maurice Richard, L. Frank Baum, Patsy Cline. Firefighting in the Chiricuahuas and playing blues guitar with a blind evangelist in New York added layers to my personality. *Germinal* and "Yo Soy Joaquín" wound their silver threads around my heart. Bertold Brecht, Fidel Castro, Malcolm X, and Crazy Horse helped to spin my political webs. Marriner Eccles, H. L. Hunt, Meyer Lansky, Bugsy Moran, Peabody Coal, Al Capone, and Robert Moses taught me more about how our society functions. From Rachel Carson and Barry Commoner I learned to weigh the environmental consequences.

I conclude, therefore, that when we separate "the West" from the whole we only belittle ourselves. The myths of "the West" are way too claustrophobic. The region is more complex than the ways in which people often try to define it. In fact, it isn't a region at all.

Nor am I, believe me.

Hence: I am a westerner, a southerner, an easterner, a New Englander, a Yankee, a rebel, a gringo, a frog, an honorary Gallego. I never specifically adopted a place or a culture or a political party, but I certainly have tried to absorb my nation, hemisphere . . . planet.

Do I interpret the so-called West with dishonest eyes because I bring such varied influences into the game? Or if we are truly one nation, indivisible under Donald Trump, with liberty and injustice for all, am I perhaps, like all the rest of us, just another addition to a much more eclectic beast?

That's what I'd like to think, anyway. And that is also why sometimes I really chafe at the regionalization of where I live. It makes me nervous when the West is viewed as a separate entity. Because it is a whole lot larger than that. And also not half as elitist as so many of us make it out to be. In other words, *don't fence me in.*

And don't tag me as a southwestern novelist, either. If you must narrow it down, I am an American scrivener, please.

And if any of you *ever* again has the audacity to refer to me as a regional writer, all I can say is:

"When you call me that, *smile.*"

Keynote speech at The Image of the American West Conference, Colorado Springs, March 22, 1996.